THE WORLD OF *TED SERIOS*

(Fig. 117) An enlargement of Ted Serios' color picture of the Denver Hilton Hotel.
See text page 234.

THE WORLD OF
TED SERIOS,

"THOUGHTOGRAPHIC" STUDIES
OF AN EXTRAORDINARY MIND

By

Jule Eisenbud, M.D.

WILLIAM MORROW & COMPANY, INC.
New York 1967

DEDICATION

To my fellow workers in psychical research, past and present, indispensable
among whom, it almost goes without saying, are Ted and my wife, Molly.

CONTENTS

THE WORLD OF *TED SERIOS*

whats in this book is true, evry word of it.
I want the story exackly as is.

Ted Seuss

CHAPTER I

The Come-on

IF anyone had told me when that first letter came that there was no use my trying to duck what Providence was plainly set on my getting mixed up with, perhaps I wouldn't have thrown it into the basket. But there were no Macbeth-like signs or portents to clue me in, not even a thunderclap. How was I to know that I was slated to spend the next couple of years—and perhaps the rest of my life—trying to make sense of an utterly fantastic series of happenings centering around a weird little man who could have stepped right out of Grimms' fairy tales, and that there was no point in my behaving as if there were anything I could do about it to the contrary?

It all came about because of a paper of mine which appeared in a parapsychological journal in the fall of 1963. Ever since its serious beginnings as psychical research more than eighty years ago, parapsychology, despite an impressive amount of first-rate evidence in favor of telepathy and clairvoyance (both subsumed latterly under the term extrasensory perception) and such diverse phenomena as apparitions and the strange effects of mind on matter (termed psychokinesis), has remained a stepchild of science. One of the major reasons for this, it has been widely held, has been the

lack of a repeatable experiment in which these so-called psi phenomena could be produced more or less on order, like hydrogen
gas or hybrid plants. In my paper, however, I argued that a truly
repeatable experiment in this field was inherently impossible. One
of the chief reasons for this, as I saw it, was that such a result
would be in essential contradiction to certain still poorly understood features, which we need not go into here, of our mysteriously
hung-together but nonetheless remarkably predictable universe.
I concluded, at any rate, that the repeatable experiment in parapsychology would take its place, alongside the alchemist's stone
and the cabalist's tetragrammaton, with those dreams of mankind
which would remain forever dreams.

And this is where our story really begins.

As was to be expected, the rank and file of parapsychologists
were anything but enthusiastic about the point of view I had tried
to argue. Most people in the field harbored the comforting faith
that the difficulties in the way of successful experimentation (and
accordingly in the way of public acceptance) and the absence of a
repeatable experiment were simply a temporary phase, as in other
sciences during their beginnings. That continued research, sparked
possibly by some Newton or Einstein perhaps still unborn but
surely waiting in the wings of history, would, step by step but
inevitably, as in research in poliomyelitis and oral contraception,
lead to effectual isolation of the factors behind psi phenomena and
to ultimate control had never for a moment been seriously
doubted. Now this messianic myth was being questioned.

Some parapsychologists reacted with anger and scorn, like children, or patients in analysis, who have a cherished fantasy exposed
or taken away from them. Others merely sulked and removed me
from their reprint and Christmas card list. One letter I received,
however, signed by a Curtis Fuller, was somewhat more annoying
than the others because the writer seemed to have missed the point
of my paper; but the letter also momentarily puzzled me. "I
should like to take issue with you," it began, "and am enclosing a
paper . . . given before the Illinois Society for Psychic Research
that does offer what I believe to be a repeatable experiment. Un-
believable as the facts set forth in the enclosure may seem to be,
it is my personal judgment that they are true." The enclosure was
a reprint entitled "The Psychic Photography of Ted Serios," a

report that had appeared in *Fate* magazine a year or so before by Mrs. Pauline Oehler, then Vice-President of the Illinois Society for Psychic Research, on a series of tests carried out on this Ted Serios, a poorly educated, unemployed Chicago bellhop in his early forties, who was alleged to be able to project photographic images onto Polaroid film by simply staring into the camera lens with intense concentration. Several examples of this 'psychic photography' were reproduced, including various street scenes, the gardens of the Taj Mahal, the Pentagon, and the dome of the White House—all rather blurred but recognizable—and the portico of the Chicago Museum of Natural History, which had appeared in a session witnessed by a paleontologist on the staff of that institution. According to the report, the conditions of a series of tests done with Mr. Serios over a period of months by "a number of scientists, photographers and other intelligent observers," were quite adequate to rule out the ordinary possibilities of fraud or collusion ("If my veracity is accepted . . ." added Mrs. Oehler matter-of-factly). The report stated that, given the usual precautions of using cameras and film supplied by others than Serios himself, and of close observation of Serios' movements—the tests were allegedly carried out in full light, artificial or daylight, and complete inspection of Serios' person was allowed at any point during the tests—there was little possibility of fraud on his part (inspection as close as desired was permitted) and only outright collusion would remain to account normally for what was alleged to occur. "By what means could these pictures have been fraudulently produced?" Mrs. Oehler wrote. "The matter is considered in detail by Stanford Calderwood, Vice President of the Polaroid Corporation in a recent letter to Curtis Fuller, President of the ISPR [Illinois Society for Psychic Research] and publisher of *Fate*. In concluding Mr. Calderwood says: '*Let me stress that while a clever man could tamper in advance with our film, I know of no way he could do it if you were to show up with the film you bought in a store at random and watched him load and shoot. Tampering with the film would be a long and complicated procedure and nothing that could be done by sleight-of-hand, especially if he had to photograph two or three pictures (or thoughts) on the same roll without reloading the camera and without an opportunity to substitute something in front of or behind the lens.' "* Mrs. Oehler then considered the hypothesis of the registration of prints or transparencies fraudulently placed in front of or behind the lens, and showed why she believed this to be impossible under the circumstances. (For one thing, the focal length of the lens was wrong for this.)

After a quick reading of Mrs. Oehler's article, I dashed off a hasty letter to Mr. Fuller thanking him for calling Mr. Serios and his 'psychic photography' to my attention but stating that he did not quite understand what I had in mind by way of a repeatable experiment. Of course, I wrote, psychics and sensitives of all stripes had been investigated for a long time, and many of these, when they here 'hot,' were able to give repeated demonstrations of the phenomena they happened to be noted for; but there was nothing in any of them that could be extracted and bottled, so to speak. I did not comment on Serios' alleged phenomena besides pointing out what I thought was a slight error in a purported matching of a photograph allegedly taken by Serios with the entrance hall of the Red Fort at Delhi, India, which was claimed to correspond to it, and stating, somewhat acerbically, that if carelessness of this sort were allowed to enter into the protocols and reports, then he (Fuller) should not expect the work to be given the hearing by serious scientists that he seemed to be soliciting. "The Psychic Photography of Ted Serios" then went right into the wastebasket, along with Fuller's letter. I had seen enough of this sort of stuff to know that despite the precautionary measures allegedly taken there must obviously be something fishy somewhere. I had no reason to doubt Mrs. Oehler's veracity and sincerity—over the years I had developed a fair nose on this level—but I thought I had every reason to entertain doubts of her (and Mr. Curtis Fuller's) scientific acumen, or at least training and competence in the elementary but absolutely indispensable techniques of differentiating genuine psi phenomena from very trickily produced normal (that is, fraudulently produced) phenomena giving the appearance of same. But what chiefly ruled against my taking the report seriously was what seemed to me the extreme unlikelihood that I and other parapsychologists would not long before have heard of this particular specialty act if there were anything to it at all.

It was not that I had any reason categorically to bar the phenomenon from the realm of the possible; indeed, my own investigations and every theoretical consideration these led to, plus dozens of well-authenticated reports in the serious literature of psychical research and parapsychology on essentially similar or analogous phenomena—various types of 'mind over matter' manifestations, both spontaneous and experimentally induced—had long since worn down whatever resistance I might initially have had to the abstract possibility of just what was claimed. What bred negative feeling in this particular instance was the glaringly suspicious absence, after several years of allegedly successful demonstrations, of any mention of investigation or even note by any of the several centers of parapsychological research in the country, to say nothing of universities or other responsible institutions, when, according to the report, a number of reputable scientists had already been participants in, and witnesses to, the phenomena. Why had Polaroid Corporation not taken an interest if its vice-president had taken the trouble to comment on it? And why had the only report to date, Mrs. Oehler's, been carried in *Fate* magazine and not in one of the recognized journals of parapsychology and psychical research, of which there were several very reputable ones published in this country? The whole thing smelled bad.

What made it smell worse, so far as I was concerned, was the curious course taken by the correspondence that developed on the matter, a correspondence that I was fairly certain, at the time of my rather brusque reply to Fuller, would not eventuate. Fuller, who evidently saw less finality in my note than I thought I had put into it, answered by stating that he would be glad to try to arrange a demonstration for me if I should ever happen to be in Chicago— "with no guarantee, of course, that results would be forthcoming." I responded to this with the conventional brush-off: "Thank you very much; if I should ever be in Chicago I shall let you know"; and Mr. Fuller's second letter also went into the basket. But several weeks later (Mr. Fuller has very kindly supplied copies of his early letters and my replies) came another letter from him, again urging me to make an effort to witness the Serios phenomenon at first hand and stressing once more the necessity of getting responsible organizations into the act. Once more I found it hard to credit his claim that he and others had had no success in trying to interest such organizations and institutions in his man, all the while failing to realize that here was I, one such responsible party, with the necessary connections with research institutions and organizations, myself playing not only hard but virtually impossible to get. Again the brush-off.

But finally—chiefly, I think, out of annoyance, as well as I can remember—I bethought myself of two days of lectures I was to give at a midwestern university in April (this was now January) and figured that perhaps I could swing around through Chicago on my way back without too much trouble and expense. I could, if it came to that, always spend a pleasant day with friends there or in the Chicago museums. I compounded this rationalization with a resigned application of the principles of Pascal's famous 'wager,' as it is known, to the situation. The seventeenth-century mathematician, and one of the fathers of probability theory, was as a young man seized by severe doubts as to the existence of God but decided to keep up his regime of prayer anyway. If there is no God, he reasoned, he would thereby sacrifice but a few minutes a day in ineffectual activity. But should there be a God and he failed to pray, his salvation might be lost for all eternity. I figured that if Serios and his alleged psychic photography proved to be a complete washout—and I had little reason to expect otherwise—I would lose very little if I included Chicago in my itinerary; but if, through some outside chance, there was anything at all worth investigating in the fantastic claims made, I would perhaps stand to lose a great deal by not doing so.

But things weren't as simple as I had tried to make them out to be in my schematized way of arriving at a decision. Indeed, if Pascal had run into a situation analogous to the one that now developed in the Serios affair, he may very well have skipped a few days at his devotions as he saw the probabilities on the affirmative side of the question dwindling fast.

At the beginning of March, I finally wrote to Fuller that I could arrange to be in Chicago if he could manage to arrange a demonstration for me. I received the following answer—eleven days later:

"Dear Dr. Eisenbud: I have delayed acknowledging your letter of March 2 because of uncertainty as to my own plans. I now find that I will be gone from the city from March 21 to approximately April 10 and hence would not be here on April 4. Is there any chance that you could be here at a later time?"

"Meanwhile I wish to discuss the problem seriously.

"There have been, as you may imagine, a succession of 'demonstrations' with their attendant build-ups and expectations, which have played emotional havoc with Ted Serios.

"In nearly every instance these were conducted by all of us quite seriously, with considerable expenditure of time and effort. When photographs were obtained, the persons for whom they were obtained turned out to be merely idly curious—or in two cases had insufficient courage or stature in their educational institutions to dare to pursue the matter to its obvious conclusions of more research.

"Now all of this brings me to my main point. I am not interested in cooperating in or being a party to another 'demonstration' unless there is a serious intent behind it. That intent, in my view, must be that if the results are positive a firm commitment of further research by a responsible organization must be made."

My suspicions were hardly allayed. When I had finally acceded to Fuller's request, he delayed answering my letter, he had to be out of town, he made impossible conditions. I wrote a curt note stating that it was obviously impossible for me to make commitments before seeing what the whole thing was about, and let the matter drop once and for all. Or so I thought.

On March 17, I received a letter from a Mrs. Freda Morris, who introduced herself as a Ph.D. candidate in psychology at the Illinois Institute of Technology and a person "interested in the Serios phenomenon." "Mr. Curt Fuller told me recently," she wrote, "that you had expressed an interest in seeing a demonstration of this phenomenon in April. I understand that he did not encourage you unless you could give assurance that you would be able to follow up with research. I fear that you may not feel it feasible to promise further research and will thus be discouraged from investigating further." She then went on to propose that since the phenomenon was not reliable anyway, and since I might "spend several hours or even days with Ted and see no picture taken which would lead you to invest time and effort in an investigation [a formal investigation, I presumed she meant]" I could perhaps undertake a survey of the work already done, which would be "almost as convincing as an actual demonstration." She herself had never seen Serios "take a 'hard' picture," she went on, and if she had had no further information she could perhaps have convinced herself that it was all a trick. She then named several people of "scientific repute" who had worked successfully with Ted and who saw no reason to suspect fraud, and suggested that perhaps I too should contact these people for further information, which would perhaps induce me to commit myself to some still unspecified but responsible research.

The thing was getting sillier and sillier. When I offered to witness a demonstration, everybody backed off and offered me a chance to talk with authorities of "scientific repute."

I wrote back that I realized that people like Mr. Serios could not be expected to produce on order. "At the same time," I continued, "I don't think it reasonable to demand that a full dress set-up be arranged for preliminary demonstrations. So far, I must confess, I am not too impressed with the reports as they now exist. On the other hand, you may be sure that if *somebody* came forth with anything even remotely looking like an authentic protocol or experimental record, full scale research could be arranged somewhere." And again I offered to meet with Serios and any other interested parties if a demonstration could be arranged.

A few days later, on March 27, Mrs. Morris wrote that Mr. Serios would be happy to meet with me on April 3. Would I please bring a Geiger counter?

It now occurred to me that, win or lose, another participant in and witness to the proceedings would be helpful, someone to take notes, perhaps, while I kept my eyes peeled for hanky-panky (not that I imagined I was capable of detecting any but the most clumsy efforts at trickery). I had just had a letter from a young cousin who, having participated in some interesting and highly successful private experimentation on telepathy and clairvoyance, was eager to go on to other things. Jonathan, a sophomore at Amherst, was just returning to his home in Cleveland for the spring holidays. Chicago was less than an hour's plane trip away. Perhaps he wouldn't mind joining me on this lark and acting as notetaker and general flunkey.

Jon immediately accepted when I phoned him. But, I hastened to emphasize, he must go into the thing realizing that the chances were very slight—*very* slight—of his seeing anything except evasions, suspicious actions, results not even remotely resembling the claims made, and excuses for nonperformance. This, I warned, was ninety-nine per cent of the history of psychical research. Was he willing to take this chance? If he wasn't, he might as well give up the notion of going further in this corner of the field; on the other hand, I pointed out, it might be valuable for him to have precisely this type of negative experience, as no one could be said to be a fully initiated psychical researcher without it.

Jon was game.

But the perils of Pauline were far from over. Just before I left for my lecture trip I received a letter from Mrs. Morris with a disturbing note. "I would like to add to your knowledge of Mr. Serios' personal characteristics: He has a problem of drinking." (Oh?) "If we assume a priori," the letter continued, "that anyone who has a drinking problem may fail to keep appointments occasionally, then you are taking that chance with him. . . . However, . . . I will keep in phone contact with him Thursday night." Then, in a most curious and confusing switch, she added: "If you would like to have a more convincing demonstration, you might bring along some pictures sealed in opaque envelopes and Ted could try to get pictures of these images. Ted prefers buildings. I hope you have a pleasant and successful trip."

Less than one hour before my departure, I now learned that the star performer might not even show! I fired off a wire to Mrs. Morris at once, asking her to leave word for me at the Chicago airport if, on the afternoon of our rendezvous, she had any reason to believe that Serios would not show up, since in that case I would not bother to leave the airport but would take the next plane out. But if there were no word from her, I'd meet her as agreed in the lobby of the Palmer House. I then phoned Jon and outlined the new turn the affair had taken. But he was still game, despite the ominous warning signals.

And that was the last I heard until I got to O'Hare field. I was pretty tired out by the time I enplaned for Chicago after two days of lectures, seminars, and conferences, not all of which were gratifying. In fact, the last formal lecture, to the department of psychiatry of the medical school, fell just about as flat as a lecture could without the ultimate indignity of the audience walking out en masse. The nice doctor who took me to my plane right afterward tried to console me by allowing as how his confreres were

not used to the kind of "high-flying intellectual wheeling and
dealing" I had indulged in, in tracing the history and symbolic
meaning of the crescent as a breast symbol in art, culture, and
psychopathology from prehistoric times to the present. And as I
slumped in my seat in the plane and gazed somewhat disconso-
lately out the window on the short hop to Chicago, I couldn't
have cared less about the alcoholic content of Mr. Serios' brain,
or whether he was planning to show or not. All I could think of
was what had been wrong with that lecture. Perhaps it had been
so far off, or out, that no one would ever get what I was trying to
demonstrate. I dozed off.

CHAPTER II

Pictures at an Exhibition

My plane came into O'Hare airport at five-thirty. I hardly recognized the rangy crew-cut young giant, whom I had last seen in the most unprepossessing of the teen years, who came striding down the ramp to meet me. No messages awaited us. So far so good. At six-thirty we were at the registration desk of the Palmer House, where I asked the clerk if a Mrs. Morris had inquired for me. He nodded toward an attractive young woman sitting a few feet away. I thought she must have been eyeing us expectantly because she looked just a little too busy with the contents of her handbag when I walked over and introduced myself. Everything was all set, she stated. Serios would meet us there, in the lobby, at eight— or at least, she added with her fingers crossed, this was the last word she had had from him that day. I registered and suggested that we all go up and have a look at our room before heading for the coffee shop. As we followed our bags to the elevator I wondered if the clerk had funny ideas as to what was about to go on in room 1320-W, and if we could expect to have the house detective popping in, in the middle of everything. This time, I said laughingly, he might get an eyeful of something *really* illicit.

Promptly at eight we left the coffee shop and headed for the

(Fig. 1) *Ted at the Palmer House*

lobby. Near the stairs to the mezzanine a slight man in a trench coat, whom I recognized as Serios from his picture in Mrs. Oehler's article, came toward us. "Call me Ted," he said with an ingratiating smile as we were introduced. We proceeded immediately to room 1320-W. Ted seemed rather disappointed that I hadn't brought a Geiger counter, but was pleased when I informed him that I had brought the concealed target pictures that he had requested through Mrs. Morris. After a few minutes of small talk I suggested that, if no one had any objection, perhaps we ought to get going, but I asked first if I couldn't order drinks. Ted looked from Mrs. Morris to me, as if undecided. "If anyone else is going to have one." He shrugged, as if it were a matter of the completest indifference. When Mrs. Morris asked for a highball, Ted ordered a Scotch on the rocks. "Make that a double, if you don't mind," he called to me as I got on the phone for room service. Aha, I thought, we're off to the races! Jon doesn't drink, and I passed one up because I wanted maximum mental acuity for observing whatever went on.

Jon acted as notetaker, as well as co-observer. I began by with-drawing a fresh film pack from its sealed container and loading the Polaroid Land type 100 camera that I had brought and which I hadn't up to that time allowed out of my sight for a moment. I hadn't had too much experience investigating sensitives or alleged mediums, but I knew just enough, chiefly from a fair acquaintance with the literature on this type of research, to realize that some of the cleverest deceptions had been achieved right before the eyes of observers who imagined that, because of conventional training in one or another scientific discipline, their methods of observa-tion and control were infallible. As a matter of record some amaz-ingly simple frauds had been perpetrated on observers of this sort, who would have taken an oath—in fact, some did—that what had been done right under their noses was impossible. It was widely felt that the only really adequate match for a talented trickster, to say nothing of some individuals who were positively geniuses at the game of deception, would be a trained, highly intelligent and forewarned professional conjuror, and that even then the odds, depending on the type of deception attempted, might not be much better than even on. Nevertheless I decided that in this prelimi-nary session I would simply try to observe as closely and as well as possible, and worry later about chinks in our methodological armor. The light was good, and Ted was perfectly willing for me to watch as closely as I might want and even to hold his hands, if I felt like it. He would have preferred a model 95 Polaroid camera to the one I supplied because he was used to it and liked the wink-light attachment for it better than the much brighter flash that went with the 100 model, but he offered no objection to going ahead with what we had. The following account of the proceed-ings is from Jon's notes made at the time and from additional notes made by me a day later.

At 8:50 Ted indicated that he was about ready to go. He pre-dicted that he would get a long, tall structure with "a sign cross-wise on it." He then removed the coins, the keys, and a rosary from his pants pocket and laid them on a nearby table top, ex-plaining that he felt that the presence of metal on him interfered with picture taking. More small talk, Ted smoking away. Finally Ted indicated that he would like to try to fog the first film without touching the camera or tripping the shutter. Would we mind if he took his shoes off? (As I was later to learn, he now and again tossed in ostensibly innocent actions of this sort, which he would deferentially ask permission to carry out, as if he were a prisoner in the dock.) At Ted's request, I held the camera about two feet from his head, pointing at it. The shutter was left uncocked. Ted sat in a chair, leaning forward toward the camera. He said he would try for a small dot and a large dot. He concentrated for a couple of minutes, complained of a headache and said that that was it, that he had finished, that he had tried for a plus sign. (He then told us that concentration was very difficult, that he sometimes bled from the mouth and anus immediately afterward, never at other times.) Print number 1, the first try, came out perfectly black on development. "A black cat on a dark night," quipped Ted, not in the least bothered by his failure. More chatter, mostly about what he could do when 'hot.' A couple of cigarettes more.

At 9:32 Ted was ready for his second try, this time in his usual manner, holding the camera and tripping the shutter himself. For this he fished out of his pocket and used a device, which we later came to refer to as the 'gismo,' that, as I was to find out, never failed to arouse darkest suspicions on the part of uninitiated observers and that indeed I myself felt called upon to examine closely on the spot. It consisted on this occasion (it was later modi-fied) of a half-inch cut section of the plastic tube which carried the chemically impregnated squeegee for fixing the prints after development. Ted claimed that this device, which he held between his thumb and index finger, or between his thumb or index and third finger, and placed more or less flat against the outer lens, was originally adopted to keep his fingers away from the lens (this didn't make too much sense to me, but I didn't argue the point) and at the same time to limit the amount of light and surrounding imagery (this I could see). He had gradually become more or less habituated to the thing, he explained, so that now he felt very uncomfortable working without it, although he would do so, he hastened to assure me, if I desired this. I suggested that he work in the most comfortable way. Ted showed me that the ends of the cylinder he was using on this occasion were covered by cellophane, and that inside one end, under the cellophane, there was a circular piece of film negative, covered by stove blacking, which covered the opening and rendered the cylinder opaque when held more

or less flat against the lens. This all seemed unnecessarily complicated to me, but I offered no objection after examining the 'gismo'
and finding nothing in or on it to justify suspicion.

For the next try, for which he himself held the camera resting
on his crossed knee and pointing at himself (as in fig. 2), Ted held
the gismo over the lens, opaque end up, between his first and
second finger. (Figs. 2 and 3 show him holding the open type of
gismo which was later used.) Perhaps I should at this point describe his more or less unvarying behavior during this and the
ensuing shots. When about to shoot, he seemed rapidly to go into
a state of intense concentration, with eyes open, lips compressed,
and a quite noticeable tension of his muscular system. His limbs
would tend to shake somewhat, as if with a slight palsy, and the
foot of his crossed leg would sometimes start to jerk up and down
a bit convulsively. His face would become suffused and blotchy,
the veins standing out on his forehead, his eyes visibly bloodshot.
The physiologist might assume that a heightened venous pressure
was being produced, with perhaps what is known as a histamine
effect, similar to what occurs in many allergic rashes and bee stings.

(Fig. 2)

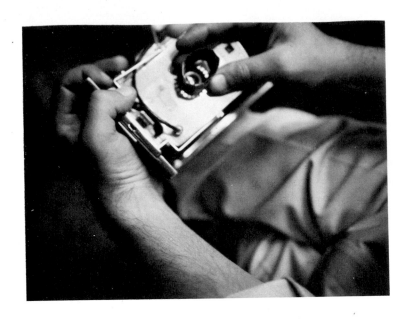

(Fig. 3)

(The proctologist would perhaps liken what was occurring to the kind of tension and pressure built up during a difficult movement.) This might go on for anywhere from fifteen or twenty seconds to a minute or more, during which time Ted would be seemingly undisturbed by noises, remarks, movements of those about him, or by people coming over and putting their faces within inches of his hands or even, as I did on quite a few occasions, putting fingers on his wrist to take his pulse. On the other hand, Ted would sometimes get started, interrupt his 'trance' for a second or two, get going again, and then interrupt or stop completely, settling back in his chair and shaking his head, much like a high jumper getting set for a takeoff and then deciding that this was just not the right moment for his run. During this time, however, whether in or out of 'trance,' Ted never, as I have indicated, acted the part of the nervous and jumpy athlete or performer, never protested anyone's doing anything he pleased by way of scrutiny and examination, physical or otherwise. It was easily possible in the middle of a try (as was sometimes done when he fell back momentarily) to suggest a different procedure—say that the gismo be turned upside down, or that his position be changed in regard to a light.

Ted never protested. His general composure and assurance were, with only one notable exception which I shall mention later, always remarkable, even when he was sweating it out and getting only failures. Sometimes he would, immediately after a shot or even during one of his interruptions, hand the camera to someone and invite—even insist upon—his examining his heartbeat by the laying on of hands. He claimed that his pulse always began to race and his heart to beat like a trip-hammer when he was hot, and indeed the poundings he experienced were sometimes palpable by others.

On trial number 2, Ted asked to be given his first target envelope. For this I had used a heavy-grade manila, with cardboard covering the image side. Ted held the envelope in front of him for a few seconds and said, as he handed it to me, "It's an entrance, a driveway entrance or a walkway." (It was a color photo of part of the Kremlin that I had taken the summer before.) I tried not to let my facial expression indicate that he had missed—an almost impossible task, of course—and held the target envelope for him next to the camera, as he requested. As he got set for the shot, his breathing became deeper and faster until the flash came. When the print came out completely dark again, Ted still showed no signs of loss of composure but merely changed his guess as to the photo hidden in the opaque envelope. "A group of buildings with two people," he suggested, but without even a trace of the question mark in the voice that is so characteristic of some psychics fishing for clues. Ted acted as if his first diagnosis, "a driveway entrance or a walkway," just happened to be wrong, but as if, with no apologies, he was now making the correction that would render his guess right. He asked, however, for a short rest.

I picked up the phone for room service and asked if anyone wanted anything. This time Ted didn't even flinch as he snapped out, "Double Scotch." (I ordered orange juice for Jon and myself.) When the drinks arrived a few minutes later, Ted went immediately for his double, saying with an arch look as he pointed to his throat, "For my cold." He looked from one to another of us for a response, which we generously supplied.

At 9:50 we got set for the next shot. The procedure was the same as for the preceding one except that for this one, at Ted's request, I held the target envelope next to the top of the camera (which Ted was holding) but not in such a way as to obscure what he was doing with his hands or to prevent my taking his pulse, which I clocked at 120. Ted almost gasped with the flash, and predicted "a little something" on this one as I took the camera for development. Again a black cat. Ted simply shook his head and lit another cigarette.

We talked some more until Ted indicated his readiness to try again, and when Jon or I had to move around we saw to it that one of us had the camera in his sight at every instant. Ted took this supervision as a matter of course. At 10:26 I got out the second enclosed target picture, another view of the Kremlin, this time with a couple of soldiers in the foreground (I wondered for a moment if this is what he got in one of his first guesses, but quickly put this out of my mind as of little consequence). With complete confidence, as if he were not even guessing, Ted stated, "A white house, white boards, green roof." Fascinated, I saw this incredibly brash self-confidence as the mark of the genuine psychic or sensitive, since I have learned that these people never quite know where their images come from but have learned to trust them as giving a high enough percentage of correct hits to override the bad impression they give with their misses. (I once saw a famed psychic say something to a woman in the audience of a television show about her mother back home. When the woman stated simply that her mother had died several years before, this man said, with emphasis and narrowed eyes, as he leaned forward, "Are you sure?")

The procedure for shot number 4 was the same as the preceding two, except that this time the target picture was held to the right of the camera. Ted again let out his breath explosively with the flash. 10:27. Pulse about the same, but pounding a bit, I thought. Again a blackie, possibly a trifle lighter but nothing to hang anything on, what with the still undetermined vagaries of the film and unavoidable variations of a second or two in the ten- to fifteen-second development time. Shot number 5 at 10:35, same target, same procedure. Gismo with opaque end up, shutter fully covered. Ted hoped to get "a white line, part of a building, white boards." Vague enough, but we got a complete blackie.

At this point, what with the evening wearing on and nothing to show, and at the rather slow rate of only five shots in about an hour and a half, I threw out the suggestion that perhaps Ted ought to change his procedure and not bother about shooting for a target, which could conceivably be inhibiting the spontaneous expression of his imagery. Ted assured us that we had nothing to worry about, that sooner or later he'd hit a target; but at this point I rather forcefully insisted on putting the target aside. Ted reluctantly agreed to let me have my way, but asked if I minded whether he took a cold shower first, as this, he claimed, sometimes toned him up. Of course I had no objection, I said, but it immediately entered my mind that this might be the point at which, in some way that I could not comprehend, a clever performer could introduce the gimmick that would turn his trick. Ted went into the bathroom and in a minute or so I heard the shower go on, and then in another minute or so it went off again. A few seconds later Ted stuck his head through the door and called to me. "Hey, Doc—do you mind coming over here for a minute?" When I came over he threw the door wide open and stood totally naked and dripping wet in a recess to the left of the door, where he couldn't be seen by Mrs. Morris. "Hey, Doc," he whispered, "do you mind if I use one of your bath towels?" The inappropriateness of this quite unnecessary request intrigued me; and I wondered why Ted wanted me to see him naked because I noted he did not turn around, which he might have done were he out to show me that no secret cache of microfilm equipment or God-knows-what was taped to his back or thigh. I thought it just as likely that he wanted me to see his natural endowment, for such a maneuver, I reflected—a maneuver supremely childish in origin and intent— was quite in line with the simple, in fact infantile narcissism that so many psychics seemed to possess and exhibit in various ways. From what I was weeks and months later to find out, this was probably the more correct surmise and, in fact, dovetailed nicely with other psychological material that was soon to come to light.

At 11:04, Ted having dressed after his shower and now claiming that his heart was starting to pound—a good sign—took shot number 6. I didn't note which end of the gismo was up. This print showed some unusual, rather amorphous, fogging and one or two lines or shadows that I didn't stop to examine at the time but which Ted thought showed beginning activity. Because his heart was pounding away at a fast clip now, a fact which he demanded

I verify by feeling through his shirt, he asked for the camera again immediately and took the next shot at 11:05. Again I didn't note (nor did Jon) which end of the gismo was up (not that we could see that it should make any difference) and in the hurry we neglected to change flashbulbs, so that there was no flash with this shot. Blackie. Ted demanded the camera immediately again and shot number 8 at 11:06, Jon and I watching intently as Ted was shaking rather noticeably now but not enough so that we couldn't see perfectly clearly in the quite adequate light what he was doing with his hands and the camera. It was nothing different from what he had been doing earlier, although this time, when Ted handed the camera back to me, I started to fumble for some reason and had some difficulty grasping the print tab firmly to pull it out for development. But when this finally got done it was at once apparent that we had something here that was a picture of a recognizable structure (fig. 4). Mrs. Morris excitedly identified it as the well-known Chicago Water Tower and started to jump up and down, clapping her hands. Young Jon, who set about to fix and number the print, as he had all the others, said nothing, as if this were the sort of thing he saw every day of the week, while I, less

(Fig. 4)

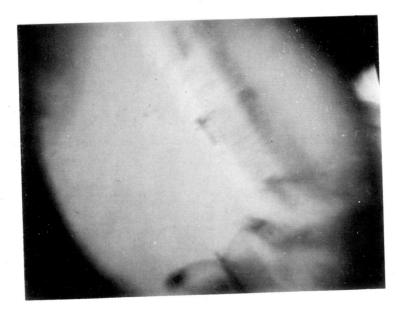

excited about the crude mechanical oddity of what had just occurred than about an interesting peculiarity of the picture that
would have meaning to no one but me, started to expound on
what had struck me so forcefully and its relation to the phenome-
nology of telepathic dreams seen in analysis. This most interesting
facet of the whole business merits separate discussion and will be
taken up later.

Ted meanwhile was sitting back in his chair and staring into
space, as if nothing of all this concerned him in the slightest. I
don't recall his even asking to see the picture, and this was an
aspect of his behavior that I noticed on subsequent occasions
when something of interest in one of his prints would become the
center of excited attention in a group of observers. On these
occasions I might glance over and see Ted sitting in his chair,
head sometimes sunk on his chest, and seemingly lost in thought,
the forgotten man.

It was some time before we got going with the next shot. Meanwhile we loaded a fresh film pack into the camera and ordered
another round of refreshments. I couldn't tell whether Ted was
exhausted or quietly drunk. So far as I could see, the headache he
complained of, which he thought was worse than the usual ones
he got during these sessions because of the flashbulbs going off in
his face, he came by honestly as a result of his chain smoking and
drinking. He refused my offer of a couple of aspirin, however,
and just continued to sit rather glumly by himself. Mrs. Morris,
who by now had got over her great excitement, lay down on one
of the twin beds and tried to catch a few winks while waiting for
the drinks to come, while Jon and I chatted of one thing and
another—his schoolwork, friends—as if the others were not in the
room. A peculiar lull had settled over the whole affair. Gone were
the tense expectancy of the beginning of the evening and the
exhilaration immediately after the seemingly miraculous appearance of the Water Tower.

At about 11:40 Ted began to stir. He had a hunch that on his
next picture he would get something that would be meaningful
to both Jon and me. He got set to shoot and went through his
usual procedure, the flash coming at 11:47 when he thought his
heart was pounding at a favorable clip. At first, picture number 9
looked like nothing much; but as Jon was fixing it with the

(Fig. 5)

squeegee he noticed something on its right margin that looked interesting and passed it over to me for inspection. Something that might have been a couple of windows and the ghostly beginning of a roof line of a building appeared to be peeping through the gloom of what would otherwise seem to be another blackie, or at least a partial blackie. (A fourfold enlargement of this is shown in fig. 5.) We put this aside and got set for trial number 10, because Ted claimed he was hot again and insisted on shooting one right after another. He *was* hot. Picture number 10, shot at 11:50, Ted's heart pounding away like a trip-hammer, was again a partial blackie, but this time there was an area of light fogging in the center of the circular black shadow and nothing else. And picture 11, shot right afterward, was again a bull's-eye, as became apparent the instant we stripped the developed print away from its backing (fig. 6). Glowing in the center of a murky but nonetheless quite distinguishable 'photograph' were the letters STEVENS on an illuminated sign over the marquee of the old, no-longer-standing Chicago Hotel (it had burned down some years before, Mrs. Morris informed us). Both Mrs. Morris and Jon flipped at this one, why I don't know—perhaps the idea of the illuminated sign added an extra touch of the miraculous to what was already quite a trick—and began excitedly pressing Ted for more pictures. And Ted, who appeared to take developments as a matter of course and was indifferently fishing some ice out of a bucket, would have gone on to try, despite the splitting headache which he now admitted to. But I called a halt when I discovered his pulse to be 132 and pounding like an angry surf. After all, we had seen enough, I felt, to indicate that something quite out of the ordinary had taken place; more we could do on future occasions.

I took another look at print number 11. Ted now identified the Stevens as the present Hilton and thought that it had not been known under the Stevens name for the past thirty or so years. He had no particular memories connected with it and couldn't imagine why it should turn up. And contrary to Ted's prediction, it carried no special meaning to Jon or me as a structure. The

(Fig. 6)

name Stevens, however, rang a peculiar kind of bell for me, and
I shall speak of this in a later chapter.

Our first session was over. Mrs. Morris couldn't understand how
I could remain so calm throughout. I assured her that I was not
far from experiencing what might be termed a quiet sense of
exhilaration, but that my more dominant feeling, in so far as I
could sort out the different components of my mood, was one of
tremendous relaxation, of complete absence of tension, such as I
had experienced at other times in my life after a crisis had passed
or something had happened that had drained from me the last
ounce of emotion. Ted had, I confessed, upset all my prior prejudices and expectations in regard to him by coming through. But
now that he had, I felt as if 'the other shoe' that I had been waiting to hear drop for almost twenty-five years—a shoe that I knew,
from all sorts of cross-checking data, must have been somewhere
around—had finally dropped with a dull but delicious thud. Now,
I told her, I could sleep.

CHAPTER III

The Morning After

BUT sleep was not for me that night. I had not counted on the double take which hit me shortly after we had taken Mrs. Morris home and parted from Ted, who promised to show up the next day about noon. As Jon and I sat over our ham and eggs in an all-night eatery, a lot of things which had been left unsaid and a lot of questions that had not been brought up while we were with the others kept pouring out of us, and by the time we got ready to turn in it was almost sunup. I'm sure I must have dozed now and then, but all I can recall is tossing about restlessly or lying on my back with my eyes wide open in the gloom, my mind a turbulent river of thought. What I still couldn't fathom was why this clearly remarkable phenomenon which, according to both Mrs. Oehler's and Ted's accounts, had been on more or less public display for over ten years before all sorts of observers and investigators, including scientists of various persuasions and competences, was still going begging as far as responsible research interest went. Mrs. Oehler had made an outspoken plea for this in her article of more than a year earlier. Fuller, the publisher, must have written to others besides me. Ted himself had stated plainly that the thing he most wanted was for 'scientists' (whom he rated only slightly below saints and supermen) to give serious study to what he was doing and to certify once and for all that it was genuine (genuine *what*, of course, was something that Ted seemed to be not too much bothered about). Why had this not been done? Where was the hitch?

I realized that I am by nature more than ordinarily suggestible and credulous, that I find it easy, both emotionally and intellectually, to accept all sorts of things that others boggle at and approach cautiously, if not suspiciously. But I am not stupid, and for the life of me, despite my intellectual awareness of the many pitfalls and booby traps besetting the inexperienced investigator of this shadowy realm (and I had to adjudge myself an inexperienced investigator in this corner of the vast field that for better or worse has been dubbed psychical research), I couldn't understand how in the *hell* anyone could produce the pictures Ted had under the circumstances that had obtained. I knew perfectly well, however, that this was precisely the reaction that tricksters counted upon and indeed were able to produce in their audiences, and that if this were not so there would be no tricks and no audiences. I recalled also the many puzzles I had tried for hours and sometimes for days to crack—how to divide a cube into so-and-so many parts with only three cuts, how to trace a course between a given number and disposition of points with only such-and-such a number of straight lines—and which I had finally given up on only to learn, when the solution was forthcoming, that what I would have sworn was impossible was as simple as truth, with only insight (that only divine gift!) as the missing link. I was aware, further, of how many problems appeared insoluble so long as a perfectly obvious but absolutely incorrect conceptual— or even semantic—framework was not replaced by one that was far out, even ostensibly insane, but nevertheless correct. On the other hand—and I went over these steps a dozen times before morning—not only was there, first, the direct and hardly to be bettered evidence of my own and Jon's senses under conditions that I could scarcely ask to be improved upon as far as control of materials and personnel was concerned (haunting refrain: Could they not, though? Was Jon or I *closely* observing at *every* instant? What about the time Ted went into the vestibule for some ice? Did I estimate what went on in the shower correctly? What about. . . . Did I, etc. . . .) but also, second, far from there being any categorical bar in physical—including physiological—law to what had apparently taken place, the very opposite was true.

In my own work, both published and unpublished, I had tried to show that it was necessary to postulate the existence—somewhere and in some guise—of phenomena on the order of what Ted was ostensibly producing before the still but poorly delineated and structured physical and biological universe, which we simply accept piecemeal out of inertia and habit, could begin to be adequately integrated. Moreover, as I had also tried to show, it was necessary to postulate that we all had latent capacities to do unconsciously essentially what Ted was doing (even though, for the most part, what 99.99 per cent of us did in this line continually and systematically escaped detection through a clever ruse on nature's part) in order to begin to close in on what to my mind was the number-one problem in science, the phenomenon somewhat inaptly called precognition, in comparison to which, as I saw it, all other problems were relatively trivial and without whose understanding nothing in the universe could begin to be properly understood.

Now here it was, just as predicted, like the planet Pluto. Here, in what Ted was doing, was the beautiful, smoothly functioning fusion of the cognitive and physical powers latent in all of us. I was familiar with the literature of so-called physical mediumship, but what Ted appeared to present was the missing link par excellence in a still only dimly discerned and poorly integrated panel of problems. If repeatedly verifiable it might yet turn out to be the most economical, the most elegant, the most stripped-down version of what, so far as I was concerned, all science implicitly pointed to as the indispensable factor in both life and also whatever it was that—ordinarily subsumed under, or even identified with, the only partially comprehended laws of probability—held the universe together and on course. Finally there was the extremely compelling testimony, which I earlier referred to in passing and shall return to more fully in a later chapter, of the *latent* content of the 'communications' (for that is essentially what they were) Ted had served up in his pictures, communications for which the pictures themselves were merely pilot vehicles or structures, so to speak, exactly as in dreams, art, and other manifestations of the unconscious. What kept turning over and over in my mind, as I lay in my Palmer House bed not even trying to sleep, was this: Even if I assumed that there could be a means of producing these pictures normally (or fraudulently, since this is what 'normally' would amount to under these circumstances), even if I assumed that I had been taken in by an extremely clever trick (which would then, incidentally, have had also to get by dozens of other witnesses and investigators over the years), there was still the peculiar and peculiarly consistent 'meaningfulness' factor to be accounted for; and this I could conceive of only as the exquisitely deft hand of the unconscious as I had come to know it over my years of clinical study and observation, or a purely chance effect the odds against whose occurrence struck me offhand as astronomically great. For a trickster, I thought, to have pulled out of his hat by chance, out of an entire universe of objects, structures, and symbols—even granting the large number of situations that I, like every other psychoanalyst worthy of his couch, could find broadly meaningful—the images that were so *immediately* relevant to me, was like winning ten Irish Sweepstakes in a row. (I pushed aside, at this time, the possible significance of Mrs. Oehler's having stated in her article that Ted had once before come up with the Chicago Water Tower for someone.)

All in all, after my long night's feverish deliberations, I found myself—emotionally, at least—in a position quite opposite to that of the great nineteenth-century German physicist Hermann Von Helmholtz who, when confronted by the data of psychical research being turned up in the 1880's by a group of which many were members of the British Royal Society, is reported to have said (or thundered) that neither the testimony of all the Fellows of the Royal Society nor the evidence of his own senses could lead him to believe what was clearly impossible. As the light came peeping through the blinds of room 1320-W, and the noises from the street below started to quicken, I kept thinking that neither the prejudices of all the Fellows of the American Association for the Advancement of Science (which had recently refused accreditation to a group of parapsychologists seeking affiliation with it) nor the weight of my own built-in biases to the contrary could lead me to discredit, without much further investigation and more convincing arguments than the mere abstract possibility of trickery, what was so clearly theoretically called for. I could hardly wait for the hour to arrive when I could decently ring up a few of the people whose names I had been given as prior witnesses to Ted's 'psychic photography.'

Promptly at the stroke of eight I began my phone rounds, while Jon went out to try to hunt up a Geiger counter. The first man I called was a psychologist who had been retained by a large industrial research corporation in the area which had had Ted under contract for several months a couple of years before and whose staff, according to Ted, had witnessed a number of successful shots under a variety of conditions. Mrs. Morris had shown me, the evening before, a copy of a letter this psychologist had written some months earlier to a well-known scientist who commanded the funds and facilities and was in a favorable position to investigate Ted. He wrote that he had had an opportunity to study some of the phenomena, that "under carefully controlled conditions . . . excellent results were obtained," and that he had, after due psychological appraisal, "arrived at the opinion that no fraud was involved." "There is a crying need," he also wrote, "for some responsible people to give this just enough moral support so that suitable organizations would become interested in investigation." (Here we were again. Why *hadn't* any responsible people come in on this thing? Why had the large industrial research corporation dropped it after several months of what was stated in the letter to have been "excellent results"?) Dr. M, whom I was successful in reaching, at once confirmed what he had said in his letter, without evasion or hedging. "Yes, indeed," he replied to my query as to whether he had personally witnessed some successful shots, "and right here in my office too." The pictures weren't always too clear, he went on to say, but there was no doubt in his mind that they were definite structures and that there was no way, under the circumstances—*his* camera, *his* film, close observation in good light— that they could have been produced normally. Why hadn't he gone on to research the phenomenon? Well, that took time and money and organization, and the best he could do was to pass it on to Professor So-and-So, who was in a position to swing it. Fair enough, I thought.

The next one I called was the chief physicist of the research laboratory that had hired Dr. M to study and give his psychological appraisal of Ted. I was lucky to catch Dr. R at his home, as he frequently traveled about, he explained, and he seemed very glad to talk to me about Ted. But at once I detected a caution, a careful—somewhat too careful—weighing of words and a sort of 'fifth amendment' stance that I hadn't seen in Dr. M. Someone was being cagy. Yes, he admitted, Ted had been studied by them for three months ("I think") and although some interesting things (which he couldn't be induced to specify) had gone on, it was difficult to evaluate the whole thing.

Why?

Well, it wasn't the sort of thing one came to an opinion about without very refined study, and one had to be cautious about making inferences. He himself, he stated, had not witnessed any successful shots, and so "could not give a very positive statement" on the phenomenon, but others, he went on with almost judicial fairness and balance, had had a different experience and "felt differently about it."

They felt *they* could give a positive statement?

Well, yes, but he couldn't really speak for them.

I felt I wasn't getting anywhere, and decided to leave this source for the time being and come back to it at a future time. I thanked Dr. R, who assured me of complete cooperation should I want to discuss the matter further on a later occasion.[1]

I next put in a call to an editor of a large weekly publication with headquarters in New York. After I had left the message that my call concerned Ted Serios I was duly rewarded by a return call in which it immediately became clear that I was the one who was expected to answer the questions and give information. Parrying this as best I could, I did manage to get out of Mr. Birch (as I shall call him) that his publication had originally been interested in Ted's phenomenon and that he himself had witnessed it several times under varying and on the whole excellent conditions but that the story was absolutely dead at the moment, as far as the top

1 I later found out that there had been at least one occasion when Dr. R was reported to have witnessed a positive demonstration. On the back of one of the prints produced by Ted under the supervision of the research staff of the laboratory, which I later had an opportunity to study, was written, "our film, our camera"—and the names of the witnesses. Among these was that of Dr. R.

brass in the organization went, for lack of proper certification by a university or its equivalent.

"Besides," went on Mr. Birch, who, pencil in hand I am sure, now threw in a leading question, "I'd like to know what the devil good the thing is. So a guy takes pictures with his mind. So what?"

I mumbled something about the immense scientific importance of a phenomenon of this sort if its occurrence could be verified, but immediately changed my tack when I could practically hear the pencil scratching away at the other end of the line and got one or two more questions that I thought no educated person, certainly no senior editor in the *Poof, Woof,* and *Spoof* class, would be silly enough or naïve enough to ask unless he was doing an article on the subject from the ground up, an article the material for which I was not yet about to provide. Instead I told Birch the story told of the visit Michael Faraday was paid one day by three exchequer inspectors on behalf of the British Government during the reign of William IV.

"Look here, Mr. Faraday," one of them began, after the three had poked around for a while and had got Faraday to show them what he had been up to with his magnets and coils, "His Majesty's government has now supported you for several years with these thingamagigs, and you still can't tell us what is the good of it all, or where it may lead?"

"Gentlemen," Faraday is said to have replied, "I'm not quite sure myself where all this is going, but who knows? Maybe some day it will be taxable."

"Maybe," I said in ending my talk with the journalist whom I was now convinced I could never beat at his own game, "it will some day be tax deductible."

The next phone interview of the morning was the real shocker. I had been told by Mrs. Morris and by Ted that a Professor X, of the psychology department of one of the large universities in the Chicago area, had had several sessions with Ted over a year before, and that even though the results had been quite successful (in Ted's view, at least), nothing further had been heard from the man. Here was something I certainly wanted to run to ground because if, as Ted claimed, the results had been successful—or even only interesting and provocative, if not conclusive—why had a representative of an institution professedly dedicated to the advancement of learning (I had never yet seen an institution of higher learning that did not proudly display terms like *lux* and *veritas* on its shield and seal) not pursued the matter further? Why, indeed, had he not pursued it to a point where, what with the research facilities of his department, a clear and definitive statement could be made? Where, I again asked myself, was the hitch? Possibly Ted was guilty here of the kind of exaggeration seen again and again in witnesses to occult phenomena, especially in instances where the witnesses are themselves the individuals in connection with whom this or that remarkable phenomenon or coincidence is supposed to have taken place. Perhaps Ted had blown up a minor irregularity on one or two of the prints into a success of major proportions. It was easy to conceive of this happening, even if the central figure had not been an untrained person of ostensibly rather weird mental makeup but an educated one with a demonstrable sense of balance in most other things. In this area the tendency to exaggeration, distortion, and retrospective falsification is so well known as to have led, since the earliest days of research in it, to the necessity for adopting safeguards and controls on verification and documentation quite unheard of in other domains.

I was fortunate in finding Professor X in his office at the university on my first try. And here, to my amazement, was no caginess, no pussyfooting, no attempt to worm information or admissions out of me, but simple, straightforward, forthright illogic of a sort I would hardly have credited had I not been hearing it with my own ears. Yes, Professor X admitted at once, he had had several sessions with Ted and had got several pictures from him. What did I want to know?

The following is verbatim from my notes made immediately afterward, but I can still hear Professor X's rather slow (not out of momentary but probably habitual thoughtfulness, I imagined), measured replies. I felt him puffing on a pipe, could practically see the smoke curling lazily around his professorial head.

Well, I proceeded, somewhat cautious myself, what did he think of these pictures? Oh, came the reply, not terribly clear, not really very clear.

Nevertheless, I asked, were there any definite and recognizable structures involved?

Well, yes, yes, he would say so.

Now I came out with it. How was it that he or his department was not investigating further?

The reply caught me off balance. I couldn't be sure that I had heard right. In one "crucial" test, claimed the professor, Ted had been given a hidden target to try for, the picture of a hospital building in Miami. He had missed. Another building entirely had shown up.

"You mean he got the *wrong building*," I queried, for the moment at a loss for anything but a kind of juvenile sarcasm.

"Exactly," came the absolutely deadpan reply.

I couldn't help thinking of the talking-horse story and of its insane "Don't believe a word that pathological liar of a horse has been telling you" punchline. "Now, Professor X," I began again, trying hard to control my rising irritation and adopting the approach one would to a backward but nonetheless earnest pupil whom one is trying to get to see some not too difficult point, "supposing you were to see someone flying unaided over the Merchandise Mart, and without any visible or inferable support . . ."

"Well?"

"Supposing you saw this. Would you just walk on, saying to yourself, 'That's funny,' but with no inclination to do anything about it, report it to anyone, or even stop and look further?"

"I see what you mean," he said, so help me, as if I had advanced some brilliant analogy that made immediately clear what otherwise could be grasped only with great difficulty.

"Then why aren't you researching the thing?"

Now came another shocker, and again this is something I would hardly have credited if someone else had given me the story. "Well, Doctor, researching the Serios phenomenon is not an easy matter. It would take at least an afternoon a week—not just for weeks, but possibly even for months."

So?

"Well, this is just not my research strategy, nor that of my department—not our dish of tea, that is."

This was the end, and the end I made it of our talk. "Thank

you, Professor X," I said as I hung up with, I am afraid, a rather
rude bang that I had to reassure myself could not be heard at the
other end.

Here was the most up-to-the-minute experimental approach in
all its glory. Every psychologist getting his Ph.D. had to go through
tons and tons of experimental reports to learn about the most
modern, most sophisticated methods of setting up research designs
that would protect him from falling into methodological errors
while at the same time giving some minimal yield of information
concerning some point about as momentous as the tendency of
persons with strong ties to mother figures to doff their hats in
elevators versus the non-doffing tendency of oppositely oriented
men. Hundreds of pip-squeak projects like this existed in Ph.D.
manuscripts all over the country, and scores were being currently
supported by research grants from a dozen large agencies, including the fabulously profligate Federal Government. I have seen
scores of young graduate students, who later became Ph.D.'s and
went on to teach in various institutions, talk just like Professor X
about "research strategy," about advanced Monte Carlo opera-
tional methods, or what not, all convinced that a course or two of
learning the ins and outs of statistical research methods, and
about Type I and Type II errors in evalution of data, were going
to equip them to be veritable Pasteurs of psychology (who any
longer wants to be a Freud?).

The last person I called was Mrs. Oehler, who later that day
brought to the hotel for my inspection a number of pictures done
by Ted over a period of time in her presence, and dozens of others
that she had collected from other sources. The pictures ranged
from shots of well-known structures like the Eiffel Tower, the Taj
Mahal, and the Pentagon, to exterior and interior shots of the
White House (including the late President Kennedy in his study),
to shots of places, structures, and people that still had not been
identified. Some were clear, many were dark and out of focus, and
a few showed interesting features—montage effects and 'double-
exposures,' what appeared to be structures developing (sometimes
in the course of a series of shots done on the same occasion) over
Ted's partially visualized face and the structures behind his head—
that I thought might be rather tricky to bring off if one were
deliberately setting out to produce these effects by normal photo-

graphic processes. Mrs. Oehler, who impressed me as highly intelligent and quite sincere, assured me that some of these had emerged from the camera in front of her eyes, and in the presence of numbers of other witnesses. What impressed me most, however, were target shots where Ted had 'missed,' as he had with Professor X, but where what came up instead bore such an obvious associative relationship to the target as to constitute a peculiar type of hit for all but the pathologically skeptical or very stupid. In one picture, where Ted was asked by the people at a photographic research organization to come up with the Declaration of Independence, he produced instead an out-of-focus but still quite recognizable picture of three Revolutionary War soldiers in full regalia ("three revolutionary GI's," as Ted put it).

Another series of pictures which Mrs. Oehler showed me (and which I hope she will soon publish) Ted got in her presence when he was asked to shoot for the Chicago Art Institute. While 'aiming' and preparing to shoot, according to Mrs. Oehler, Ted remarked that he saw the lions in front of this building looking at each other. He was told that these lions did not face each other but were both facing forward, parallel to each other. Nevertheless, Ted claimed, he saw the lions facing each other, and that was the way he was going to shoot them. When the print was developed something showed up that was later identified as a view through the gardens and courtyard of a Jain temple in India, and on the print, not too clear but still readily identifiable, were the two lions on the gates of this temple—facing each other. (This is one of the pictures that were built up in successive shots.) On the same occasion, reportedly observed by several witnesses, Ted shot one picture which, before it was pulled from the camera and developed, he claimed to be of "a pile of rocks." This particular rock pile happened to be the Lion Gates of Mycenae, as was immediately verifiable from a comparison of Ted's shot with a picture of the original ancient 'rock pile.' It seemed that when Ted got on a target—in this case a 'lion kick'—there was no stopping him; and whatever was going on was beginning to look more exciting (to me, anyway) than Heinrich Schliemann's discovery of the Lion Gates themselves and of the vast storehouse of treasure in the buried site (which he had thought was ancient Troy) that ushered in a whole new era in archeology. The importance of the sort of thing Ted was doing in these 'misses,' if verifiable, I thought, was that it was right along the lines of the way the mind worked in dreams and other areas, and mirrored exactly the type of substitution of ideas through association demonstrable repeatedly in ordinary cognition and perception, and in creative thinking. It was particularly close to what is seen repeatedly in telepathic drawing experiments. In these experiments, one person, the so-called experimental agent, is asked to concentrate either on a picture chosen at random from a book, magazine, or other source, or on a drawing composed by himself, while another person, the so-called experimental percipient—stationed anywhere from a few feet away in the next room or, as was the case in experiments done in 1925 by Professor Gardner Murphy, then of Columbia University, and René Warcollier, a French chemical engineer, separated from his opposite number by a considerable distance—is asked to draw at the same time the image that comes to his mind. Surprisingly enough, a respectable percentage of these experiments are successful, but quite often the percipient's image bears less a direct configurational than an ideational or associative relationship to the target. As is true of ordinary perception, the data of extrasensory perception are filtered through the associative processes of the mind before they emerge in consciousness. I shall go into this more fully in later chapters.

Throughout my discussions with Mrs. Oehler of the pictures she had unloaded from a suitcase and spread out on a bed, Ted, who had shown up about noon, sat quietly in a corner, chain-smoking and looking vacantly into space, with no more apparent interest in what was going on than if Mrs. Oehler were showing samples of children's ware to an out-of-town buyer. I decided not to press him for more pictures that day, as I had enough to think about already. Besides, Jon had had no luck trying to locate a Geiger counter, so that Ted's somewhat extraordinary story of what happened when one was brought into the picture couldn't have been checked then, anyway. All this could wait, I felt.

CHAPTER IV

Roundup

A WEEK later, at my urging, Ted arrived in Denver. From the moment I saw him coming off the plane, obviously stoned, I knew we were in for trouble. With somewhat uncertain gait Ted was trying to keep up with a pair of priests who were hurrying along, facing grimly ahead as if to avoid seeing the portion of the Lord's work that lay right to hand. He was mumbling something to them, accompanied by a weird leer, that I didn't catch but which the brothers of the cloth apparently found not at all amusing. When he spotted me—and I could almost see the process of my taking shape out of the mists as his eyes struggled gallantly to fix me—he immediately started apologizing for the way things were. He hardly ever drank, he burbled, but it had just happened that his very good companions hadn't touched the drinks they were served en route and so, at their invitation, and because he needed something to steady his nerves aloft, he had had a couple of snifters in addition to the ones he had ordered for himself (and in addition, I concluded, to what he must have had before boarding).

It was all too horribly plain, I thought to myself as I went about trying to locate Ted's luggage, why no one had been able to develop an effective research plan with him, and I saw the collapse of my efforts before we even got started. It was just like everything else in this frustrating, hopeless, doomed field of research, I mused, trying to derive some comfort from the fact that I had at least described the almost uncanny way things could go wrong at crucial junctures in parapsychological research in the very paper that had brought me Fuller's letter about Ted in the first place. Now I knew why Fuller and the others in Chicago had called for some "responsible" organization or institution to work with Ted. Perhaps they had had the Department of Public Welfare or the Marine Corps in mind.

I drove Ted down to the apartment hotel where I have my office and where I had engaged a small furnished apartment for him. He'd get himself to bed, he insisted, so I left him sitting groggily in a chair and went home.

The next morning at ten, the rather hazily agreed upon time, I knocked on the door of Ted's apartment. When no answer was forthcoming I let myself in, as he had requested me to do in such a case, claiming that he tended to be a tight sleeper and often needed vigorous rousing. My man was nowhere around, as I quickly verified with hurried looks into the bathroom and dressing room. The bed was still made up and apparently had not been slept in. Ted's bags and trench coat were just where we had set them down the night before. On a coffee table in front of a couch was a card presenting one Gene Sorenson, sales representative of an industrial machinery concern with offices in Denver. I assumed, with sinking heart, that Messrs. Serios and Sorenson had been on the town and that the only problem now was to find out where Ted was sleeping it off. Very likely, I thought, his memory had become thick, not quite able to summon up the name or address of his apartment building, and he had stayed over somewhere with his buddy. Unfortunately it was Saturday; most industrial offices were closed, and no Gene Sorenson was listed in the phone book. I couldn't very well go to the police and ask them to look for a slight man with features somewhat like Voltaire's who may very well have told people in various bars a fantastic story about some top-secret mission that had brought him to Denver (and which, in fact, I regretted that I myself was not at the moment free to divulge).

All I could do was wait, so I trudged up a couple of flights to my office to see a patient to whom, I am afraid, I must have given

less than my keenest attention. With no sign of Ted in his apartment by eleven, I went down to the drugstore in the building to
make inquiries; and there he was, chatting gaily and gallantly with
the girl behind the counter like an accomplished boulevardier. He
greeted me cheerfully and explained that he had slept like a top,
had got up early and made his bed and had gone out to look for a
church where he could hear mass. I had little reason to doubt this,
as he was clean-shaven and tidy and looked as clear as an ad for
vitamins; but I couldn't quite comprehend his amazing powers
of recovery. This, as it developed, was merely one of the few
strange things about Ted that I would never quite be able to
understand. But there he was, anyway, ready and eager for work;
and from that time on, I am happy to report, his drinking, though
always considerably in evidence, rarely seemed to interfere too
much with what we were trying to accomplish. But other troubles
soon developed, which I shall mention in their place. I was to find
that my thesis about the inherent unrepeatability of psi experiments was far from washed up.

The first thing I did was to arrange for Ted to have a complete
medical and laboratory checkup. Everything turned out negative
except for one finding of undetermined significance, an elevated
blood sedimentation rate, frequently found in infections of various
origins but of no great significance if the clinical picture does not
bear it out. There were no active signs of an old pulmonary tuberculosis, for which Ted had spent fifteen months in a Chicago
municipal sanitarium some years before, and no signs, I was happy
to find, of any damage to liver or kidneys, despite years of what
would ordinarily be judged as drinking on a heroic scale.

For Ted's first working session in Denver we decided to aim
high. Since he kept harping on his desire for scientific vindication
and recognition—he had taken a lot of abuse from people, including 'scientists,' who had somehow managed to convince themselves
of his fraudulence without any kind of direct personal investigation (and I had come awfully close to this myself)—I thought it
would be helpful to his morale if several people in different fields
of science who were sympathetic to parapsychology, or at least to
me, could be present at our first rather simple and still more or
less informal test. Besides wanting to provide a stimulating audience for Ted, however, I thought it would be valuable to begin

immediately corralling witnesses of stature who might be willing
to testify publicly to whatever extraordinary findings they might
be lucky enough to observe. If nothing remarkable were to occur,
very little would be lost, since I would see to it that each of the
people I invited was well aware of the chancy nature of sessions
of this sort; but if Ted came through, we could immediately
capitalize on the public testimony of the witnesses to arrange for
broader participation in the still, I must confess, somewhat nebulous
program of investigation that I had more or less committed myself
to undertake. In addition, of course, I wanted people of competence
in several lines to aid me in controlling and observing the conditions of test.

I therefore invited for a session at my office to begin about
seven P.M., Thursday, April 16, five days after Ted's arrival in
Denver, the following people, to each of whom I tried as best
I could to explain in advance—and this took some explaining,
even with the help of reprints of Mrs. Oehler's paper which I sent
around—the nature of the problem: Dr. Paul Polak, Director of
Psychiatric Research at the Fort Logan Mental Health Center in
Denver; Dr. Joseph H. Rush, a physicist, specializing in optics,
with the National Center for Atmospheric Research, Boulder, Colorado; and Ray M. Wainwright, Professor of Electrical Engineering at Colorado State University, Fort Collins, Colorado, whose
specialty was electromagnetic theory. Dr. Rush and Prof. Wainwright I felt I could count upon to provide critical faculties of
high order, even though they were quite sympathetic to the psi
hypothesis, and Dr. Polak, a former student of mine whom I knew
to be a skeptic, albeit a benign one (I didn't think it wise to invite
a militantly hostile one to our first session), would provide a certain counterweight to the positive bias of the others and myself.
Prof. Wainwright asked if he might bring along another benevolent skeptic, Dr. Ralph Baker, Professor of Botany and Plant Path-
ology at Colorado State University, to whose participation I was of
course happy to agree—provided, I made plain, Dr. Baker would
have no objection to making his testimony, whatever it turned out
to be, publicly available. I requested each of the four to bring his
own camera and several rolls or packs of fresh, unopened film.

At seven on the appointed evening the invitees started arriving at my office. I had asked Miss Leslie Vandegrift, a graduate student at Denver University, who, while an undergraduate at the University of Colorado, had written a splendid critical thesis on problems of parapsychological research for a course in the philosophy of science, and who, I thought, might appreciate getting a firsthand look at some of these problems, to be on hand as a notetaker. My son John, who might best be described as at that time an ambivalent skeptic, I asked to be present to look after the development, fixing, and notating of the trial prints.

I had planned to stay as much in the background as possible once the participants had agreed upon conditions and procedure; but I wasn't prepared to find myself and my initial briefing on minimal conditions of control totally bypassed as everyone began frenziedly fiddling with tripods, flash equipment, and various extra props he had brought and ignoring the fact that at odd moments the cameras and film were left unguarded, and that either Ted or I could have switched films on them a dozen times in the first five minutes. I had to stop camera, call for order, and give a stern lecture on the necessity for absolute vigilance at every moment. Much chastened, the group settled down to a slower pace and promised sharper attention to detail. But it was immediately apparent that I had miscalculated in imagining that even those participants who were professedly sympathetic to the possible existence of phenomena such as we were hoping to witness could comport themselves as calm and, to at least some minimally necessary extent, detached observers. The atmosphere was electric with tension. Everyone looked as if he were momentarily about to witness Mephistopheles spring up out of a hissing sulphurous cloud. Only Ted seemed relaxed as he sat in a centrally placed chair and amusedly watched the fumbling preparations. He had already had a couple of double Scotches by the time we were ready to begin.

The following is from Miss Vandegrift's notes, after her listing of the participating personnel and cameras.

"Note: All pictures were taken in room light (two table lamps, two ceiling lights) unless otherwise noted. Mr. Serios used the cylinder in all pictures taken. Pictures are numbered according to the camera used and the number of pictures which had been taken previously on the roll in that camera.

"8:15. Dr. Eisenbud explains Ted's cylinder to witnesses.
"8:20. Ted has a 4 x 5 film from camera No. 3 out of the camera
which he wants to try getting a picture on.
"8:20. Dr. E. opens four factory-sealed film packages under the
eyes of witnesses; he loads camera No. 1. First casualty—Dr. Baker
cuts self on camera. Dr. E. searches for Band-aids. Ted still trying
for picture on 4 x 5 film in holder while Dr. E. bandages Dr. Baker.
Ted asks for wink light, and Wainwright brings No. 4 camera to
him."

I won't proceed with Miss Vandegrift's fairly detailed summary
of what was, on the whole, a very confused and most unlaboratory-
like set of procedures. Cameras were placed in Ted's hands in
more or less random sequence, with every now and then someone
taking a picture of Ted or the group or of himself in an attempt
to duplicate the conditions of Ted's picture-taking with the use of
the gismo, since no one knew exactly what a 'normal' picture under
the circumstances was supposed to look like.

The gismo used was the one Ted had used in our initial Palmer
House session, and which he had cheerfully let me keep after the
session. In the interval I had examined it closely and found it to
be exactly what it was claimed to be, merely a plastic cylinder,
about one-half inch in diameter and in height, with one end
covered with plain cellophane and the other with cellophane over
a piece of film darkened by stove black. There wasn't much in or
about it, so far as I could see, that could be used as a lens or for
the concealment of trick devices, but it was nevertheless comforting to have the others examine it from time to time. At times Ted
would hold the gismo a bit eccentrically over the lens opening, so
that a certain amount of light and some imagery—perhaps part of
his face or shirt—would show up, and at other times he would
manage, despite a good deal of straining and shaking, to hold the
gismo tightly over the lens opening, so that a complete blackie
would result. Several times the prints would emerge totally black
when one would expect, from observing the angle of emplacement
of the gismo, that some light would enter, and several times vague
patterns would emerge that seemed difficult to account for in
terms of the amount of light ostensibly available under the conditions of this or that trial (and which one or another of the observers seemed unable to duplicate in control shots), but on the

whole nothing of major interest turned up to stem the growing tide of impatience on all sides. People started wandering about the room aimlessly, getting Cokes or Seven-ups for themselves—I had barred alcoholic drinks on the grounds that I wanted everyone to retain maximum acuity for observation (all too plainly, however, the unspoken query after about an hour and a half, during which less than a dozen completely uninteresting shots had come forth, was, "Come, now, observation of *what?*")—and although the initial tension seemed to have abated, so had anything that looked like respectable interest or expectation. Only Dr. Baker, I noticed, kept a quiet but hawklike vigil over every movement Ted made, never once, so far as I could see, allowing Ted out of his sight and inconspicuously shifting his position or craning his neck when this became necessary. At length Ted himself became somewhat irritated at his lack of success, insisting that he needed another drink or two to insure a decent performance. At this point—he had already had an amount that would have put anybody else present under the table (but this, curiously, never got into Miss Vandegrift's notes)—I put this aspect of our experimental procedure squarely on a *quid pro quo* basis: no picture, no more drinks. A recess of fifteen minutes was called, during which Ted was allowed to go to the bathroom, with Dr. Polak detailed to accompany him and to watch closely for suspicious movements.

When we resumed at 9:40 Ted's first try was for something simple, just a plain plus sign, and it was agreed that if he got this he would have earned his drink. Dr. Rush's Graflex with a 4 x 5 Polaroid attachment, camera number 4, was used for this, and Ted gave it everything he had in the way of intense concentration. What came up was what the notes referred to as an "embryo structure" —something suspiciously a bit out of the ordinary, and not reproducible when an attempt was made to duplicate the conditions of shooting, but still not a recognizable structure or scene. No drink. Ted gave vent to various expressions of disgust, moderately pitched, he explained apologetically, because of Miss Vandegrift's presence. "If I only had a target—that picture I was looking at yesterday in your waiting room, Doc—I betcha I could get a building." I had forgotten all about the picture Ted was referring to, but I told him now that I had it right there, in a locked drawer in my desk. Would he like to have it?

This, now, is the story of how this picture had gotten into my desk drawer. Just before six P.M. on the day before, after my last patient for the day had left, I came into the waiting room to find Ted looking appreciatively at a full-page picture of Westminster Abbey in a 1961 issue of the British Travel Association magazine, *Coming Events in Britain*. "Doc, this is the kind of thing I know I could get." "Fine," I said, "maybe you will someday." While Ted stepped into the bathroom for a minute I took the magazine into the adjoining consulting room and shoved it into the top drawer of my desk, after having first stuck it into a clasp envelope. I relocked the desk (which is ordinarily kept locked because it houses notes on patients) and went out to join Ted in the vestibule, saying nothing to him of what I had done.

So out came the envelope enclosing the magazine carrying the picture of Westminster Abbey when Ted brought it up the next night. When I started to pull the magazine from the envelope, Ted insisted that I reinsert it—it was still folded closed—and put the envelope back in the drawer. Then he changed his mind and asked if he could have the envelope in order to sketch on it his impressions of the picture he had seen the night before. This done (fig. 7), he again asked that the envelope be put back into the drawer. I did so and locked the drawer once more. At this point I shall allow Miss Vandegrift's notes to take over.

"9:50. Dr. E. seals magazine in envelope; Ted will attempt to get a picture of cathedral shown in magazine. Ted decides to draw on outside of envelope picture he is seeing mentally.

"9:55—(3-5). [Fifth shot on camera number 3] f 8, 1/50, focus approx. 2 ft. Cylinder close to lens and vibrating above it; ordinarily a blob should show in center of film. Black cat.

"9:58—(3-6). Same setting as 3-5. Test picture (control). Ted asked not to try for anything, just to take picture under conditions of 3-5 shot. Bl. cat.

"10:11—(2-3). No wink light. Cylinder touching lens, but at angle. Bl. cat.

"10:20—(3-7). Ted attempts plus symbol using cylinder with transparent end toward lens and almost touching. Focus at 2 ft., 1/25, f 8. Bl. cat.

"10:25—(4-4). Attempt for a building."

Ted by now was far off course again, and the thrice-forgotten

(Fig. 7)

Abbey was still locked in the obscurity of my desk drawer. (Miss Vandegrift, it will be noticed, had neglected to mention that it had been put back again.) He had gone back to trying for a plus, on the seventh picture on Dr. Rush's Graflex, and five minutes later, at 10:25, he tried for a building—any building—on Prof. Wainwright's model 95. This fourth shot, on Wainwright's camera, showed considerable fogging and, in terms of my later experience with the limits of variation of normal shots, would have been adjudged as presumptively paranormal, as a sign that something was cooking. At this time, however, with long intervals between shots and with hardly anybody paying much attention any longer to what was coming out of the cameras when Ted did bestir himself for a try, it passed unremarked and simply took its place with a dozen or so other prints on the processing shelf in the adjoining kitchenette, which, with the separating fold door pushed to one side, opened full upon the main room. Ted himself made no comment on 4-4 but, still holding Wainwright's camera, asked if

he might change his chair ("Do you mind if . . ." was his usual
way of putting these requests), stating that this sometimes helped
in getting pictures. He then went to a corner of the room and
plunked himself down in my analytic chair, Dr. Baker watching
from where he was sitting on the couch about three feet away, and
asked if we would mind his turning off the table lamp on his right.
We had no objection, since there was still ample light for close
observation from an overhead light several feet away. He then
asked Dr. Polak to place his finger on the gismo while he shot,
and instructed him just how to do this, stating that this too sometimes helped in getting pictures, especially when he felt *simpatico*
with one of the audience. Dr. Polak obliged, with an embarrassed
grin, and as Ted got ready to shoot he stated that he was again
going to try for a building. Here, once more, the official notes:

> "10:30—(4-5). Ted sitting in SW corner of room with lamp off; asks
> Polak to touch cylinder as he tried for a building. After shot, Ted
> says the picture was delayed slightly—evidently [sic] wink light and
> film button not synchronized."

For the first time, now, something really interesting emerged,
but no one could quite make out what it was. Everyone agreed that
it was a structure of some sort that definitely would not be expected to result from normal exposure under the conditions employed, and that what appeared to be straight lines in it—the print
was turned this way and that (fig. 8) for inspection, while I
anxiously cautioned everyone to hold it only by its edges—might
even suggest a building. We finally gave it over to John for num-
bering and fixing, and it took its place with the others on the
drying shelf. Ted, meanwhile, got set for more shooting and it
was not until almost fifteen minutes and three prints (out of three
different cameras) later, with people wandering at intervals into
the kitchenette to take further looks at the puzzling 4-5, that it
occurred to anyone that Ted after all had, if we were charitably to
allow a certain latitude, met the minimal conditions for another
drink. It was certainly *something*. So Ted got his Scotch on the
rocks and we settled down to further shooting, feeling considerably
encouraged and revitalized by a sign that the evening had at least
not been a complete failure. Ted went back to trying for plus
symbols, and at 11:10 said he would try again for Westminster

(Fig. 8)

Abbey, this time asking that the magazine in its envelope be taken out of the drawer and held in front of him. The flash failed on this one (3-9) and only a black cat was pulled. Ted rested for a few minutes, took his socks off ("Do you mind if . . .") and began to complain of headache, although he did not want to give up, feeling that he would get something yet. The magazine went back into my desk.

Suddenly came a yell from the kitchenette, "Hey, this *is* a building; can't you see?—look at it this way . . ." John stepped out of the kitchenette holding print 4-5, which had now dried, and all at once it became apparent to all of us that it was indeed a building. But I saw more. "Wait a minute," I exclaimed, and immediately unlocked my desk once more to get out the envelope with the picture of Westminster Abbey. After fumbling to get the magazine out and open to the correct page, I held it up for everybody to see (fig. 9). Ted's picture was a beautiful match for one part of the clock tower of the Abbey (fig. 10).

Great excitement! Dr. Polak, who had hardly been able to suppress his feeling of utter foolishness a little while before when the picture was shot, was now dumb with amazement. The others

WESTMINSTER ABBEY, whose Christmas Eve peal follows a short time after the bells of St. Paul's have started to ring out over London. Another peal is rung on Christmas Day. The Abbey's eight bells hang in the left-hand tower.

(Fig. 9)

(Fig. 10)

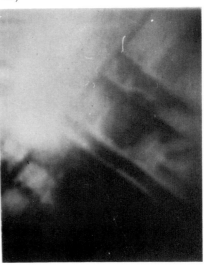

were equally affected—all, it seemed, but Dr. Baker, who still had his eyes glued on Ted and who could hardly be induced to steal a quick look at the triumphant print. I ordered grog to all hands.

When the excitement had abated somewhat, everyone began scrutinizing Ted's picture more closely. It was noticed right away that the image Ted had produced was not an exact copy of a portion of the target picture but rather—however this came about (no one presumed to offer a speculation as to the mechanism of what was going on)—an image shot from a slightly different angle and with distinctly different shadows showing up. I shall say nothing about this curious circumstance now, but will return to it in a later chapter. Here I will remark only upon the curious fact, which impressed itself on everyone, that the print did not seem to present itself as a definite structure immediately upon being pulled, but rather as a series of lines suggesting merely that something other than an image within the narrow range of hitherto observed configurations was coming through. The lines did not at first arrange themselves into a pattern which the mind took in as one of light and shade on a structure conveying the information: building. It brought home to us the well-known fact, which I was to see illustrated many times in the months to come, that without some sort of implicit set of expectations, perception and cognition are very variable and infirm functions and not just matters of physical sensory stimulus and automatic mental response. The vagaries of perception were here compounded by the shock effect of seeing any organized or meaningful pattern at all emerging under the 'impossible' circumstances obtaining, and no doubt also by the distracting highlights from the still drying, liquid print-fixer.

After a short rest Ted once more called for a camera; but everyone soon agreed, what with Ted now well into a sloppy phase and scarcely able to make a direct hit on the trigger when he felt ready to fire (much less, it was felt, on any target he may have had nestling somewhere in the deeps of his mind), that any further yield would be highly problematical. This, as later sessions under very much the same conditions were to demonstrate, was a most unjustified assumption, but it was decided, at any rate, to call an end to the session. No one felt cheated, least of all I, but Ted grumbled some about his having failed and about our not having given him a chance to prove himself. The more he was reassured that he was far from a failure and that he had, in fact, been a dazzling success, the more he kept mumbling dejectedly. I could see that he was lapping it up.

For my part I felt that the magnificent payoff warranted my having risked so much on this first throw. I had won what I knew would be the unqualified support of four strong figures who would stand staunchly at my side in the many battles ahead. Drs. Baker, Polak, Rush, and Wainwright, each without demur, signed testimonial statements regarding the conditions of trial—camera status, film loading, and so forth, and the conditions of observation—visibility, opportunities for inspection, and other things that might have appeared relevant along this line. Each stated that he was unable to formulate a specific hypothesis as to how the Westminster Abbey picture might have been produced. Only Dr. Rush added a formally correct note of caution to his statement. "So far as one can judge from a single experience," he wrote, "the production of the one recognizable photo seems inexplicable." I sided with him when the others took exception to his emphasizing that we had only one instance to go on. The problem, as I saw it, was not the validity of the well-known syllogism to the effect that it takes only one white crow to demonstrate that not all crows are black, but the difficulties in the way of proving that what you had was in fact a white crow. However, the witnesses were not in this instance required to come to any opinion as to the normality or paranormality of what they had seen but merely to state the conditions of test as they had observed them, and whether they could or could not account for the data observed in terms of plausible hypotheses.

Nevertheless, I felt that I had now to point out to my guests that they had been guilty of a more serious breach of circumspection than in the area of merely making formal inferences, a breach which would vitiate their observations and conclusions for some and completely nullify their value for others. The breach lay in the fact that the print, which, as I remarked earlier, was at first regarded merely as a conglomeration of lines of indefinite significance and only later recognized as a definite structure, had been allowed out of sight for some lapse of time before it was marked for subsequent identification by their signatures. Even though the print in question had gone no farther than the little kitchenette directly off the main room and thus was potentially within everyone's line of vision at all times, no precaution had been taken to insure that it actually was in someone's sight at every instant until the signing had taken place. It was thus hypothetically possible, even though people kept wandering over to the table in the kitchenette at odd moments to have a look at the puzzling print, for a switch to have been perpetrated at some instant when the print happened to be totally unguarded. No one experienced in the standard methods of investigation in this field would under the circumstances have accepted the evidence as anything but suggestive yet also inexcusably deficient in those safeguards which have become the hallmark of good investigative procedure. Since to my knowledge I was the only one who could have pulled the switch in this instance, I dropped the matter. A first-rate investigator, under other circumstances, would not have. He would have carefully considered the hypothesis of each of the others, down to my son John, having attempted, for whatever reason (the irrelevance of the ostensible lack of motives in such situations I shall have occasion to touch upon later), to perpetrate a fraud and would have studiously examined the possibilities of his having done so.

I made a mental note thenceforth never to permit observers to take their eyes off a possibly or presumptively paranormal shot until someone other than myself had witnessed it with his signature; nor have I ever done so.

CHAPTER V

Alarums and Excursions

DR. RUSH took the gismo along with him that night for home study. His report, which I received a few days later when he returned the mysterious object, more or less eliminated it as a justifiable source of suspicion. There was, he stated, no discernible break in the cellophane covering the open ends of the thing to enable it to provide a pinhole camera effect, nor did he discover anything else about it that might provide or play in with any normal system for producing images of photographic appearance. Besides, he concluded, there simply was not enough light getting through, when the gismo was held even loosely against the lens, to permit the normal reproduction of any image source that might have been concealed in it, quite apart from the fact that a lens of very much greater refractive power would have been necessary at the close range at which the gismo was being held.

Dr. Rush's report was reassuring; but it did not still the quivering doubts which started to rise in me as soon as I got some distance away from the test experience. Moreover, I found myself quite unprepared for the strength and pernicious quality of these doubts. Certainly an attitude of canny caution and systematic skepticism should be expected of anyone undertaking to test a hypothesis according to conventional canons of scientific inquiry. But not the kind of gnawing, festering doubt—for the most part doubt of nothing I could even put my finger on, doubt in the abstract, doubt accompanied by feelings of resentment, as if I had been rudely tricked, duped, outwitted—that took possession of me as soon as the aura of triumph produced by the emergence of the Westminster Abbey print wore off. It was suddenly as if the earlier pictures I had witnessed, even with the peculiar meaningfulness factor that I have already alluded to and will come back to later, counted for nothing, as if I had to start the long steep hill all over again. This kind of almost obsessional doubt—which oddly co-existed with an attitude that at peak moments was, justified or not, its exact opposite—I was to observe in myself many times in the months to come, many times before, I might say, the cumulative force of the data reduced it finally and for good to the vanishing point. I can compare this doubt qualitatively only to the kind of morbid suspiciousness seen in lovers and pathologically jealous married people that I have often seen in my practice, a suspiciousness that is lulled only by continual and never wholly successful attestations of fidelity on the part of the suspected partner only to renew its painful beating at the mind sometimes after only a few hours, requiring ever stronger proofs. This doubt had nothing to do with logic or evidence; it was just an ache, a spasm of the fractured mind.

I was aware that similar reactions were not uncommon among experienced investigators of psychical phenomena and had led some of them, in fact, to leave the field because of their inability to resolve them. The irrationality of this kind of morbid doubt was beautifully expressed by a brilliant British investigator, Everard Feilding, in his delightfully written notes on a series of sittings (carried out in 1908 with two other experienced investigators) with the noted physical medium, Eusapia Palladino. This illiterate but quite remarkable Italian peasant woman, who on occasion had been caught in flagrant fraud, nevertheless on other occasions could be observed under conditions of most stringent control to cause objects to move by means unknown—that is, without physical contact of any discoverable sort, and to cause other strange things to happen that I won't even mention here for fear that the reader with all his buttons will lay this book down and

turn to something like good science fiction or a James Bond bit of
nonsense. "If Eusapia's psychology is a puzzle to us," Feilding
wrote, "we find that our own is scarcely less so." He observed
that so marked was his and the other investigators' need to
resolve the painful ambivalence occasioned in them by the
contradictoriness of what they saw when stacked up against ordinary experience and their habitual ways of regarding things that
they hailed with relief some minor break in control technique that
theoretically made it possible for their already mentally indicted
culprit to outflank some precaution, and kept looking hopefully
for the definite indications of fraud that would once and for all
put their minds at rest. Again and again their eagerness to resolve
an almost unbearable emotional confusion tricked them into believing that such signs had been found, only to discover, upon
reference to the notes carefully dictated to a shorthand stenog-
rapher present at the sittings, that what they had hoped would
prove to be a lapse in some condition of control was in fact not
such at all. (I was later to find exactly this sort of thing operative
in witnesses to Ted's phenomena.) On the other hand, they tended
to minimize and even to blot out altogether the recollection of
certain very positive data, which again later emerged only from
study of the carefully compiled protocols of the séances. Even
then, upon study of the records immediately after or shortly
following certain sittings, Feilding and his collaborators found
themselves emotionally unable to take in what they were forced
intellectually to admit they had witnessed. "It is nevertheless a
satisfaction to me," Feilding wrote, "that these notes exist as a
record of our critical, indeed hostile state of mind . . . We preferred to believe that we had been deceived in some way unknown,
that we had been hallucinated, or had wrongly observed. We
doubted our senses rather than our experience; were guided, in
fact, by our emotions rather than our observation."

I soon found myself wondering if Ted could not in some way
have fraudulently produced the image that matched, even if it
was not an exact copy of, a portion of the Westminster Abbey
target picture. It wasn't as if I were able to come up with a concrete proposal as to *how* he might have done this, any more than
Dr. Rush or the others could; but the very fact that he had seen
the picture in a magazine at least twenty-four hours and possibly

several days before the test and had been, when one came right down to it, himself the one who had suggested this as a target at the time of the session, introduced certain notions that seemed to take off on their own, quite apart from any question of the still-unsolved and indeed seemingly insoluble physical mechanism of producing fraudulent prints under the conditions that obtained. Was it not possible for him, even in twenty-four hours, to have availed himself of pictures of this face of Westminster Abbey from which he could have made a microprint? And could we neglect the fact that just before this print had emerged he had, in his innocent if slightly disingenuous way, asked if we minded if he changed his position, whereupon he had somehow got himself over to the chair in the southwest corner of the room and even— again, of course, after asking if we minded—managed to turn out the lamp that would normally have been shining over his shoulder? Who had observed his movements as he went over to this new position? The notes said nothing about what he was carrying in his hands (it was my recollection that he had the camera with him), or in fact about how many of the five of us were closely observing every single movement. These things were not positively noted in the record because no one, naturally, had the slightest inkling that the Big Event was about to occur. But was it enough, in retrospect, to rely simply on the fact that no suspicious-looking movements had been positively noted, or that a couple of observers had claimed afterward that they had watched every single step? What about Dr. Polak's finger touching the gismo? This is just the sort of thing I imagined might be introduced by a trickster to allay suspicion. Was it possible for something fishy to have taken place under cover of this ostensible proof of closeness?

As I look back at this period, it is of course apparent, as I have already indicated, that my doubts and alarms were nowhere near as rationally grounded as they then appeared to be; but then I didn't have at that time the benefit of the months of observation, data gathering, and rumination that later settled certain issues. So let's get on with the story.

It was obvious after the session that produced the Westminster Abbey print that, despite my nightmarish doubts, there was no place to go but forward. But how? What sort of plan of action could be formulated? Thinking up things to try experimentally

with Ted, assuming even the alleged going rate of one out of three
sessions with a positive yield, was not terribly difficult to begin
with; on the plane back from Chicago after our initial session I
had jotted down a number of hypotheses which could be fairly
easily tested. But even these would require some organization and
help to be done right, to say nothing of more sophisticated experimentation, especially in which instrumentation of some kind
might be required. On the other hand, if I kept Ted doing the
same things, the things he was habituated to doing, just to insure
at least his minimally expected rate of success each time he exhibited his 'thoughtography' to people whose interest and support
might sooner or later be of value, we wouldn't get very far beyond
the point we already were and by the time we got the support we
needed lined up, his powers might have waned or disappeared
altogether, as had all too often been the case with other gifted
psychics.

Meanwhile there was the problem of how to keep Ted happy
and occupied in Denver. At the moment he seemed perfectly
satisfied to go along from day to day; he even talked of leaving
Chicago and settling in Denver permanently. But how long this
mood would last was problematical since it was already plain that
Ted's inner resources (paradoxically, in view of his presumptive
abilities) were very limited. Away from his usual haunts and
cronies he would probably soon get bored. The hours when he
was accustomed to hit his familiar beer joints in Chicago, from
midnight until four or five in the morning, were usually empty
for him here, and when he did try making the rounds one night
he succeeded merely in getting picked up and questioned by the
police as a suspicious character, which hardly endeared the pride
of the Rockies to him. During the day—he generally rose at one
or two in the afternoon—he showed no interest in doing anything
beyond lying around in his apartment and guzzling beer when I
wasn't with him; and although he occasionally glanced at *Popular
Mechanics* or printed material having to do with model railroads,
which he claimed as one of his hobbies, reading was obviously not
one of his major diversions. Nor were movies or television; in fact,
it was impossible to get him to go to a movie or to look for more
than a few moments at television. Sometimes, when several of my
family were watching a program, Ted could be seen sitting near

the set but facing the other way, the typical faraway look on his face as he chain-smoked in silence in the semidarkness. It struck me, after a number of unsuccessful attempts to get him interested in some movie or other program, that he was just plain bored with anything outside of himself, since talk about himself, his powers, his ideas, what other people thought and said about him, was the one thing he would spontaneously join in. Indeed, at the dinner table, or at other times, it required a certain skill on the part of those with Ted to lure the talk away from him as its subject and to keep it in play for any length of time in some other corner of the conversational field. As to anything ordinarily referred to as a gainful occupation, this was nothing that Ted felt any inclination to look into. He pointedly ignored every hint I dropped about the great advantages of his holding a part-time job which, besides perhaps providing something of interest to do, might even supplement his pocket money while the financial picture was (hopefully) getting straightened out. Ted's indifference to these issues was something lordly.

I had no idea at this time of how often Ted could or would care to work at his thoughtography. According to him, the effort he put out in his sessions was so prodigious that he usually ended up coughing blood and frequently bleeding from the rectum, and for this reason the most he felt he could comfortably work at picture-shooting was once a week, twice in a pinch. This, if adhered to, would of course impose such a glacially slow time scale on any research effort that it was difficult to see how experiments in which certain conditions were systematically varied, in order to test specific psychological, physiological or physical hypotheses, could be effectively designed and carried out. I could begin to see why no firm opinion of even the genuineness of the phenomenon had been arrived at by Dr. R and his staff at the industrial research laboratory after three months' study.

The ideal thing, it seemed to me, would be to have some department at the University of Colorado Medical School take Ted over and to have the full-time researchers there worry about how to take care of him and what to do with him (I, of course, being retained in the capacity of consultant emeritus). I felt that even on the basis of the reports of others and what I myself had already witnessed (and despite my middle-of-the-night broodings to the contrary) Ted should by rights be put on a par with a nuclear reactor as far as his possible importance to biological research went. Yet how many of my colleagues at the school would see him in this light, I wondered, or even recognize in him another Alexis St. Martin, the Canadian woodsman who over one hundred years ago became one of the most valuable subjects in the history of medical research by virtue of having suffered a gunshot wound in his abdomen, enabling William Beaumont, the United States army surgeon in Vermont who took him in charge, to keep open a window into the chemical laboratory of the stomach? St. Martin could very well have expired in committee today were he to come stumbling into one of the hugely complex research organizations that go in for teaching medical students as a sideline, and I knew that Ted could easily suffer the same fate, even granting that I could get one of the departments to take an initial look at what I thought Ted might offer, a prospect, judging from the entire history of psychical research, which was by no means rosy.

I thought nevertheless that it would be worthwhile having the Dean of the Medical School, Dr. John J. Conger, take a look at Ted on an unofficial basis—somewhat like getting a friend who happened also to be a judge to comment during a poker or golf game on how he might be likely to rule on your case. I also felt that Conger was a natural for a front-row seat because, besides his academic and administrative position, he was an experienced researcher in psychology and might even be seduced into taking a personal interest in the matter. The problem was how to put it to him. Despite his knowing all about my psi activities—like others of my friends he managed to preserve a benevolent but still quite skeptical tolerance of them—I could hardly ring him up and ask him casually how he'd like to take a look at a chap who projected photographs from his mind onto Polaroid film. Besides, I realized that in his capacity as representative of the university he had to watch his p's and q's as far as the public, the state authorities, and various public and private sources of funds for administration and research went. (I was once told by an administrative officer before Conger's time that the Medical School couldn't chance having me doing psi research officially for fear of jeopardizing funds for cancer research.) Still, I felt that it was due him, in both public and private capacities, to be advised of what I thought we had in Ted.

So I rang him up and very simply asked if he could come to my home some evening "on a matter of considerable interest and importance." He had to leave town for a week, but he named a date about ten days away, which was fine, as it would give me plenty of time to prepare the scene. My plan was to have the original Four Horsemen of the New Apocalypse, Drs. Baker, Polak, Rush, and Wainwright, present as backup men when I made my presentation, to have Ted go into his act—and to see what happened. It would not be like risking everything on the turn of a card; if Ted came through, I could count on a powerful, if perhaps at the moment necessarily rather hog-tied and inactive ally. If he didn't, we were simply back where we started from. Instead of formulating a positive blueprint for action, thus, I was merely stirring the broth.

Luckily I was able to get the Four Horsemen for the evening the Dean was free, and I set about grooming Ted for his official debut into the big time. For the next ten days I watched over him as if he were an Olympic athlete. Certainly no queen or princess of the blood, to switch metaphors, ever had better prenatal care. I watched his diet and his bowels (he claimed that he tended toward constipation, and that when he was really stopped up his pictures either didn't come or were very hard to make out) and tried to limit his alcohol consumption somewhat, seeing to it, nevertheless, that he got only the best stuff for his daily ration, which was still considerable according to my standards. I had him rechecked medically and saw to it that some long-needed dental work was begun. (Ted had to be restrained from jutting out his lower jaw when impressions were made; he wanted to come out, he insisted, looking like Barry Goldwater.) Since he was of the opinion, which later proved quite erroneous, that he did better with the camera when he had been off the girls for a while, I didn't have to concern myself immediately with that aspect of things; but I did get an earful about his likes and dislikes and his overall philosophy in that sphere, which, while somewhat less wordy, was not too unlike that of *Playboy* magazine. I took long walks and drives with him, got him on a horse in the mountains ("Boy, breathe that air! Get ridda all that cancer!") and even dropped into a beer and billiard club with him once or twice to shoot a couple of games of pool. I found out that he was—or could be, if he weren't always giving his queen away—a clever chess player, when I could induce him, that is, to turn his thoughts to something other than himself for a while. But this wasn't often, and for the most part, whether walking, driving, dining, or just sitting around, we talked of nothing but Ted and the Big Day, which, despite my all too deeply felt cautions against unwarranted optimism, he insisted on viewing as the gateway to immediate acceptance by the scientific world. He spent hours talking about how he was going to make a certain newspaper woman eat (and perform other functions with) her article about him in the *Chicago Tribune* in which she had more than hinted that his whole act was nothing that a skilled photographer couldn't master with a little patience and a small mirror. He vowed that he'd get a picture of her in the bathroom, on the toilet, and that he'd insist that it be carried on the first page of the *Trib;* and there were just as deadly salvos against other people who had denied or doubted him, who had snubbed or slighted him. He was going to get them all. Wait till they had heard that the Dean of the Medical School had witnessed his performance at first hand. Just wait.

I waited. Every day Ted would pick me up at the end of my office hours and we would drive to my home where another evening of nervous waiting began. Once I thought the whole venture was about to explode when Ted flung out of the house in a rage because a teenage son, obviously jealous of the amount of time and attention I was devoting to Ted, had spoken sharply to him over some minor matter; but I hurried after him and managed to calm him down, and as the hours neared for the final countdown Ted never appeared in better shape. I deposited him in his room the night before D-day with the suggestion that he sleep late and not bother to get together with me for lunch but simply pick me up as usual at six the next evening before going home with me to meet the Four Horsemen and the Dean. And that, my friends, was the last I saw of Ted for quite a while—the last, in fact, that I thought next evening I would ever see of him.

When six o'clock rolled around I was already somewhat anxious, because I hadn't heard the faint opening and closing of the outer door to my office that usually signified Ted's slipping into the waiting room to be ready for me when my last patient had gone. He was not there when I went in to check. Sprucing up no doubt, I thought hopefully as I recalled that Ted liked to shower and shave at this time. I waited another couple of minutes and then decided to walk down to his floor, thinking that I might meet him on the stairs coming up. I didn't, and when I got to his apartment there was no answer to my knock. It couldn't be, I told myself, but with mounting anxiety I let myself in and at once saw that the place was empty. The closets were bare; no bags or clothing lay around. Ted had cleared out. On the desk was a simple note to me, alongside one he had evidently left for himself the day before which said, in big block letters, NOTIS TO ME— GET SHIRTS FROM LONDRY. The note to me, which I read in blank dismay, said simply: "Dear Doc—Id miss on the test any way Didn't want to Dispoint you."

That night the Four Horsemen and I regaled the incredulous Dean with a blow-by-blow account of what he was missing. I had discussed with them the unfathomable ways of gifted psychics, and everyone took Ted's defection in good part; but the question now was where to go from here. The dean promised a rain check if ever I could get Ted back again, and that's where we left matters. The following morning a telegram from Ted in Chicago stated simply—as if he had completely forgotten about the note he had left—STOP TEST TONIGHT (sic) MOTHER IS SICK.

For the next couple of days I seriously considered turning my back on Ted and the whole business. I foresaw endless troubles ahead. Continuing was tantamount to signing over several months or years of my life for a mess of pottage that might turn out to be very thin gruel indeed.

Nevertheless, I finally phoned the nursing home that Ted's mother ran in Chicago, in order to inquire about her. I couldn't delude myself into imagining that I could do anything other than go ahead, or that I was anything other than wholly committed, win, lose, or draw. (Why should I expect nature to offer up her secrets in gift-wrapped packages?) Mrs. Esther Serios herself got on the phone and for a few minutes we engaged in double-talk as I introduced myself and she, sensing something amiss and evidently quite used to covering up for her son, adroitly tried to fish out of me what the situation was. She seemed utterly blank when

I asked about her health, offering only that she wasn't getting any younger but that for her years—I had gathered from Ted that she was in her mid-seventies—she wasn't doing so badly.

The next day Ted phoned. He had simply gone home, he stated, to collect his things, and he'd be back as soon as he had taken care of a few pressing matters. He mumbled something about having to sign some papers for his mother (or was it a wife or an ex-wife somewhere in the incredibly, maddeningly murky picture?). No mention of having stood me and the others up, of his note or his telegram. When I asked directly about his mother's illness, he seemed to go blank for a moment but quickly recovered. Illness? Yes, she had been ill, in the hospital, with a heart attack. She was fine now.

It was now perfectly clear, if I had somehow conned myself out of this insight earlier, that I was dealing with a very strange person indeed, and that any question of how to proceed—scientifically, promotionally, or on any other front—was largely academic so long as my understanding of and technique for keeping Ted effectively in tow were lacking.

I wired Ted some money and hoped for the best. In a few days he came boiling into town in a borrowed car that had broken down several times en route. Piled high in it appeared to be everything Ted owned in the world, including sets of tools, a miniature lathe, parts of model trains, and various books on mechanics, World War I aces and airplanes, and model railroading. He was through with Chicago, he claimed, and wanted to look for permanent digs in Denver so that he could be near me and continue to experiment. This sounded like a windfall to me; but what I didn't know was that he was far from through with Chicago or vice versa, and that the only reason he had cleared out was that he was hoping in this way—by being out of state—to escape a somewhat bothersome problem that had developed back in Chicago. Several weeks later, when I was asked to arrange for Ted to give power of attorney to lawyers whom Curtis Fuller had brought in on the case (but who later withdrew when the confusion, the double-talk, and the aura of bewildering unreality that usually surrounds Ted and his doings proved too taxing for their talents), I found out that Ted, who claimed that he had only been looking for a place to hear mass after all the bars in town had closed, had got into a tussle with the police when he was caught driving without lights or license, drunk, speeding, passing lights and stop signs, and proceeding the wrong way on a one-way street. From what I was later able to piece together from several sources, Ted had also been charged with resisting arrest and assaulting an officer, both these charges being more or less technical. The former charge had been the consequence of his having led the cops a Keystone-comedy chase before being run up onto a sidewalk and cornered ("Where'd the goddam street go?" he is reported to have said at this point) and the latter of his having grabbed the keys from a turnkey just as he was being ushered into a cell and, according to the charge, pushing the officer into the cell and locking him in.

Another meeting was arranged with Dean Conger, but this time I let the Four Horsemen out to pasture and invited only Dr. Martin Alexander, a physician who had examined Ted medically, and Mr. Joseph Igo, a keenly interested friend. This time I decided to introduce a cautionary measure that hadn't been employed in the earlier session, even though I still wanted to keep everything as informal as possible. Since the gismo was always and inevitably a source of suspicion, I asked those present to examine it closely (I used the one that Dr. Rush had returned) and to sign a piece of paper which was then taped around it with cellophane. This was to eliminate the possibility that they could examine one gismo only to have another similar-looking one slipped in as a substitute when their attention was diverted. To make doubly sure that the gismo they had examined would be the one used, a string was put through it and tied into a loop that Dr. Conger was then asked to wear around his neck, which would tether it with about a two-foot play. Conger thus always sat close to Ted, and when Ted wanted to shoot he would simply reach for the gismo dangling from Conger's neck. To complete the precautions used at this session, Ted was stripped to the waist and examined, after which he put on a black sleeveless knitted sport shirt. Alexander supplied the camera. Randomization, this time, was achieved with the aid of a table of random numbers.

Ted started out quite casually, smoking, drinking, chatting, and joking, and asking that the camera be handed him only at five or

ten minute intervals. Nothing out of the ordinary showed up. At
first the witnesses were anxiously expectant, tensely leaning forward with each shot and looking, as had the Four Horsemen at
the start of their session, as if the Evil One himself were about to
materialize. After the first hour, they began to relax and even to
show signs of boredom. Ted, whether he sensed this or not, kept
assuring everyone that they had nothing to worry about, that he
felt as hot as a pistol and would get something. When he had to
go to the toilet one of the witnesses was delegated to go along to
see that no hanky-panky took place. He was ecstatic when he
emerged after Conger's turn to accompany him, claiming that
this would have a high place in his memoirs—the Dean of a Medical School supervising his taking a leak.

During the second hour, with Ted again shooting only every
five or ten minutes and spending the rest of the time telling everyone of his past successes, of what he had done that time for this one
and for that one, of the beauty he had got for Dr. R of the industrial research laboratory, of how he had foxed Dr. P, who thought
he had swallowed some uranium, still nothing showed. He was
now well aloft on alcohol. The invitees were getting restive and
beginning to look at their watches, and I started to wonder somewhat anxiously how long I could keep them there at this rate. I
had already written off the evening as a failure, and I'm sure the
others had too but were simply waiting, like guests at a dinner
party, for the moment when they could decently take their leave.
By ten o'clock Ted was in the mumbling and muttering stage, his
eyes bleary and hooded, his utterances getting progressively of-
fensive and unfunny. When, at one point, I banned further drinking, he lashed out, wanting to know if he was boring me. He
insisted that we were rushing him, not giving him a chance, and
started lunging around the room looking for the Scotch. I shoved
him back into his seat. In my mind the impossibility of the whole
project was now obvious. How could I get others to sit in on Ted's
sessions once word got around that the evening amounted to
watching a witless drunk go through the motions of trying to bring
off something that only a witless drunk and his deluded impresario
could believe to be possible?

No one was amused. I was furious at myself and Ted for having

(Fig. 11)

allowed things to come to this pass. I suggested that we quit. Ted wouldn't hear of it. "Goddam it," he exploded, "gimme a camera! I'll show you that I can get one. Here put your hand over mine," he said to Dr. Conger as a camera was handed to him and he prepared to shoot. "Now just hold it there." Conger had his palm flat over the gismo, which Ted was holding with his two fingers. "There," he exclaimed as he shot, "put that in your pipe and smoke it."

This time there was no question about identifying what emerged. The double-decker bus that Ted had managed somehow to come up with (fig. 11), and which I doubt he was sober enough at that moment to have boarded at the right end if it had stopped squarely in front of him, was perfectly clear. Its effect, of course, was electrifying to an audience which, including me, had been just a moment before restless, bored, and irritated. Conger immediately started examining the gismo, which was still hanging from a thread around his neck, as if he half expected to see Aladdin's genie materialize from it. He was too dumbfounded to say anything, but I could see that he was thinking that he had enough to worry about without *this*.

I did not on this occasion ask my guests to sign statements as to what they had witnessed, but each signed the bus print on its reverse side.

CHAPTER VI

Trials and Tribulations

DURING the next several weeks I did a few informal experiments with Ted, a kind of playing around which every investigator knows to be strictly invalid in so far as making reliable inferences from the data goes, but which most people given to research have always indulged in anyway. Needless to say, it is and always has been the backbone of science. Unfortunately, one never knows whether the answers one gets from this kind of impatient short-cut—whatever they are, positive or negative, in the usual sense—will stand up when test conditions are laid down in which every identifiable variable is taken care of and every conceivable alternative hypothesis to the one which you think your shortcut favored, including of course the hypothesis of chance, is taken into account. But this is difficult to arrange when the material and facilities available for investigation are limited. I would have needed ten Teds, ten times as much time, and at least ten of me or my weight in assistance in order to carry out well-prepared experiments along the lines I had in mind.

I still had to decide, too, whether to deploy Ted and my time with him in the immediate future chiefly in the direction of propaganda, promotion, and proselytization or in trying to gain

whatever information I could about what was happening on a
process level. In so far as the two goals might not always be com-
patible, which one should be given priority? Without a certain
amount of promotion, which, as I have indicated, meant allowing
Ted to go on as before and sticking to the kinds of routines he
worked best with, the chances of getting the kind of help needed
for further and more substantial work appeared to be slim. On
the other hand, if Ted's powers deserted him (or he me) before
we ever had an opportunity to attack certain problems—and this
could very well happen if we concentrated chiefly on making con-
verts—a lot of potentially valuable information might never come
to light. In either case, it seemed to me there would be little lost
in devoting a modest amount of time trying to hit upon something,
some psychological trick or device, which might increase Ted's
yield beyond the one or two paranormal prints out of about three
working sessions, totaling perhaps twelve or fifteen hours, that
were alleged to be about his average. (My batting average of three
successful sessions thus far I took to be within expected limits of
variation and would, I presumed, sooner or later be balanced by a
prolonged slump.) The fact was that without a substantially in-
creased yield the chances of being able to deepen the investigation
were slight anyway. It was thus in this spirit that, while trying to
think other problems through, I engaged in the kind of informal
experimentation referred to.

But none of these 'quickie' experiments panned out in the positive sense. I tried simple hypnotic suggestion and also hypnotically
induced hallucinations. Ted was a willing and susceptible subject,
but nothing got on film from these maneuvers. I tried inducing
sudden amnesia after flashing certain target pictures in front of
Ted under hypnosis, on the hypothesis (which I had had some luck
with in other types of telepathy experiments) that repression of
ideational content and visual imagery facilitated psi functioning.
Again nothing, much to my disappointment, since I felt (and still
feel) that there is something in this area—that is, something connected with the change of phase of consciousness or awareness—
which is very close to the core of whatever goes on in psi functioning. I even took a fling, during this period, at trying to catch Ted
hot off the dream griddle by watching his telltale eye movements
when he was asleep, but without benefit of the automatic electrical

registration of these movements which is now used as an indicator of dreaming. One night I sat by Ted's bed, long after I should have been in mine, and, when I thought from certain signs that he might have been hallucinating in dreamland, I pointed a camera at his head—I had to point it *somewhere*—shot, and, of course, bagged nothing. I even woke him up at one of these points with the command that he shoot from the hip, which produced nothing beyond a slightly irritated response from a beer-and-sleep-sodden subject. Finally, just by way of pure gamble (and for kicks, since this was not particularly with the hope of increasing the yield), I took brief flyers with color film, X-ray film, movie film, and film pack. Ted's thoughtography didn't show a flicker of life during this period of fun and games, and the net result of all my playing around was to prove not that some connection between the variables I had toyed with might not have showed up had better experiments been designed and carried out (by ten Teds and ten mes) but only that I am a person incorrigibly given to wasting my time on wild hares and foolish hunches.

Curiously, the one thing that paid off—and this was not calculated to increase the yield but to fill in one chink in the evidence—was the suggestion, made by Dr. Leo Szilard, shortly before his all-too-untimely death, that we see if Ted could get anything with the lens removed from the camera. We didn't get around to trying this until early July, when Ted and I were beginning to wonder whether anything would ever again pry a picture loose from whatever recesses in Ted's mind his images were conceived in. Then one warm evening, at my office, I handed Ted a Polaroid camera from which I had removed both parts of a dual lens system and suggested that he try for a concealed target, which had been enclosed in an opaque clasp envelope. Before we began I put him briefly under hypnosis during which, besides making positive suggestions for success, I addressed a few words gently but firmly to the inner 'infant' who, I felt, was rebelling at taking orders and sabotaging our work. Suspiciously, the infant did not answer with the usual sign—a movement of the right index finger for 'yes' and the left for 'no'—when I asked if I was getting through. Thus after shooting a couple of rolls of film with nothing much coming through I concluded that the obstructive demon inside, or whatever it was that presumably had blocked our efforts for the past six or seven weeks, was as resistant to 'producing' as ever.

Shortly after nine—we had started about seven—Ted gave up in disgust, insisting that he just didn't have it in him that night. I took the target picture out of its envelope—it was a rural Austrian church with a clock tower—to show him what he was supposed unconsciously to be aiming at. "I'd never a-guessed it," was his response as he opened another can of beer. He agreed, however, to try another couple of shots, with no target in mind but simply by way of running out the half roll or so of film that was left in the camera, as soon as he had a couple of cigarettes and perhaps another beer or two. "Might as well get *good* and loaded," he said, shrugging.

At 10:10 (neither of us had been out of the room in the interval, and hardly out of our chairs) Ted indicated that he was ready to resume and picked up the camera. "Wouldn't it be funny," he said, "if I got the clock with the same time on it." With the first shot, number 18 of the evening, it was apparent that something was happening. Ted suddenly became transfigured. He began breathing in gasps, his body shook, and his eyes took fire. As soon as he had shot he shoved the camera at me forcefully, demanding that I pull the film and give it back to him at once. I did as he commanded, and he again started shaking violently as his eyes blazed at the lens through the makeshift open black-paper gismo he was using. I put my hand on his wrist to judge his pulse and noted—curiously, in view of what appeared to be major physiological ructions—that it was comparatively slow. Suddenly Ted jammed the trigger down and jumped from his chair, after practically tossing the camera at me, waving his hands in the air to show that they were empty. "It's a clock, a clock," he shouted. I held the camera in my lap for a few seconds, dubiously. "Develop it, develop it—you'll see," he commanded. I pulled the tab and waited the usual development time, during which I told him that I thought his pulse had been too slow for anything to happen. "But I saw it," he insisted excitedly. "It's there."

He was dead right. What emerged was indeed a clock tower (fig. 12a), even if it wasn't an exact match for the target picture that had been lying indifferently on a table a few feet away (fig.

(Fig. 12 a, b, c)

(Fig. 13)

12b).[1] (The best match, later found for it, was Big Ben, fig. 12c.)
Fig. 13 is a control picture I shot from several feet away (with the
camera set at the usual 3 opening and infinity setting) of Ted
sitting in his chair and illuminated by both overhead and side
lights, strong enough to produce a well-exposed picture if the
camera had had its lens. I might state that there was no clock
tower of any sort in the immediate neighborhood, even if Ted had
tried to sneak a shot out the window.

I quickly discovered that the success of the lensless camera experiment, even with the added factor of the near hit on the target,
did not impress everyone equally. (I wondered whether it would
even have allayed Szilard's suspicions.) Upon discussing this new
thread in the strengthening fabric of evidence with colleagues, I
found that, when it came to second-hand reportage (the effect of
which I was trying to gauge—after all, it would never be possible
to have *everybody* present at a firsthand demonstration) it was
going to take more than simple maneuvers of this kind to produce
a major effect. Indeed, it became apparent that, to meet all objections, we were ultimately going to have to get rid of the gismo—
invariably the first object suspected of being the innocent-looking
hat out of which all the rabbits were pulled—the camera (another
magician's prop; why couldn't Ted affect unexposed film in sealed
containers?) and even Ted himself, who to some would remain
suspect as long as he was allowed to be even in the same room as
the camera.

When I mentioned these demands to Ted several days after the
experiment, he was furious. "What in the hell am I knocking
myself out with them scientists for?" he grumbled. "All I have to
do is convince a couple of magicians and everybody is gonna be
happy, huh?" Nor could he understand how anybody in his right
mind could possibly imagine that year after year he would waste
his time trying to deceive people, with abuse and ill-health as his
only rewards. Nevertheless, he insisted, give him time and practice and he'd meet all requirements; and in principle, I felt, he
could. The only question in my mind was the practical Archime-
dean one: Did we have a lever long enough and a place to stand?
How long, at the current rate of working, might it take to realize

[1] Courtesy Austrian Trade Promotion Association. Photo: Franz Hausmann

even the simplest part of a training program aimed at ultimately separating Ted from his gismo and his camera?

But I hadn't correctly gauged the extent of Ted's rage and of his disenchantment with me and the entire scene in Denver. When I came to pick him up for lunch on the day following our discussion, Ted's apartment was empty, cleaned out except for a pair of Italian-made shoes I had presented him with and which he had no doubt left as a sign of his displeasure. He had evidently piled everything into his car during the night or early morning and had taken off for points unknown, probably Chicago. There was no note, nothing.

One morning a few days later, after a restless night, I hurriedly arranged a conference with several of the top research brass at the Medical School. I had only a flicker of hope that something would come of this confrontation, but I had to start somewhere. All I would ask for would be some expression of interest, something I could put forward to Ted as a promise of future developments.

I had the feeling that the people who came to the meeting had already got wind of my doings with Ted, and that only the fact that their curiosity had been aroused could account for their showing up for a nine o'clock meeting on such short notice. But whatever curiosity may have been astir before the meeting seemed completely absent when I presented my data and my modest requests. One man, one of my good friends whose cooperation might have saved us a lot of trouble, leaned forward nervously as I began to show Ted's pictures and describe the circumstances under which they were obtained, but suddenly got up in the middle and, with a solemnly pronounced "I don't believe it," walked out. Another good friend and colleague started riffling through some papers he had brought to the meeting, as if all he could spare was his peripheral attention. His only comment when I got through was, "I'd strip him," as if he were thereby suggesting *the* crucial experiment which could not fail to ferret out the truth or falsehood of the matter. A third man, also a friend of long standing, seemed to be more interested in discussing his own latest research interest, a new approach, via communication theory, to the psychophysiology of the anus. No one present spontaneously asked to see Ted at work. When I suggested that this might be a helpful way of getting the facts, the only response I got was the request, made by The Stripper, that I first prepare a written presentation of the essential data of the situation, which would then be given careful study. Later, in the corridor, I buttonholed my friend the anus investigator for the use of certain facilities in his laboratory. His attitude was so preposterously humiliating that I had to back off.

I was not greatly surprised at the outcome of my tilt with the academic windmills. Still, had these not been good friends of mine, the downright discourtesy shown would have been nothing less than shocking. But then again, these men were not the shifty-eyed bad guys of a movie script, the narrow-minded bigots who refused to allow the doctrine of evolution to be taught in schools; top-notch scientists every one of them, people of outstanding breadth of intellect and vision, they were simply in the grip of powerful resistances that had yet to be adequately identified and understood. Unfortunately for what I—and many others—was trying to accomplish, the entire development and the complexion of modern science were in some way intimately related to these resistances. We shall return to this in a later chapter.

I finally got Ted back with the offer of somewhat better financial terms and the promise that, even if I couldn't deliver anything like official Medical School support, I would do everything possible to have a steady stream of people from the school and other academic institutions in the vicinity privately witness his performances and, as private persons, sign affidavits attesting to what they had observed. I made it plain, however, that there was no point in simply going on as we had been if, when the smoke had lifted, we were going to meet the same objections and if, despite first-hand observation under excellent conditions, people continued to entertain the suspicion—and how well I knew the mental processes at work here—that there might still be some normal explanatory factor which had escaped their thinking and observation at the time they had witnessed Ted at work. Somehow I convinced him also that a program of training and development was in order. He agreed to begin by allowing me to place over the lens a single thin layer of masking tape which would allow light but no form to get through to the film. The plan was to add successive layers of tape, Ted hopefully taking one hurdle after another, until the camera was virtually a light-tight box. Then, perhaps, we could substitute a simple film holder for the camera and ultimately get even this out of Ted's hands.

I will telescope my report of the sessions devoted to this program, carried out over a four-week period and witnessed by over a dozen people, to a brief account of its main feature, the 'whitie,' an effect which had shown up sporadically in earlier sessions but which I have ignored up to this point because of the greater value, if only from a dramatic standpoint, of the other material. (A counterpart of the whitie, the 'blackie,' I shall take up in another place.) Here the whities have to be dealt with because, much to our distress, this is all we ever got from Ted with the masking tape over the lens turret. And we never got beyond the single layer.

The whitie is a film which emerges from development more or less completely white, as white as the borders of this page, in many instances without a trace of shadow on it. Such a result would, under normal circumstances, indicate that the film had been exposed to a light source strong enough to reduce chemically all the molecules of the silver salt in the emulsion coating to the state where they are not transferred during development to the facing print paper, which then emerges free of dark areas. (The Polaroid development process differs from that of ordinary film. In the latter, the emulsion-coated film becomes the negative, and the light-sensitized molecules of silver salt remain while the others are washed away during development.) Normally, the greater the degree of light sensitization the greater the degree of silver-salt reduction, as it is termed, and in a finished Polaroid print one sees bright areas and highlights, where the molecules thus affected have not been transferred to the print paper and therefore allow the underlying whiteness of the paper to show through, and different degrees of darkness, representing the shaded or dark areas of the external scene to be imaged, where less or no light hits the film and the unaffected molecules have been transferred to the print paper. From the varying combinations of light and shadow brought about in this way come the print configurations which we see as mountain scene or Aunt Tillie, or Aunt Tillie against a mountain backdrop, or what not. Ordinarily, when a film comes out very light it is said to have been overexposed; and should it come out entirely white some mechanical accident, such as the shutter having inadvertently been left on a time-exposure setting, or careless loading of the film while exposed to a strong light source (although it is not easy for this to happen under ordinary conditions), would be suspected.

The whities that Ted produced were in no way different from the whities that can be and in fact were produced in control shots taken during these trials by pointing the lens at a seventy-five or one hundred watt light bulb several inches or a foot away. The difference lay in Ted's whities being shot with the camera pointed at himself, in no case near enough to a light source of sufficient strength—even with whatever reflected light came off his face or body—to produce anything other than a varying configuration of light and shadow, depending on whether his closed gismo was being held flat against the lens, held a millimeter or so above it, or tipped so that it was resting on edge. Sometimes, at Ted's invitation, an observer would hold his palm over the gismo, which was itself being held against the lens. A whitie in the latter case is entirely unexpected—and, needless to say, cannot be produced in control shots—because light from no detectable source whatever is entering the camera and impinging on the film.

In the first trial session, which was witnessed by four members of the Medical School faculty whom I had dragooned into unofficial participation in our masking-tape experiment—I made it plain to them, as I did to all subsequent invitees who agreed to sit in on this basis, that no matter how tedious and uninteresting the session became because of the lack of positive results we would not backslide to the older, open-lens way of doing things—six more or less perfect whities were produced, several of them with the palm of one of the witnesses over the gismo, apparently blocking out the light, and one with a slow-speed film. In five of these six instances Ted felt that he had produced a picture and, immediately after triggering and handing the camera to one of the observers, showed his hands around, fingers spread and palms exposed, by way of indicating that there was nothing in or on them to account for the picture that was about to emerge. His statements on these occasions were "That's it!" or "This is the one," or something of the sort. Of several dozen whities thus produced in this and subsequent sessions, Ted ran about 80 per cent correct in his predictions (if you can term this a prediction of a sort) and very rarely predicted a positive result on a trial that turned out negatively. Sometimes his whities came out with a bit of graying on the film, especially in one or another or all of the corners, but there were numerous films which emerged from the usual ten- or fifteen-second development (we tried to keep this as constant as feasible within these limits) unrelievedly, absolutely white. Control shots made under a variety of circumstances by numerous observers, and at specified intervals derived from tables of random numbers, failed in each instance even to approximate Ted's results.

After the first couple of sessions, it occurred to me that Ted was conceivably managing in some way to flip the little time-exposure knob during his manipulation of the camera before shooting, and, after some experimentation, I managed to do this myself in a way that would produce fairly good approximations of whities without detection. I had to assume that Ted, like practically every other big-time psychic known, was not above a bit of 'fooling around' for kicks when the paranormal powers failed, for whatever reason. I also had to assume that there was nothing about the camera and its capabilities which Ted was not aware of, after ten years of playing around with it. Unfortunately for this hypothesis, and much to my relief, Ted had no trouble producing his whities under the same conditions as before when the time-exposure knob was taped down (I had had apologetically to explain to Ted that this was purely for the record) and impossible to dislodge.

The effect of the whities on the people who had a chance to observe them during this period appeared to be uniformly strong. All were willing without demur to sign statements. Witnesses were particularly impressed when Ted made one of his generally correct predictions or when he asked one of the observers to cover with his hand the gismo being held over the lens. When he did both together the effect was, naturally, startling. But although the witnesses seemed to feel that whities were remarkable enough—they were all trained scientific observers of one sort or another, up to at least this level of appreciation—and did not seem to be too disappointed that pictures didn't appear under the masking condition, Ted himself became increasingly frustrated by being unable to get through the barrier, and more and more despondent over what he considered his failure. His letters to his friends and side-line quarterbacks in Chicago became progressively more complaining and maudlin, from what I was able to glean from letters some of these people wrote me suggesting—even demanding—that I let up on Ted. Why was I being such a tyrant by insisting on the masking-tape routine and not letting all the little ghosties in as they were used to getting in? Ted had also implied, I gathered, that his health was failing fast, that he was coughing up dangerous amounts of blood (I had yet to see a drop), and that he was eating next to nothing and had been reduced to sleeping in the car because I had tightened up on money.

The climax of this period came during one session at my office with two fellow psychiatrists. Out of about thirty tries, Ted got sixteen whities, practically every one of which he felt sure would turn out to be a picture. His despair at flooding out this way, after a few quarts of beer and several double shots of Scotch had begun to tell, was in the classic heroic mold; he began to blubber, wail, bang his head on the floor, and moan that he was a failure. To crown this performance, he finally got around to divesting himself of every stitch of clothing and prancing about in all his phallic glory, demonstrating, by appropriate gestures, an open-crotch policy that apparently was supposed to be the counterpart of the open-hand-see-I'm-concealing-nothing flourish that he had used on other occasions. My colleagues were duly impressed.

Two days later Ted again took off. This time I had seen it coming and I had pleaded with him the night before not to give way to his Huckleberry Finn streak until we had thoroughly discussed his grievances and considered what could possibly be done to get things going the way he wanted them to go. During this talk, in which he opened up to me about the seamy aspects of his past more than he ever had previously, he stoutly denied any intention of decamping; but seven weeks later, upon his return (after I had practically offered him heaven and hell on a platter), he insisted that this denial had had no force because he had had his hand behind his back with his fingers crossed at the time he had made it.

Ted's major beef, which, as I have already indicated, rendered highly academic my ruminations on questions of promotion versus progressive experimentation and took the problem of what to do and how to proceed next right out of my hands, was that by my insistence on doing things my way I was impeding his acceptance by the scientific world, specifically by the Medical School, which he envisaged as a compact, streamlined executive body which, if handled cleverly, could quickly be brought into line to put its seal of approval on the genuineness of his phenomena. He didn't see why I couldn't herd the entire faculty into one room, with perhaps the State Board of Regents and the Governor thrown in, and have them witness the performance to end all performances, after which, with everybody on his knees crying hallelujah, we could just pass around affidavits for everybody to sign. Nor did he really see why he couldn't be accorded some sort of official status at the school—it didn't necessarily have to be a professorship (although he thought that *would* be nice) but something that would amount to official recognition of his place in science, a Ph.D., maybe.

The deal I arranged by way of compromise was not really what Ted wanted, but it was the best I could do; and, complemented by still more acceptable financial arrangements, and my guarantee that I would forget about doing a quiet monograph or two on the data (my original and, I am willing to acknowledge, somewhat unfair and unrealistic plan), and concentrate on a book which would put his name in every household and make some money, it succeeded in getting him back. This compromise was a guaranteed full-dress performance, in one of the auditoriums of the Medical School, before the District Branch of the American Psychiatric Association. I arranged it with my fingers crossed behind *my* back, with full awareness that I was putting the association on the block in what was no doubt the most underhanded horse trade in its history but salving my conscience (and hedging against what might otherwise well turn out to be a nightmarish flop) by agreeing to provide, at the same time, a lecture on thoughtography, a fetching subject which, I calculated, not one of the 160-odd members, unless he was already clued in, would have dreamed to consist of what it actually did. I felt a little like Mr. Garrick of the Royal Nonesuch, rafting down the Mississippi and ready to get my Shakespearean posters out at the next sucker town, but justifying the action to myself on the grounds of my certainty that everybody would have a riproaring time no matter what.

Not until I had sent Ted the printed announcement mailed out to the membership of the association did he return. This time it was understood, as one of the fringe benefits of our agreement, that he would not be expected to stay in town longer than he felt comfortable in so doing, and that, when his strange inner tide began to run, he would not have to sneak off, but would be allowed to go back to his haunts in Chicago—and stay drunk and disorderly for weeks, if that's what he felt like doing—with dignity and decorum.

On the night of the big event Ted was in the kind of high spirits that Heifetz or Horowitz would probably give anything to be able to achieve before a recital. He was charming and witty and brimming over with ideas for horseplay. He thought of concealing a bunch of photos and mirrors in his underclothes so that these could be discovered, much to his mock consternation, when he was examined. At the dinner table he entertained us with a rendition of Adolf Hitler, *Deutsche Sprache und alles,* and asked how we thought it would go over if he came out on the stage looking like Der Führer and making the Heil sign. (Afterward he actually made me take a picture of him doing this.)

By eight the auditorium was full. Monitors were posted at the entrances and exits to turn away persons whose faces were not familiar (we were afraid that word might have got out to the press). A committee of four, chosen by the association, was on stage to supervise everything. Ted was stripped and searched, given fresh undergarments and slippers provided for the occasion, and sewed into a monkey suit. Two cameramen were provided to get whatever happened onto movie film from different angles. All other arrangements were according to the book—method of randomizing control shots, control of cameras (three) and gismo (a new open cylinder was provided) and of anything else that might have appeared relevant. I was not allowed near Ted during the evening but gave my talk, at the start and at subsequent intervals when Ted was resting after periods of sustained shooting, from the other side of the stage. By the time Ted started with his first trial shots, after I had delivered my explanatory introduction, the place was as hushed as any Big Tent after the roll of the drums and the dimming of all lights but the glaring spot announce the one and only world-famous death-defying triple somersault with a full twist without a net. The only difference was that nobody gasped or shrieked when Ted missed the bar and, as far as the effect of his performance on most people went, sailed clear out of the ring. It was all very dull.

One might think that anything but a complete failure would have almost automatically been ruled a success, but this was not so. The audience, not knowing quite what to expect and, despite my talk, not entirely certain that the whole thing was not some sort of science-fiction extravaganza, very early became restless. By the time Ted had shot about forty prints with nothing to show for it, people started to talk quite audibly among themselves and a few walked out. Ted went for his Scotch. The official notes read: "At picture 35 and thereafter the subject, Mr. Serios, ingested several ounces of alcohol on several occasions." (No mention of Ted's mugging and hamming as he gave the audience his this-is-for-my-cough routine.) Shots number 42 and 43 were whities, the latter with a member of the audience's hand over the lens, but neither the audience nor the committee seemed to realize that something quite out of the ordinary had taken place. The most interesting shot was number 59 (fig. 14), which came a few minutes after one of the committee had suggested a crescent as a target (he

(Fig. 14)

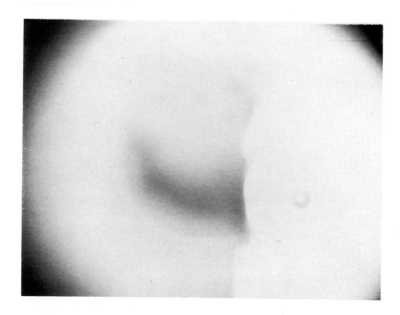

had in mind my lecture to the society of about a month before on
this subject) and offered to bet Ted a quarter that he couldn't get
it. By this time the audience had thinned out considerably, but a
few members, gathered near the stage, finally seemed to grasp that
something very extraordinary had occurred, and a little while
later, when Ted got whities on a couple of the last shots of the
evening, again with someone's hand over the lens, the remaining
members seemed ready to agree that they had witnessed something pretty remarkable after all.

Ted was jubilant. The world was his. He foresaw the word
spreading to different research centers and all sorts of offers pouring in. He went back to Chicago for a triumphal homecoming
and, despite my warnings that no judgment could be considered
final until the committee had carefully examined the data and had
given its verdict, he let it be known in various quarters that he
had finally won official acceptance from "the scientists."

Unfortunately, he had not. After some days the committee announced its verdict: unproven. They had found, on examining
all the prints, that number 47, shot as a control with the lensless
camera, had something sufficiently crescentlike on it to render the
significance of number 59 highly questionable; and, upon examin-

(Fig. 15)

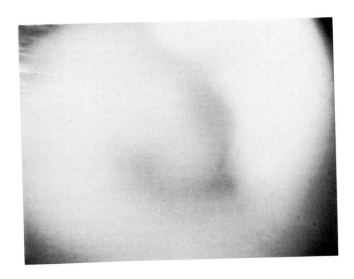

ing this print (fig. 15) myself, I could only agree. Incredibly, there it was, quite indistinct and blurry, to be sure, but for that matter so was number 59—or almost so. The curious thing, to me, was that shot number 47 had been taken by the very committee member who a couple of minutes later had proposed the crescent as target but who, on questioning, now disclaimed any awareness of his having shot anything like a crescent on 47.

Following this verdict, which I had no alternative but to accept, I returned to the auditorium and shot several rolls of film with both regular and lensless cameras in an attempt to duplicate either crescent, but especially the one with the nipple and breastlike overhead light superimposed upon it. I was not only unable to do this, but was unable to get the light alone to show exactly as it had with the setting at the regular 3 opening that had been used in the test. This was of particular interest because it was conceivable to me that Ted had not only got the crescent on demand but had also, in a way that was familiar to me from many presumptively telepathically conditioned dreams that I had studied over the years, managed to incorporate in the finished product, for which he had used a structure lying ready to hand—the overhead light (which he must have got over his shoulder as he shot)—the one configuration which gave his effort its special meaningfulness in relation to the idea I had put forward as being behind the symbol of the crescent, the breast. We shall return to this in another connection later on.

Fortunately, three of the four official committee members were, in their private unofficial capacities, sufficiently impressed to volunteer to proceed with similar tests if I could get Ted to cooperate, and several other offers of cooperation came from members who had stayed through to the finish of a wearing evening and had managed to be attentive enough to what was going on to form an opinion. The ticklish problem was breaking the news to Ted of what, from an official standpoint, could only be called a debacle, and getting him back on the scene. This I managed, in another unconscionable fingers-crossed-behind-my-back maneuver, with some salving double-talk in which, without straying too far from the essential truth, I convinced Ted that 'the committee' (three of the members anyway) was much impressed but desirous of nailing the thing down with actual photographs, which they were sure he could produce if we continued with a few more or less official tests.

So Ted returned, and over the next few weeks the nucleus of the original committee, Drs. F. Bruce Merrill, Aaron Paley, and David Starrett, and several other interested colleagues who had been present at the original shoot, went through the same test routine in the auditorium, monkey suit, prepared random numbers, official photographers and all. Even Scotch and cigarettes were supplied by 'the committee' so that, if anything major occurred, no one could say that Ted had ingested or inhaled anything radioactive.

But nothing terribly interesting occurred. We made several passes but never quite cleared the bar as far as what everybody wanted was concerned. A number of whities emerged, some with the camera held and triggered by one or another of the participants, all duly recorded by the movie cameras, and a number of blackies—perfectly black takes, as if not a photon of light had entered the open lens, which would normally have shown Ted's face through the open cylinder—which were, of course, just as interesting as the whities. There was nothing that even faintly resembled a recognizable structure, however.

One of the difficulties, it later occurred to me (and I don't know how I could have been so obtuse at the time as to have goofed on this point) may well have been our insistence each time upon sewing Ted into his monkey suit so that his cuffs and collar were more or less tightly fastened around him. Ted did chafe a bit about this, but since he didn't make a big issue of it I thought we might as well let it stand, since it would look fine for the record should anything of importance eventuate. Somehow it never struck me, in this connection, that Ted's feelings about being held in and restricted in any way, even to his manner of wearing clothes, were being rudely violated and that the effect might be just as inhibitory as if we had asked a virtuoso performer of any other sort not only to depart markedly from his regular way of working, with all its magic little mannerisms and crotchets, but also to do or wear something extra that he would feel even at less critical moments to be burdensome. I should have remembered that Ted, with his great difficulty in enduring constraints of any kind (right up to his great need periodically to go on the bum), characteristically never wore a belt or garters and customarily either left his shoelaces untied or removed them altogether, going about with empty flaps where laces should have been. Even when he wore a tie, which was invariably a clip-on because he couldn't endure anything around his neck, his top collar button was generally open to give him the feeling of freedom he craved. (I recall once seeing the manager of a fancy gentlemen's apparel shop, with coat of arms on the door and all, stiffen up and go visibly livid— he reminded me of an English butler in traditional comedy—when Ted walked in with his unlaced shoes slapping and one wing of his clip-on tie dangling in the breeze. And I thought he'd have a stroke when Ted walked up to the sport-jacket rack, flipped back a sleeve to look at the price tag of one of the garments, and remarked in his cab-driver brogue that he could get a whole trousseau for less.)

At any rate, it never occurred to me or the others, until we had finally given the project up as a bad job, that we were being a bit harder on Ted than was strictly necessary for our overall objective.

Meanwhile, Ted, when he was in town (I never knew what was happening when he was back in Chicago) was in and out of scrapes of one sort or another, and I was constantly afraid of his busting loose in a major way. Several times he was picked up at night as a suspicious character wandering around neighborhoods he had, according to the police, no business to be in, and his pursuit of females tended at times to be, what with one thing and another, rather on the risky side. Once I discovered that he was borrowing the family car, which was always at his disposal, to go off on jaunts with a young lady who was not only a poor, confused out-patient at the psychiatric clinic (whom he had picked up in a nearby park) but also about sixteen and technically, thus, prime jailbait.

On another occasion I received a call early one morning from the downtown jail where Ted had spent the night. It seemed that after the bars had closed on the previous night, he had gone in search of more acceptable game and had wound up in an apartment building that he had mistaken for the nurses' residence, where he had prowled up and down the halls with a match in hand, examining letter boxes and cards in doors, and making known the object of his quest in fairly direct terms. One of the male residents finally called the police, but when the squad cars

came growling to the scene Ted already had things well in hand.
"Officer, arrest that man," he commanded, pointing authoritatively
toward the informer. At the jail, where he registered as "medical
photographer" in my employ, he was put in a cell "wid a common
drunk." But by the time I got down to bail him out next morning,
he might well have carried the precinct had there been a spot
election for alderman or even sheriff. Cops passing in the corridor
hailed him warmly by name, and Ted might even have retained
a soft spot in his heart for the force had he not become convinced
that somewhere between his being taken in tow and the clearing
of his wits he had been rolled for about thirty-five dollars.

The thing that had me most worried, however, was the alarming
regularity with which he managed to get the hell beaten out of
him in tavern brawls. Once he picked on a drunk about twice his
size who was trying to undress a woman at the bar. "I thought I'd
play the hero so I could pick up where he left off," he remarked,
"but the dame only tol' me to mind my own goddamn business."
He got laid out and stomped on. About ten days later he tried a
bar mate about half his size, whose presumed private dimensions
Ted for some reason felt himself called upon publicly to ridicule.
After disregarding a couple of quietly and calmly delivered warnings to cease and desist, he was invited to the center of the floor
and ordered to put his dukes up, and was duly knocked flat. Two
weeks later he almost had his brains beaten out with a board.
"This has got to stop," said Ted after this last, in which, in addition to his head injuries, he damaged his hand and shoulder and
got a few severely bruised ribs which kept him trussed up for
weeks. "Them hospital bills are killing me."

In between incidents of this sort, when Ted felt himself in not
too bad shape and up to a bit of work, we would round up whatever members of the committee could be on hand on short notice
and have another go at putting something on film that would
stick for the experts. The end of our formal auditorium trials
came after one session when Ted collapsed following the tremendous effort of producing a whitie, a blackie, and another
whitie in rapid succession, on shots 36 to 38, between 10:19 and
10:21. The movie reel ran out just as he hit the floor and Dr.
Starrett, who had been holding and triggering the experimental
camera during Ted's trials, ran over to a table in the corner of the

room to grab a freshly loaded camera in order to get a picture of Ted laid out. Each one of the eight shots he made turned out to be a perfect whitie.

Later that night, at my home, Ted was in tears, inconsolable. The next day he remained at his place, incommunicado. On the following evening he showed up for dinner but sat through the meal, still virtually incommunicado, with a faraway look on his face. Suddenly he asked why we couldn't cut out the auditorium sessions, why he couldn't take on the committee one by one at the individual members' homes.

I called Dr. Paley on the spot, and within an hour we were at his home making trial shots, in the presence of his wife Evelyn, a graduate psychologist, and his two teenage children, Judy and Bobby. There was nothing formal about the way we conducted the session. Dr. Paley happened to have on hand film left over from our auditorium trials. Notes were minimal—just enough for basic identifications and descriptions of who did what where. We forgot about randomization from preprepared random-number lists but just took our control shots when the spirit moved. Dr. Paley, at Ted's request and under his direction, fashioned a gismo on the spot by folding the black opaque protective paper that comes in each film roll into a strip about one inch high, rolling it into something like a napkin ring, with a diameter also of about an inch, and taping it around with cellophane.

Ted began by very quickly clearing the scene of all light, just as if, despite the open gismo, which should have allowed his face to show through on all prints (it did on some, of course), he had put up an invisible barrier or as if, like Moses commanding the sea to part, he had somehow managed to push aside whatever photons would normally have been streaming in. After a couple of perfect blackies, slight suggestions of light and highlight started appearing on the prints. These imprints, on otherwise perfectly black films, and first spotted by the children (I discovered then and subsequently that children are invariably more perceptive, quicker, more curious, and more questioning than adults), soon began to take on the beginnings of form. At first we looked around the room to see if some of the suggestions of lines that seemed about to emerge couldn't have been ceiling beams or other structures, but control shots exhibited nothing like what was showing up.

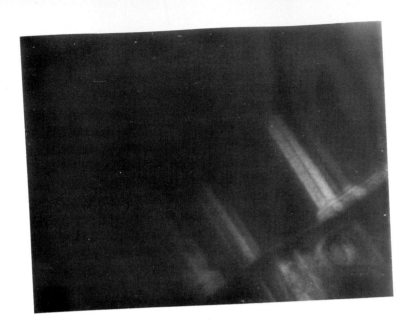

(Fig. 16)

Finally, on number 18, came a full-fledged structure (fig. 16) which, bathed in a ghostly light, was definitely not in the room. (I still have not succeeded in identifying it.) Dr. Paley revealed at this time that the concealed target of our auditorium trials the evening before had been the Arch of Triumph in Paris, which he promptly took out of the envelope he had had in his desk. This was apparently not it, but who was going to quibble?

The story from here on is very simple. The session at Dr. Paley's marked the beginning of a series of more than forty working sessions at different people's homes over a period of the next few months which, interrupted only by Ted's trips back to Chicago for his on-the-bum periods, without a single exception produced successful results under a significant variety of conditions. At his peak Ted got up to seventy presumptively paranormal shots a session, with from ten to over forty perfectly distinct pictures centering around two or three different themes a session, some of them selected for him by witnesses. Let me state here, however, that I soon gave up my fatuous dream of being able to control, as in a textbook of laboratory procedure, the fine conditions under which we did our work. Ted, in various stages of besottedness (he developed a routine of drinking his beer directly from quart bottles), became the impresario, the field commander, giving every-body orders sharply and authoritatively as to what they were to do, where to stand, what to hold, and so forth. As far gone in drink as he sometimes was, he improvised distance experiments, experiments with two or more cameras, experiments with cameras out of the room and at queer angles. Sometimes he'd work himself into a frenzy, ordering cameras to be handed him one after another—he almost never reached for one himself or handled cameras between trials—even though, as it sometimes turned out, the film in them had run out. Sometimes our notes were perforce bare and telegraphic, and the notation and development lagged while Ted produced at a rate too fast for our bookkeeping. As soon as I got it through my head that there was no point in trying to hold Ted down, or draw cobwebby lines of preferred procedure around him when he was hot, we got better results. This does not mean that our vigilance was relaxed, or that all restrictions or controls went by the board. On the contrary, vigilance was, if anything, more hawklike because we all realized, during these periods of furious shooting, that there was nothing for it but to catch-as-catch-can, skip nimbly and not only observe with utmost attention but keep well in mind exactly what was being done in order to fill out our sometimes skimpy notes at the first break. At any rate, as soon as I realized the futility of trying to swim against the strong under-tow that dragged everything and everybody along with it when Ted became master of magic ceremonies—for magic it most certainly was—I never again questioned Ted's basic prerogatives while he, from his Olympian eminence, graciously accorded me control of certain conditions when, at crucial junctures, I strongly urged him to do so. "Just so long as we know who's boss around here," he'd say. Fortunately, there resulted from this period of intense activity, despite occasional breaches of conventional research technique—inadequate randomization and sometimes too few controls, for instance—that scientific investigators with all their methodological bolts and nuts screwed down tightly might (as some did) shudder at, a body of first-rate data that will probably keep me busy long after this book is in print. Some of these data I shall now try to sort out and present from various points of view.

CHAPTER VII

Kinds of Data

I THINK it will become plain as the data develop that an exhaustively detailed description of the conditions of trial and observation for each separate experiment will hardly be necessary or even, in some cases, relevant. To put the reader at his ease, however, lest he find himself unduly concerned, before the relevance or non-relevance of certain factors has been established, that major precautions may have been neglected, I shall provide here a once-over-lightly review of conditions that obtained generally and assure him that whatever may be lacking in this treatment for a final assessment of the evidence can, if necessary, be taken up later.

I should like to state at the outset, however, that I shall exclude from this presentation all data resulting from situations where I or others felt that the conditions of observation and especially of note-taking left some doubt or ambiguity as to the exact circumstances surrounding the production of a particular picture. I shall describe later, as we take up different categories of data, certain instances in which such strictness became absolutely essential.

Perhaps we should begin by giving the general form of the statement that most witnesses were asked to sign after observing Ted work, and the names and positions of some of those who witnessed pictures, and not just whities, being produced. (In several instances, witnesses who signed pictures or protocols, or volunteered statements of their own, were not asked to sign these prepared statements.) With insignificant differences in the wording of the first paragraph in certain instances, these statements were as follows:

Dear Doctor Eisenbud:

On .... beginning at about .... at .... in the presence of the witness(es) named below, I, the undersigned, observed the following evidences of extraordinary activity on Polaroid film contained in a Polaroid camera (modified as specified below) handled by Ted Serios in his usual manner (pointing at himself) or as specified below.

The number of prints showing distinguishable structures ....

The number of prints in which other evidences of presumptively extraordinary activity (which would ordinarily be expected from photochemical activity) could be seen ....

The conditions of trial as to camera status, film loading, randomization, etc. (specify below if necessary) were ....

The conditions of observation as to visibility, time allowed for inspection and other relevant factors (specify below if necessary) were ....

I am able to formulate the following specific hypotheses as to how these effects might have been produced in a normal manner:

Remarks:

You have my permission for the use of this statement for dissemination or publication in responsible media of communication of scientific information.

(Signed) ....
(Position and Title) ....

Witness .... Witness ....
Witness .... Witness ....

Date ......

A partial list of signatories follows. (The statements of individual signatories are, of course, in no way to be taken as reflecting the attitudes, opinions or involvements of the institutions with which these persons may be affiliated.)

could be normally produced under the conditions obtaining during Ted's trials. (I should add, however, that most witnesses, despite their signed testimony, probably went through the kind of doubt that I described in myself; and many, who participated in only one session, may very well still feel that some unthought-of normal explanation is possible. Not one, nevertheless, ever sought to recant his testimony as given.)

Witnesses were asked, whenever possible, to provide the cameras to be used for the experiments, and when this was actually done it will be so stated. (Unfortunately, not everyone complied.) When witnesses did not own cameras that could be used, which was the rule, they were asked to borrow or rent them, the place of rental, of course, being left up to the witness (to minimize the probability of a 'plant'). The cameras used were ones that did not have the electric eye for automatic light adjustment, which might have been a drawback in keeping certain background conditions constant, but had aperture-shutter arrangements of fixed-light value at different settings. On the model 95 series camera which was chiefly in use, the aperture number invariably used was 3 (equivalent to exposure value 12 in some 95 model series cameras), representing a setting of 1/30 second at f 11. Except where otherwise noted, a wink light was used.

In all cases, after the initial experiments, the setting disc regulating this aperture was taped down so that no movement was possible during the trials. In all instances in which one or more cameras in use were provided by me, the participants were asked to inspect these inside and out before and after the sessions and also were given the option (which Drs. Chapin, Metcalf, Paley, Frey, and others accepted) of afterward impounding them for further inspection by themselves or others. When more than one camera was used, all were plainly labeled and initialed, so that substitutions could easily be detected. As already noted, after the beginning experiments the time-exposure knob was always taped down and could not be flipped. The focusing-lever setting was always at infinity, which was simply the way Ted had always had it.

In all experiments (except in the one instance already noted, and others to be mentioned later) the film used was high-speed (3000 ASA equivalent) Polaroid type 47 black and white. Except where otherwise noted, this was provided by the witnesses, who were asked to seal and initial each film package before the sessions (to insure that the film packages later opened and used were ones provided by them) and to either carry out themselves or supervise the opening of the outer packages and the sealed protective inner wrappings and the loading of the film into the cameras. (One witness insisted, in addition, upon carrying all his initialed film packages inside his shirt.)

In all experiments it was understood that witnesses were accorded the privilege of full inspection of anything and everything that appeared relevant, as closely as desired, in any light desired, and at any desired times. The open paper gismo which was used was always subject to inspection and, where desired, was made up and initialed by the witness prior to beginning a session. Sometimes two or three gismos were in use during a session. Control shots were carried out at the option of witnesses, but it was seen to that this was done at least several times with each camera during each session and, when feasible, at least once for each roll of film with which a positive result was obtained. In one or two instances, however, where a witness wanted to hold up proceedings to do repeated controls at a time when inordinate delay might have interfered with Ted's mood, he was asked, if it would have made no apparent difference, to put this off until a later time. On all trials the prints were pulled and developed by me or other observers in the presence of one or more witnesses, who were requested to sign or initial any print that looked interesting, either on the margin or tab of its face or on its reverse side, before it was allowed to go out of sight. Where initials were used, the full signature and sometimes date were added, either on the front or the back, after the print was fixed and dried. Ted was never allowed in contact with the camera or prints during the developing, pulling, signing or notating process (indeed never, even in private sessions with me, did he indicate any inclination to be).

Before reviewing the basic conditions under which direct observation was carried out in the trial sessions, it will be of value to run over the possible ways in which an image can be imprinted on the film in a Polaroid Land camera of the model 95 series. A diagram of the camera of this series (the 95, 95 A, 95 B, and 94 C differ slightly in ways that do not concern us here) is shown in fig. 17. It is essentially an opaque box through which light impinging directly or indirectly on the film, which moves from print position to print position through a pair of apposed rollers as each print is pulled, can enter from the outside only through the lens aperture, when the shutter is momentarily opened in being snapped, or through apertures already existing or specially made, through accident or design, somewhere in the rigid frame or the cloth bellows. In either of these latter cases, if a leak through a small aperture were to provide a pinhole camera effect, this would tend always to be in evidence on each print made, unless an additional mechanism were provided to constitute the equivalent of a shutter.

(Fig. 17) *The Polaroid Land Model 95 Camera*

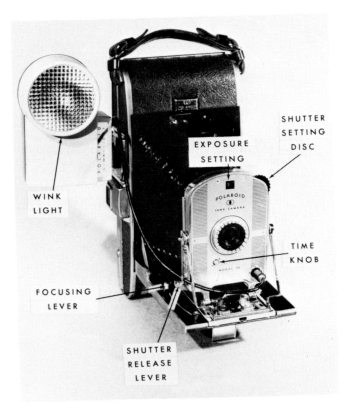

In addition to this, if the hinged back of the camera were left ajar, it would be possible for light to pass through the semitransparent print paper and to affect a still-sensitive film in the few seconds immediately after it had been—with movements perfectly obvious to everyone, of course—pulled through the rollers and before full chemical development had occurred. It is virtually impossible, however, to produce a whitie this way without detection, and still more difficult, under these circumstances, to place something like a transparency between the light source and the exposed back of the print paper, in order to produce anything like an image without detection. If the hinged back plate is left open *after* a film has been pulled and development allowed to proceed in normal fashion, no light can ordinarily enter the camera to affect still-sensitive film inside. Uninformed people are apt to get needlessly nervous about this.

In order for a recognizable image other than what would normally be registered by the camera to be produced on film from light entering through the lens from the outside, such light would have either to pass through something like a positive transparency held within an inch or so of the lens but with an additional lens of high refractive power interposed, or be reflected from a positive print under the same circumstances. If this lens and transparency or print were not held close to the lens (or right at the opening of the gismo held over the lens), other and easily identifiable parts of the surrounding scene would be imaged on the film in addition to whatever was produced by means of it. Thus if the transparency or print plus the extra lens were held in the hand or elsewhere some distance from the lens of the camera (some have suggested that it could be concealed in a contact lens or artificial eye), one would get, in addition to the surrounding scene, the image of a hand holding something suspiciously like a very small lens (or of a face with a very funny-looking glass eye). In any case, although getting an image on film with a system of this sort can obviously be managed, no one has suggested that it can be done in a rapid sleight-of-hand way that could pass detection under close scrutiny, no matter how minute the props. As far as this goes, Mr. Billie W. Wheeler, Director of Audio-visual Education of the University of Colorado Medical Center, wrote in his statement: "I have been a professional photographer for twenty years and, in my opinion, the pictures Mr. Serios obtains cannot be gotten by normal or even trick photography."

The possibilities of producing images on the film in the camera through some sort of inside job are, of course, manifold. There is no doubt that a clever machinist or instrument maker could contrive a means not only of arranging somehow for a single preprepared image to be produced on freshly inserted film but also of doing this with several images, without having to reload his mechanism or having in any grossly detectable way to alter the outside arrangements of his trick camera. A concealed inside shutter, to block off the outside light when the trigger is snapped, as well as an adequate inside light source, is not beyond the bounds of possibility; nor would it be utterly impossible to contrive something that might pass cursory inspection when the camera was examined and the shutter snapped prior to the camera being loaded for use. (Witnesses in experiments with Ted are invited to look through the open lens when this is done, or even, if desired, to hold the shutter open on time exposure for prolonged scrutiny.) In no case, however, were cameras used in trials with Ted that were not provided by me or one of the witnesses, wherever feasible, naturally, by the latter.

Now let us go over once more the basic conditions under which direct observation was carried out in the trial sessions. When he handled the camera himself for a shot, Ted almost invariably asked that a camera be handed him and practically never reached for a free-standing one himself. He sat on a chair or sofa, usually with one knee crossed over the other, and usually near or under the light from a standing lamp but in any case with enough light from additional (e.g., overhead) sources to insure perfectly adequate visibility of his hands and fingers. As far as this condition went, the statements given by witnesses on their affidavits varied from "adequate" to "excellent" (sometimes by witnesses to the same session), but so far as I could see these ratings represented less the differences in the adequacy of lighting than in the degree of testamentary circumspection on the part of witnesses; some evidently thought it the part of scientific caution to key their designations as low as possible. In no case, however, was there any question as to the satisfactoriness of this condition (or any other, incidentally).

Nevertheless, persons who have not witnessed Ted work at first hand sometimes express doubt that the eye alone is equal to the task of following the movements and disposition of his hands and fingers, and suggest that strategically placed cameras would be better suited to the job of registering what takes place. I can only assure these cautious persons—and I believe that most if not all witnesses would agree with me—that this is not so, and that as far as simple observation goes, the eye is infinitely better adapted to the requirements of the situation. For the most part Ted's hands and fingers, despite the tremors which sometimes affect his body, are pretty much at rest on the camera and holding the gismo for at least several seconds before he shoots, and when one or more pairs of eyes are trained on him under full light, at distances as close as one or two feet or less, there is very little that can escape detection so far as Ted's being able to conceal and thrust in front of the lens anything of any conceivable relevance to the situation. Of many hundreds of feet of movie film of Ted's performance taken from various angles and under varying lighting conditions, none has been as adequate from the standpoint of registration of what goes on, as simple direct observation. One advantage of the movie, of course, is that what is registered can be restudied repeatedly, but this is something else again.

As for those times during which, as noted, Ted rises to a pitch of great excitement and demands one camera after another for shooting, direct observation is still, I believe, entirely adequate, if only for the reason that, as I have already indicated, attention on the part of the observers is apt to be more concentrated at these times, and there is still always time for an observer to get himself into position to look right down at Ted's hands holding the camera and gismo, as in fig. 3. I can only advise the reader with doubts about the validity of these statements, the reader who may feel that the art of prestidigital illusion is so highly developed as to itself border on the occult—some people appear to be almost superstitious, if not paranoid, in their abstract faith in, and fear of, the limitless capabilities of a competent illusionist—to hunt up the nearest certified magician, sit him down with a camera and makeshift gismo, and see what he can get into the camera or in front of the lens in full light while being closely scrutinized for any movements at all out of the ordinary.[1]

However, in this and succeeding sections I shall concentrate mainly on types of data which do not depend for their evidential force solely on the adequacy of direct observation. Proceeding as if there were no one single type of datum which could alone rule out the possibility of normal means of image production under the conditions of our trial sessions I shall—even in the absence of a concrete hypothesis as to such a possibility—present several types of data which could only add to the difficulty of execution of just about any means that might exist.

The first example is from a session at the home of Dr. Laurence B. Hall. (Present: Dr. and Mrs. Hall, the three Hall children, my wife and I.) Ted held the camera—the same one throughout—and an open paper gismo on all of the following. On shot number 49, Ben Hall, fourteen, was given the job (by Ted) of signaling when to snap. The picture that was pulled (fig. 18) was one of a series of nine differing shots of an unidentified building, one more and others less distinct than those shown. (In this, as in other series of a similar kind, it was as if the camera had panned vertically and horizontally over one area of a building, with very little, if any, measurable change in the size of corresponding images.) On shot number 50, with Ben actually triggering the camera still held by Ted, an indistinct image of another type, of which we had six versions during the evening, appeared (fig. 19). On shot number 51, Ben again triggering, another version of the building produced by shot 49 appeared (fig. 20); and on shot number 52, Ben still

---

1 Efforts to enlist the participation of officials of the Society of American Magicians in sessions with Ted were not successful. Dr. James C. Johnson, Jr., of Hartford, Conn., National President of that organization, was, finally, kind enough to agree to observe Ted in the summer of 1966, but, because of an airlines strike, his visit to Denver had to be cancelled.

Just before this book went to press Mr. W. E. Cox, of Southern Pines, North Carolina, an associate member of the Society of American Magicians who had been a professional conjuror for many years, had an opportunity to observe Ted produce some blackies under the same conditions as he produces images when he holds the camera and gismo himself. "I say absolutely and unequivocally," he stated, "that no lens or microfilm could be hidden in a gismo barrel under these conditions." In addition, he wrote on his statement: "No conjuring techniques are remotely conceivable under the conditions."

#49 Lawrence B. 2#22 3/10/65

(Fig. 18)

(Fig. 19)

#50 Lawrence B. Hall 3/10/65

triggering, a somewhat clearer version of the picture struggling to get through on shot 50, identifiable as someone with one leg over a bicycle, apparently mounting or dismounting, with something like part of a wicker chair in the background, appeared (fig. 21). It should be noted that the image on 52 is vertical on the print (the arrow indicates the direction of the pull tab) while its counterpart, number 50, is horizontal. In all cases the camera was held horizontally, which was Ted's invariable custom. The time elapsed between shots 49 and 52 was about five minutes. Ted did not stir from his chair in this interval.

Another series of the sort occurred at the home of Dr. John L. Chapin. (Present: Dr. and Mrs. Chapin, the three Chapin children, a neighbor child, my wife and I.) Shot number 24, with John, Jr., thirteen, triggering, was an indistinct version of an image—unidentified man and woman walking at an unidentified

(Fig. 20)

52 Laurence B Hall ↓ 3-10-65

(Fig. 21)

place (fig. 22)—that turned up several times during the evening. Shot number 25, with Annie, ten, and Johnnie manning the camera (one holding, the other triggering), showed a normal image of Ted's face. Shot number 26, taken with another camera, again produced a normal; but shot number 27, taken with the camera and with the same roll of film that produced 24 and 25, gave an indistinct version of a group of buildings near St. Peter's Square in Rome (fig. 23) that showed up six times during the evening. Dr. Chapin, at my request, impounded for further inspection the camera that had been used. Nothing suspicious was found.

In the examples given above, the images, while sometimes differing in their placement on the film, as if the camera were panning from one spot, are essentially the same in size, shape, and geometric projection. In other instances, successive versions of essentially the same image have differed slightly in size, as if the camera were at varying distances from the object. In certain cases,

(Fig. 22)

(Fig. 23)

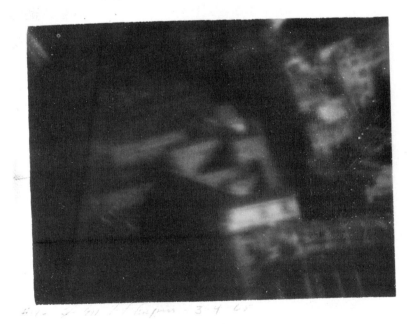

however, the successive images in a series centering around one scene differ more radically from one another. In one series, witnessed at their home by Dr. and Mrs. Lewis Barbato, Ted got thirteen different versions, from thirteen completely different camera angles, of the top of a windmill. Three are given here, figs. 24, 25 and 26, and two or three others will be shown later in other connections. The print shown in fig. 24, as several others in this series, was shot without the wink light. Thus a good deal of reflected light was not present.

Another example occurred in a series shot at the home of and witnessed by Dr. and Mrs. Jerome Gersten. (Present, besides Dr. and Mrs. Gersten, my wife and me, was the Gersten's son Steven, a medical student.) Here, unlike the case of the couple in the

(Fig. 24)

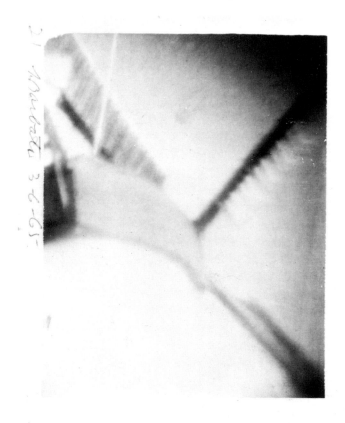

series witnessed by Dr. Chapin, who never took a step forward despite our entreaties, at least one of two people in a repetitively shot scene seems to have changed position quite perceptibly, along with the camera. Five of the six pictures in this series appear to be more or less identical, differing in only minor detail (fig. 27). But in the fifth of the series (fig. 28), the person seen from the rear at the left, in the striped shirt, with what appears (in fig. 27) to be a camera strap around his neck, seems to have bent his head forward and downward—what looks like his ear shows fairly clearly on the right of the three-quarter rear view of his head—completely changing his position in relation to the buildings seen in the background. The couple, according to Ted, who 'saw' this image coming up, right down to the striped shirt, before the first of the series appeared, are supposedly standing on a hill and looking down on the scene (a European town?) below.

The types of data just presented appear to be such as would place a burden upon any person, however skillful and whatever the mechanical means at his disposal, who tried to manipulate

(Fig. 25)

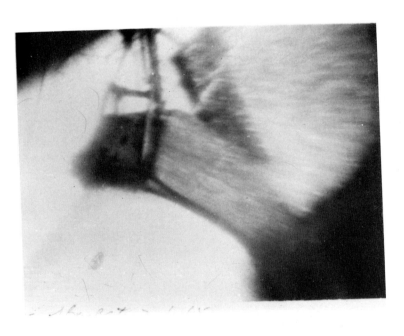

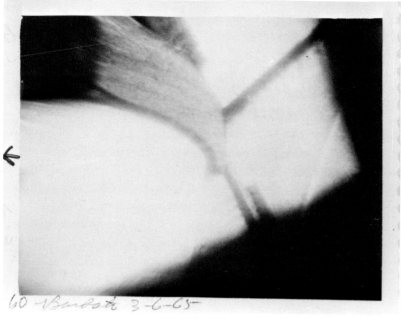

(Fig. 26)

(Fig. 27)

(Fig. 28)

some hypothetical apparatus for producing prints by normal means while under close direct observation, if only from the standpoint, in certain instances given where one print after another was shot (several of the Barbato series, for example), of the rapidity of the changes that presumably would have been required. Nevertheless it will be worthwhile to mention a few other types of data produced by Ted which, I believe, add to the evidence weighing against any concrete hypothesis (that I can think of or has been suggested to me) purporting to account for the data under the conditions described.

The first, not necessarily in order of evidential importance but simply by way of giving it brief mention before passing on to other types, consists of pictures taken with a camera from which an essential part of the lens system had been removed. Unlike the camera from which Big Ben, cited earlier, was pulled, only the lens component behind the diaphragm had been removed from the camera used for these pictures, the one in front having been left in place as a dust shield. The only picture of this type that I shall cite here (others will be given later in different contexts) is one of the aforementioned series of thirteen windmill pictures taken under the supervision of myself and Dr. Barbato. This one, shown in fig. 29, was actually snapped by Dr. Barbato while Ted held the camera and open gismo pointed at himself. To add to the interest of this picture (which, indistinct as it is, could not possibly result from any type of shot taken normally by the camera used) there is what appears to be a duplication, as if by double exposure, of one of the toothbrushy looking windmill blades, seen on the right. Fig. 30 is a shot taken normally with this camera of a person sitting on a couch under a lamp.

I think I ought to state here, by way of letting the reader in on some of the problems encountered in work with Ted, that one of the difficulties with the lensless camera was not in getting interesting pictures from it, but in verifying that what had ostensibly been shot with and pulled from it was so in fact, especially where more than two cameras were in use and things were moving at a brisk pace. It was found advisable always to supplement direct

(Fig. 29)

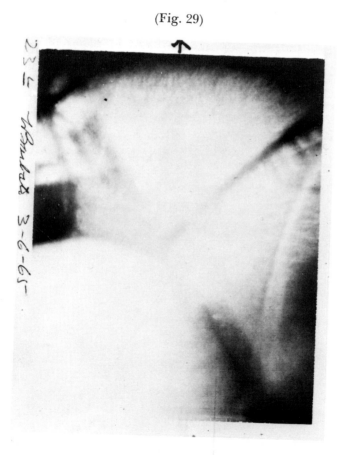

(Fig. 30)

(Fig. 31)

observation with examination of the batch, run, and roll sequence numbers on the back of each print before transferring to somewhere on the print proper the symbol of the *L* with the horizontal line below it, used to signify 'lensless,' that was first put on a tab when a print was pulled.

A type of data of some (although minor) evidential importance under the conditions obtaining consists of pictures in which two more or less mutually contradictory images appear. In the print given in fig. 31, one of several shot at a session witnessed by Mr. William Reynard, an attorney, Ted happened to hold the camera pointed over his shoulder at an overhead fluorescent light fixture. The two barrels of this fixture can be seen superimposed on the château-like structure that emerged. A control (fig. 32) shows only a portion of the fixture (on the right) whose light can be seen flooding the print. (The film for this session, incidentally, was supplied by me.)

(Fig. 32)

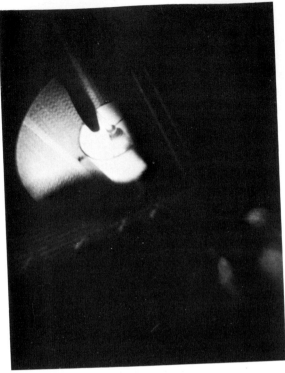

(Fig. 33)

Another picture of this type occurred at a session at the home of and witnessed by Dr. and Mrs. Bruce Merrill. (Present, besides me, and very much part of the proceedings, were the three Merrill children, Lynn, Susie, and Dave.) Fig. 33 shows one of a series of shots of the same scene. The lamp, superimposed upon the image, was over Ted's right shoulder. By rights it too should pretty much have flooded out any other image. (The image of the lamp itself, incidentally, could not be reproduced with this clarity on control shots taken with the opening and setting, 3 and infinity, that were used.) By way of adding to the interest of this series, Dr. Merrill switched in the middle to his own model 80 Polaroid camera, which produces prints half the size of those of the 95 model, and got the two unidentified images shown in figs. 34 and 35. (These were shot two days after the print shown in fig. 16 that was shot at Dr. Paley's. Ted was on a chiaroscuro kick at this time.)

At times images would appear that incorporated either all or

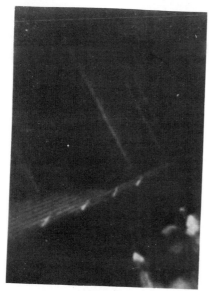

(Fig. 34)

(Fig. 35)

(Fig. 36)

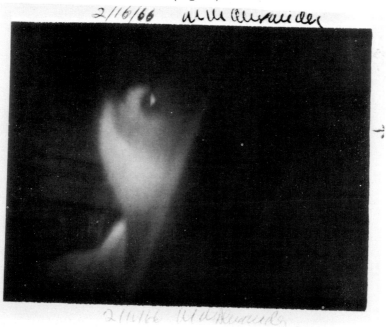

part of Ted's face (which would normally be expected to show if
nothing else were coming in) and at the same time part of other
images that may have emerged, or would later emerge, in more
complete form on other shots. Fig. 36 shows more than half of
Ted's face obscured by what a few shots later on turned out to be
part of a more or less completely developed image of another sort
(fig. 37). In the background of fig. 36 a portion of the drapes behind Ted may be seen. (Dr. Martin Alexander provided the film
and camera for these shots witnessed by himself and Dr. Lloyd
Joshel.) Fig. 38, witnessed by Dr. James Galvin, shows part of
Ted's dissolving face—his left eye and part of his nose are visible—
seemingly in front of an image which later developed into a more
complete version (fig. 67).

Perhaps one of the more important pieces in the mosaic of
evidence bearing on the question of hypotheses conceivably relevant to the production of the data is supplied by a group of
pictures produced with Ted somewhere in the vicinity of, but at
no observable time in direct physical contact with, the camera.
Because of the obvious significance of images produced in this
way, I shall present several examples of them while devoting a
few pages to a discussion of some of the problems involved in the
evaluation of a special group within this class.

From the very beginning of his uninterrupted streak of sessions
with a high yield, Ted himself began to move away from the
camera, at first timidly, by asking people to trigger it while he
held it, then moving on to asking them to hold the gismo and to
trigger while he held it, and finally relinquishing the camera
entirely. At the start he allowed it to be held only a few inches
away, then several feet and at his peak, finally, at distances up to
sixty-six feet, which was simply the distance at which we could
conveniently carry out this procedure in the corridor of the Medical School building we happened to be working in at the time.
Almost always it was Ted who indicated that he was ready for this
kind of trial, which he did by pointing at someone nearby—it
might have been a faculty member or one of his children—and
ordering him into action. "You, grab a camera—it don't make no
difference, either one," or "You, bring the lensless camera here
and hold it in front of me." But sometimes he responded to a
child's plea, "Can I hold the camera? Please let me!" by accord-

(Fig. 37)

(Fig. 38)

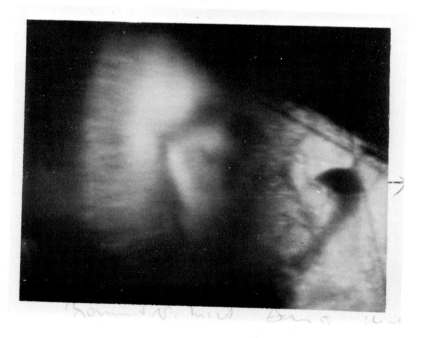

ing this privilege as he would a royal favor. Children, far from
disturbing him, seemed to draw him into his finest flights of
improvisation. For one thing, the feedback, communicated on
their part by uninhibited shrieks of astonishment and delight
when a clear picture emerged—they had no scientific self-image to
preserve—and groans of disappointment when the images began to
fade or become blurred, seemed far more direct than with adults.
Invariably, Ted and whatever children happened to be about
seemed absolutely delighted with each other.

In the usual situation, with others manning the camera and
gismo a foot or more away, neither Ted's hands nor any other part
of his body would be in direct contact with the camera, and he
would indicate by gesturing to the person holding it just how he
wanted it angled so that he could stare directly into the lens.
(Seemingly absurdly, however, he might then shut his eyes, look
away, or direct someone to place his finger or palm over the gismo
when ready to shoot.) Sometimes Ted would deploy one person
to hold the camera, another to trigger it, and often a third to hold
the gismo, resulting in as complicated a setup as can be found
outside of the Pompeii murals or the Place Pigalle in Paris.
Finally, with everything the way he wanted it, Ted would take off
as suddenly as a jet plane thrusting forward. If he were sitting,
he might begin squirming in his chair, his eyes staring wildly and
his hands running frenziedly through his hair. If he were standing, as was most often the case, he might simply keep his hand
(most often his right) or hands poised to snap. This would keep
up until he exploded with his "Now!", usually snapping his finger
as a signal for the triggerman to trip the shutter release. Then
would start the business of Ted's snapping his fingers and incant-
ing, in best crap-game fashion, sometimes with a chorus of children and adults chiming in, "Be there, baby, be there!", which
might keep up—unless Ted had, in his frenzy, gone right on to
another camera—for the ten or so seconds while the print was
developing. Fig. 39, from a movie film, shows Dr. Johann Marx
(foreground) and Dr. Henry Frey each holding a camera and
gismo and getting ready to trigger at Ted's signal. Fig. 40, from
the same film, shows Dr. Marx holding and triggering the camera
with Dr. David Starrett holding the gismo, his finger over the
open end. The prints that emerged from these shots are some of

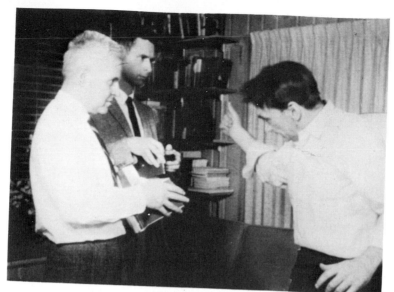

(Fig. 39'

(Fig. 40)

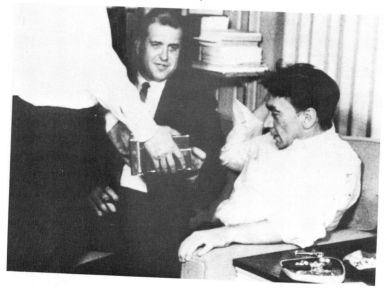

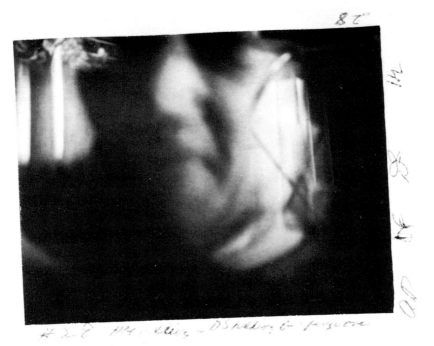

(Fig. 41)

(Fig. 42)

the ones that happen to show structures superimposed on or merging into Ted's face. (The structures shown in fig. 41, the print obtained with Dr. Starrett's finger over the gismo, could not be identified from anything in the room or elsewhere.)

Curiously, the fact that some of the people on the trigger were sometimes a bit slow in responding to Ted's signal to snap (children, incidentally, rarely were) never seemed to interfere with the production of sometimes very clear images of things other than Ted's face that might come in, any more than the fact of someone's finger or palm ostensibly blocking the light from entering the lens. But we will return to some of these anomalies later.

An instructive sequence of pictures that emerged when Ted was in no contact with the camera occurred at the home of Dr. Henry Lehrburger. (Present: the Lehrburgers, their five children, three neighbors' children, my wife and I.) Ted started by holding and snapping the camera and getting mostly blackies. On number 6, one of the children was given the camera to hold and trigger while another held the open gismo over the lens. The picture that was pulled showed Ted's face (which was entirely normal with the open gismo) and one of the Lehrburger children, curiously inattentive, in the background (fig. 42). On number 7 Ted took the camera and got another blackie. On 8, Ted designated one of the little Lehrburger girls, Florrie, eleven, to snap the shutter while he held the camera and gismo. A faint beginning of some kind of form (the notes read "? squarish form") could be discerned. This became a little clearer, after a perfect blackie on number 9, on number 10 (fig. 43), Ted having meanwhile moved to a couch a few feet away, where he again sat under a lamp. On number 11, Carl, thirteen, the distracted child in the background of number 6, held the camera and the gismo while Florrie snapped, and what appeared to be the squarish form on number 10 emerged over a still-visible light source in the center as a fairly definite structure (fig. 44). For the next six shots the same team worked at holding and snapping the camera. On number 12 some kind of a new theme emerged, as yet not too distinguishable (frequently the form and structure of unclear images could only be definitely made out in the light of later images of the same thing), but definitely something. Thirteen, with one of the other

(Fig. 43)

(Fig. 44)

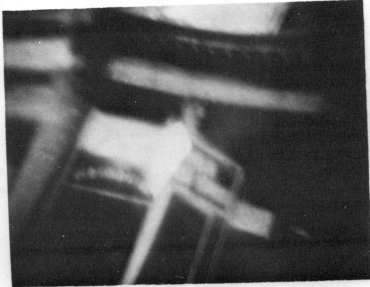

children designated to give the signal for Florrie to snap, was a return to a dark version of 11 (fig. 44). Fourteen was the new theme, a bit different this time but still not really identifiable, of which number 15 (Carl and Florrie still manning the camera) was the first clear statement (fig. 45). Sixteen was a blackie with only a trace of fogging on it, and 17, where one of the other children was called in to pinch-hit on the gismo in an effort to revive the magic (they were all howling with disappointment as the images began to recede, but Carl and Florrie bravely stuck to their camera) showed Ted's face again. At this point, the insubstantial pageant having faded (leaving not a wrack behind), Ted took over, but it was not until number 31, with himself holding and Florrie snapping, and with several *formes frustes* of the two themes in between, that Ted got a fairly clear version of the to-this-day-unidentified structure in number 11 (fig. 46). It is as if this had been shot from a slightly different position from the image shown in fig. 44, if the directions of the parallel lines near the top of the picture are compared.

On another occasion at the Lehrburger home—same conditions but with no neighbors' children present—Ted started out by getting what appeared to be a ship emerging from the mists on number 14 (this is something he had been supposedly aiming to get) with Florrie holding the camera and gismo and brother Gerry, twelve, snapping (fig. 47). On number 26, with another theme (dancing figures—see later) and a few blackies and whities in between, Ted got a clearer version of the ship (fig. 48) with Carl holding and triggering the camera and Dr. Lehrburger holding the gismo. (The camera used on this one had been delivered by Dr. Paley only a few minutes before, after having been subjected to examination.) The ship finally revealed itself as a Matson liner by the fairly clear *M*'s on the smokestacks on shot number 32, Dr. Lehrburger on camera and Ted holding the gismo (fig. 49). (The children had just requested that Ted give them some positive identification of the ship.) A normal shot obtained during this session, and given here for comparison, shows a very interested child (Gerry) behind Ted (fig. 50).

Several pictures shot with Ted in no contact with the camera occurred at the already-mentioned session at the home of Dr. Jerome Gersten. One of these, fig. 51, was the most blurred ver-

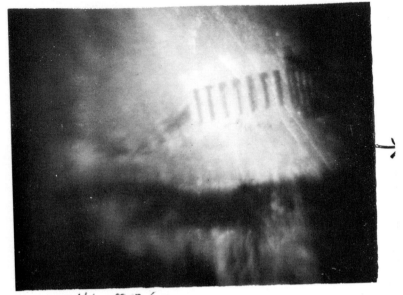

HL 5-13-65

(Fig. 45)

(Fig. 46)

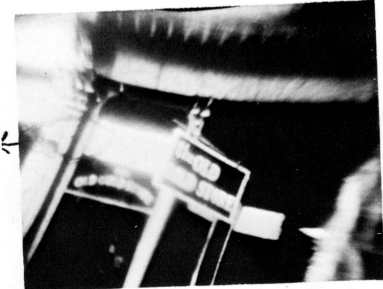

#31 HL 5.13.65

(Fig. 47)

(Fig. 48)

sion in the earlier-mentioned series of six in which someone appeared to have moved (figs. 27, 28). It was shot by Steven Gersten while standing about fifteen feet from Ted just beyond the archway to another room, with the unobstructed lens pointed away from Ted and into this room. Ted, sitting in a chair, simultaneously shot an empty dummy camera.

The special group of pictures, referred to earlier, that occurred with Ted in no observed contact with the camera, consisted of images of persons or objects in the room which would not normally have been expected to show up under the circumstances ostensibly obtaining. Precisely because of the fact, however, that more or less similar images could sometimes be produced by perfectly normal means, even if not under the specific conditions observed or assumed to have obtained in the case of the original, data of this sort are apt to present particular difficulties from an evidential standpoint. A good example of this occurred during a session at the home of Dr. Henry Frey. At one point, after several pictures of another variety had been obtained, Ted asked Mrs. Frey to hold and trigger a camera while pointing at him as he stood a couple of feet away facing her in the middle of the room. He then asked my wife to place her palm flat over the gismo being held by Mrs. Frey. At his signal "Now," Mrs. Frey snapped, and the picture that emerged was that of a chair, table, window drapes, and part of an upright piano behind her (fig. 52). The best of the controls (fig. 53) done in an effort to duplicate the picture that Mrs. Frey had snapped (and with the camera moved to various positions—it certainly could not be duplicated from the position it had been held at by Mrs. Frey) failed to get exactly the relations of the objects to each other that were shown on the original print, which seemed conceivably to be on a different projective scale. In these controls, if the size of the chair was approximated, the figures on the drapes came out a different size and in a different parallactic relationship to the chair; and if both these were angled closer to the relationship shown in the trial print, then the piano didn't show, and so forth. Nevertheless, one could not be certain, without an almost exhaustive number of control shots—which was decided to be simply not worth the trouble—that a fair duplicate could not finally have been made.

#32 Lihu 3-4-65

(Fig. 49)

(Fig. 50)

(Fig. 51)

(Fig. 52)

(Fig. 53)

The difficulty arises, however, if we assume that an exact duplicate is possible, right down to the tonal qualities of the original print, that we have no way of assuring ourselves—especially if two or three cameras were in use, as they were at Dr. Frey's—that neither Ted nor anyone else, possibly for a gag, had not shot the original while it was thought that no one was observing. If, in instances of this sort, on the next shot someone's hand is placed over the gismo or the lens, thus blocking out any light and any possibility of another imprint, or if the camera is so angled that little light enters anyway, the image that would emerge would, of course, be the one that had just before been shot on the sly.

As it happens, this is not just an hypothetical possibility. Once, at a session at the home of Dr. James Galvin, I observed Ted picking up a camera (which, as I have stated, he rarely did) and moving to another part of the room with it. On his face was a look of pure mischief. As he passed in front of a lamp, I saw the index finger of the hand carrying the camera begin to fish for the trigger and then with a deft movement trip the shutter. I immediately took the camera from him and quietly but meaningfully pulled the print and, without bothering to develop it, crumpled it up and tossed it into the wastebasket. Ted, looking on with an amused gleam in his eye, got the message without my having to say a word.

I never had occasion to catch Ted up on anything like this again. Nevertheless, it is impossible to assure oneself, when examining or re-examining the data on the circumstances surrounding a shot such as that done at Dr. Frey's before everyone's eyes, that all movements before, during, and afterward were perfectly covered, and that neither Ted nor the camera in use had been out of sight in between the trial print in question and the one immediately before it. When one tries to reconstruct the situation even minutes later, to say nothing of trying to flesh out the cold notes days or weeks later, one is aghast at the possible, if not wholly probable, loopholes. Minutes later, the slightest hesitation of memory looms up as a painful and unresolvable doubt; and days or weeks later, when one's notes begin to look as bare as Old Mother Hubbard's cupboard, one decides, regretfully but with a definite sense of relief from oppression, to scrap this or that print as evidence of anything except the difficulties and risks of making inferences from imperfectly controlled or notated experiments.

Another example of this class of data, which I should like to cite by way of an introduction to what will surely emerge as one of the standard formal objections to the data *in toto,* occurred at the already-mentioned session held at the home of Dr. Hall. At the time this occurred Ted had already shot over thirty presumptively paranormal prints under a variety of conditions, including seventeen definitely structured pictures. The print under discussion was produced following the series of shots 49 through 52 described earlier (figs. 18 through 21). For shot 53, immediately following, young Ben disconnected the wink light, at Ted's suggestion, and held the camera and gismo while he also, at Ted's suggestion—Ted was beginning to improvise freely now—did the triggering when he himself felt ready. The result was a blackie. During this entire series Ted had not been out of a chair on one side of the room. For shot 54, immediately afterward, with Ted still not having budged from his chair, Ben was directed by Ted to take the camera, which Ted had had no contact with, into the study, shown to the left of the two vestibule walls jutting up vertically in the diagram made immediately afterward by Dr. Hall (fig. 54). Ted then asked that an empty camera be handed him, which he held pointed at himself. Dr. Hall (LH), stood in front of him at *A*, holding the gismo. Mrs. Hall, at Ted's request, joined Ben behind the far wall and covered the lens of the camera being held by Ben with her hand. At the moment when Ted snapped his own empty camera and yelled "Now," Ben triggered the camera he was holding. Immediately I requested Ben to stay where he was. I went over to him and, in everybody's sight, took the camera from him for immediate development of the print. At the same time I directed Ted, who allowed me at such times to take command, to remain where he was until the print had been developed. The print that emerged, causing Ben, who had been peering over my shoulder, to exclaim, "Oh, my God," is shown in fig. 55. A somewhat blurred Dr. Hall is shown standing at the place where I am designated as sitting.

Now here we have a situation where we can be as certain as direct observation will permit that Ted could not have taken the picture. But Ben and perhaps Mrs. Hall could have, perhaps a minute or so before Ben's 'official' triggering, and when this formal

(Fig. 54)

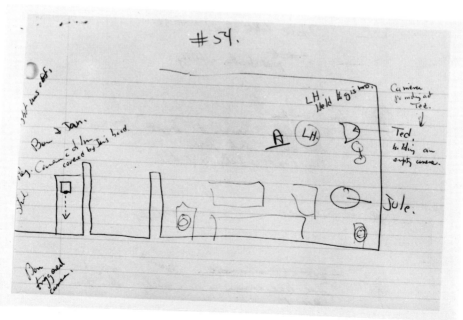

(Fig. 55)

objection is raised, as it should and as it inevitably will be (if we can judge from the entire history of this subject), their disclaimers, or my faith in them, will have little weight. Unfortunately here again controls done at the time and later were near enough to the original print, even though none—we took about thirty—was able to come up with a good match for its peculiarly velvety quality, or with anything even faintly resembling the shadow at the upper right-hand side (for which to this day we have no explanation), to force us to keep the aforementioned formal objection firmly in mind. But the fact is, nevertheless, that, except for the shadow of debatable significance, the picture is more or less duplicable and thus under the circumstances described had to be eliminated as evidence.

A number of pictures of this general type—that is, of objects or persons in the room—had to be ruled out on the same grounds, because Ted had asked that someone's hand be over the lens or gismo, and because the pictures were, in principle, reproducible. Nevertheless, this particular issue should not be closed without one or two points of possible relevance being touched upon. The first is that though it may be risky to make firm judgments about *some* pictures that turn out to be replicable by normal means, the fact that a picture can be so reproduced in major part may not by itself be taken as a presumption of how it *was* produced. I should like to cite in this connection two of at least a dozen 'in the room' pictures that, so far as I am concerned, could not conceivably have been produced by normal means, unless I and in one case two other people were not only in trance while this was done but had also, while in such a state, managed somehow to get onto film certain details that could not later be duplicated. In both cases, however—and this is the essential point here—the main geometric features of the images produced were capable of being more or less exactly duplicated on controls, indicating that the planes and angles represented were, as in those 'hand over the lens' pictures we have decided to rule out, on the same projective scale as other pictures done by the cameras in use. The first was taken by me on an evening when I was working alone with Ted in an electro-encephalograph laboratory, trying to see, before he went to bat in a full-dress runoff under electroencephalography scheduled for a couple of nights later, if he could overcome his aversion to working in hospital settings. After several interesting results in different positions, I seated Ted in a corner of a little cubicle while I stood a couple of feet in front of him, holding the camera and gismo pointed at him. At his signal I triggered, and produced, for our first shot this way, a blackie. A control done immediately showed only slight fogging, which was not too unexpected as I had detached the wink light and there was little light in this corner. On the following shot, which I took again pointing at Ted and without the camera having been out of my hands in the interval— we were using only one camera this evening, and there was thus no chance here for Ted to pull a fast one—the print that emerged shows the screened window between the room we were in and the adjacent room, and an open door to the corridor beyond (fig. 56). All this was behind my back as I shot, over my right shoulder. Over my left shoulder was the light which shows up in the print

4/12/65 Ted in NE Cor chair EEO #

(Fig. 56)

(Fig. 57)

#6 ~ John M Wadsworth 3/12/65

as a bright square (and which I was not so good in duplicating in attempts at double exposures).

A second picture whose main features could be reproduced but which, in my judgment and in that of two other witnesses could not have been normally produced, occurred at a spur-of-the-moment session at my home when Dr. John Wadsworth unexpectedly dropped in, was introduced to Ted (about whom he had heard a great deal), and asked if it would be possible for him to witness some trials. Despite my protests, because we had an important trial session arranged for the following evening, Ted insisted on going into his act. Film was freshly opened and inserted by me under Dr. Wadsworth's supervision. At first there came only a few blackies and whities, perfect but disappointing to Ted, who felt that this was no way to treat a guest. But then, without moving from his chair, and with no break in supervision between the last picture and the following one, Ted asked that the camera be handed to Dr. Wadsworth, who was standing about four feet away. He next ordered my daughter, Joanna, to hold the open gismo over the lens, which he directed to be aimed at himself in the fully lighted room. Clearly, what should have emerged on the print triggered by Dr. Wadsworth was a picture of Ted. What did emerge was an image of Joanna standing where she was but seemingly shot from the angle which would have resulted had Ted taken a picture of her from where he was sitting (fig. 57). Superimposed on her was the faint image of an unidentifiable triangular structure. This picture (except for the triangular structure) was more or less replicable from where Ted sat; but a control shot from Joanna's position showed, as was expected, only Ted. (Outside of French doors some six feet behind Joanna and a window the same distance to her left, there were no mirrors in the room.) Additional controls attempting double exposures in both directions, both with and without wink light, showed the expected double images.

We see thus, just to keep the record clear, that not every picture of persons or objects in the room that was capable of being reproduced on a control necessarily had to be of normal origin. Naturally, speaking for myself, I grant Mrs. Hall and young Ben full cogency when (nonchalantly inspecting their nails, no doubt) they bring up the fact that the formal objection which I had to take account of in their case will surely be brought up in mine and the others' too, the possibility, that is, that what we did and what we say we did might not actually coincide. They are quite right. We shall return to this and similar matters very shortly because they are certainly germane to the entire question of the evaluation of any of the data given.

The second point I should like to bring up before categorically tossing out all pictures of persons or objects in the room with Ted that were taken with someone's hand over the lens or gismo, is that a presumption that Ted was probably up to no good every time he requested—or ordered—someone to place his hand over the gismo is not justified. The fact is that in numerous instances when Ted did this the expected blackies *did* eventuate when the camera was triggered, and in one very dramatic instance when the camera was not triggered. On the latter occasion, Ted had just finished a successful series of shots while under electroencephalography, for which he had had to have about twenty electrodes pasted to his scalp, with wires coming from each one. Beginning to improvise, he suggested that Dr. David Metcalf, who had been supervising the electroencephalography, stand in a corner of the room, about four feet from where he (Ted) was sitting, and with his hand over the gismo hold and trigger a camera pointed at him. The picture that emerged, which appeared to be a peculiar montage of different parts of the room and objects in it rather than a simple multiple exposure, Dr. Metcalf is still, so far as I know, trying to duplicate on controls. (I gave up trying even to approximate it after twenty-four tries.) A couple of trials later, and after I had alerted him to the methodological dangers of this particular situation, Dr. Metcalf got ready again to do the same thing, at Ted's behest. He stationed himself in the same corner, held the camera pointed at Ted, with his hand over the gismo, and was just about to shoot when he abruptly changed course and, instead of triggering, pulled a film tab out to start development. "Perhaps we ought to make damned sure that nothing funny is going on here," he explained. I was immensely relieved when it was a blackie since, apart from any dereliction on Ted's part, it would not have been at all outside the limits of possibility for a result other than a blackie to emerge. (We have no way of determining the moment of imprint and merely make the working assumption, ordinarily, that it occurs when the trigger is snapped.) However, I didn't have much time to reflect on these matters as, with fascinated dismay—I believe that my jaw went slack as I sat paralyzed, completely unable to head off what I recognized perfectly clearly as impending disaster—I saw Ted beginning to go into one of his demonic rages. For a couple of seconds after Dr. Metcalf had come out with his blooper about making damned sure that nothing funny was going on, Ted didn't perceptibly react; but suddenly, as if the chemical reaction in his hypothalamus (as the neurophysiologists would have it) finally got to completion, he began slowly rising from his chair, his face getting purple with rage, and his eyes began to take on the look of such crazed malevolence that all I could think of at that moment, oddly, was an old movie of Dr. Jekyll and Mr. Hyde in which John Barrymore changed before one's eyes into one of moviedoms all-time-great fiends, fangs and all. At any rate, I no sooner had uncurled my toes from the threat of one possible disaster, Dr. Metcalf pulling something other than a perfect blackie, when I found on my hands a profane and violent madman the likes of whom I had not seen in all my dealings with psychotically disturbed patients. "Funny! Funny!" Ted screamed as he started yanking wires from his head, great clumps of hair coming along (his scalp looked moth-eaten for weeks afterward). "I'll show you goddamn sonofabitchin' bastards what's so funny!" Before we knew what was happening he had started to flail his way out of the cubicle, tearing violently at various wires as they ran into their insertions in the wall and ripping out whatever he could get his hands on. By now I had risen to action, as I foresaw thousands of dollars' worth of damage to specially constructed electronic equipment if I didn't restrain this madman, but there was no holding him. He simply fought past me and, thank God, without touching one of the machines, took off wildly down the corridor, cursing foully as he lurched along with a couple of wires still trailing rather festively from his head. I found him later sleeping things off in one of the trash bins in the basement.

The point, in any event, whether Ted was protesting too much or not, is that there were numerous instances when Ted had asked someone to put his hand over the gismo where no fakery occurred because nothing but the expected blackies occurred, so it may not be assumed that this maneuver in itself justifies suspicion. But now I can present a case where quite definitely the presumption of fakery would have a hard time being defended because what did occur, hand over the gismo notwithstanding, was just not reproducible, even though, for the most part, the image in question consisted mainly—but only mainly, as it happened—of persons and objects in the room. This occurred at the home of Dr. Aaron Paley. Present were Dr. Paley, his sixteen-year-old son Bob, Mr. Billie Wheeler, Chief of the Medical School's Department of Audio-visual Education, and Drs. Henry Frey, Johann Marx, and Henry Lehrburger. (Dr. David Starrett, who was present at other pictures that came in on this evening, was out of the room taking a phone call.) Three cameras were in use simultaneously on this occasion. Ted sat on a couch pointing

(Fig. 58)

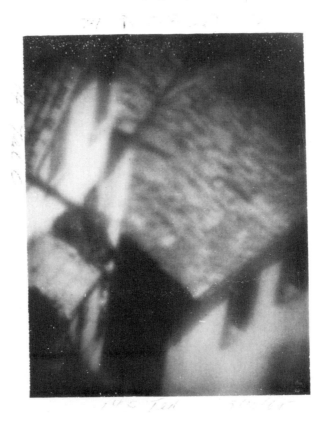

one camera at himself while Drs. Frey and Paley stood about three feet in front of him pointing cameras they held at him. Between them stood Dr. Marx, who held his hands over the gismo each was holding in front of the lens. At Ted's signal they all shot. Dr. Paley got a blackie, which would have been expected under the circumstances. Ted got the unidentified picture shown in fig. 58 (clearly distinguishable embryonic forms of which were got on two earlier trials with Ted about two feet away from the camera and gismo being held and operated by Dr. Marx), while out of the camera held by Dr. Frey emerged the picture shown in fig. 59. The triple shooting was nicely caught on movie film by Mr. Wheeler. (This was the session during which the pictures in figs. 39 through 41 were produced.)

The importance of the picture at the production of which Dr.

(Fig. 59)

Frey officiated (we shall not discuss here the question of how we are to determine who was the instrumental agent behind it) lies in the fact that not only was it impossible to duplicate the production of certain parts of it—for instance what appears to be something like, but was nevertheless plainly not, antlers being held by an arm(?) covering the upper portion of someone's (Bob's?) face—but in the fact that even the parts of it representing objects in the room—pictures, table, and Bob himself—could not be duplicated on multiply exposed control shots in anything like the way they emerged on the trial print. The image under the 'antlers' is of an abstract painting on a wall at right angles to the one on which the other pictures can be seen. Note that the board ceiling of the room and the beams emerge for the most part without any superimposed details of other structures that come through on multiply exposed control shots, and that the inexplicable 'arm,' lower face, and 'antlers,' also show no evidence of being crossed by other images. Even in attempts to heighten the contrast of the original print in reproduction, such crossing lines did not emerge. The conclusion we are led to, thus, is that the print represents not a multiple exposure but a kind of montage that, under the circumstances, could not have been produced by any known means.

Now the advantage of the movie-film record, in an instance of this sort, is not just in providing a means of repeatedly re-examining some of the circumstances in which the print was allegedly produced, but in also providing a clear demonstration that the parties to the event in question were not deluding themselves in trance at the time. This hypothesis, which has been offered in connection with the evaluation of many types of allegedly paranormal occurrences, must be taken seriously if only because it will assuredly be brought up when most other critical objections have been dealt with as fully as possible. Since we can confidently expect this to be the case with the present data, I think it will be in order, before going on to the evidential significance of other types of data, to devote a few pages to this and to its empirical, if not logical, successor, the ultimate in counter-hypotheses, that of wholesale fraud and collusion.

CHAPTER VIII

Certain Objections

I HAVE no categorical objection to what is loosely termed the trance hypothesis as applied to the question of the authenticity of allegedly paranormal data. Indeed, I myself, as well as hosts of others, have experimentally produced, by suggestion and hypnosis, all sorts of illusions (hallucinatory and other) as well as distortions of judgment and anomalies and monstrosities of belief, with and without the immediate knowledge and consent of the parties involved. Every person experienced in the theory and application of hypnosis knows, moreover, that it is sometimes extremely difficult, if not impossible, to discern where a state of fairly light suggestibility, very casually induced, leaves off and where what amounts to deep trance, with its enormously expanded horizon for the evocation of an almost unlimited universe of reality contradicting illusion, begins. I can hardly protest, therefore, that something along these lines may not have been going on in our sessions with Ted. I am ready to concede that Ted and I might have so influenced the mental processes of witnesses that they may have stoutly testified to having observed what they did not in fact observe and, what is just as important, vice versa. It may be, thus, that only a few instances, such as the one just presented and

several others that are registered on movie film, will survive this
formally admissible objection.

I strongly feel, however, that if this hypothesis is going to be
brought in at all it should, by rights, be brought in on both sides
of the fence so that it will apply equally to the case of witnesses to
an allegedly paranormal event claiming that they *failed* to observe
such an occurrence or, as is more relevant to the data presently
under discussion, that they failed to observe such-and-such precautions being taken. (There were one or two such instances.) Such
witnesses might be asked to demonstrate, if possible, how they
know they were not in trance, or at least not compliant victims
of an insidious but effective process of suggestion on the negative
side of the ledger. Curiously, this is never brought up as a purely
logical consequence of entertaining the trance hypothesis—that it
has, rightfully, to be applied to both sides of an event whose
occurrence, or the circumstances of whose occurrence, is in some
question.

I recall an amusing story in the fascinating book about ESP
among the Australian aborigines by Ronald Rose who, in his
research among these last of the stone-age people, showed that not
only was the incidence of ESP in ordinary card-calling tests about
twice as high among these people as among populations whose
ideas of time, space, and causality had been developed in the late
Western scientific mold, but also that the distribution of the high
and low scorers was comparatively stable over a three-year period,
one pipe-smoking old aboriginal lady being the high scorer of the
group at both testing periods. However, Rose had no luck in
running down the factual basis of stories told by these primitives,
and apparently accepted as part of their world view, about certain
feats of materialization by their "clever men," or witch doctors.
On one occasion, when Rose had finally succeeded in tracking
down one of the reputedly most potent of these (a feat which
apparently was scarcely less difficult than getting led to the faceless
chief operative of a complex counterespionage hierarchy) and
wangling a demonstration out of him, what he saw was not a
respectable cloud of ectoplasmic material emerge and take form
out of the Clever Man's mouth, as two aboriginal witnesses present
swore was the case, but just a thin trickle of spittle running
down the old fox's chin. Clearly, he concluded, the two had been

in some sort of hallucinatory trance. It never occurred to him that *he* might have been the victim of autohypnosis, and that his failure to perceive something might have been just as spuriously based. Here we had two opposing world views in clash, with no neutral Einsteinian observer, outside of both of them, to point out at the time how devilishly difficult it might be to say what was *really* what.

I am forced to agree, in view of the formal relevance of the trance hypothesis (which some may feel, wrongly I hold, to be somewhat on the frivolous side), that an ideal system, coming back to our own data, would have been on all occasions to have all participants in the trial sessions covered at all times by cameras grinding away from several angles—cameras concealed, perhaps, in walls and ceilings, as in banks and supermarkets. I have no doubt that some agency like NASA, or even its poor relation, the Armed Services, will institute such a system if they ever find someone like Ted to work with. Meanwhile we shall have to limp along with only partial coverage and, for the rest, leave the reader to his own judgmental devices as this issue hangs in the balance.

Before going on to further data of evidential significance, however, I think we might as well meet head on and deal with the ultimate counterhypothesis to the authenticity of data purporting to provide evidence of so-called paranormal occurrences, the hypothesis that not only the principal subject being investigated (in this case Ted) was guilty of fraudulent acts—and in sufficient quantity and variety to account for the data in question—but also, if required, as many witnesses (including, of course, the chief investigator, in this case I) as testified to the occurrence of the data as reported. Obviously there is little point in adducing data that, in the absence of a simple- or collusive-fraud hypothesis, might provide the really clinching evidence if, in its presence, these data completely lose their force.

There are no data in the history of psychical research that have not, either directly and specifically or implicitly, been subjected to this counterhypothesis, on occasion with a virulence that has gone considerably beyond the professedly purely logical framework that its proponents sometimes claim to be its *raison d'être*. The fact is that, when the chips are down, organized science, through some of its more articulate spokesmen, whose printed words come to have an effect far beyond the arena in which they first appear (so that this is sometimes about all some otherwise-well-informed scientists know of the field), has no hesitation in bringing in this argument to stop all arguments.

Logic alone, unfortunately, has very little to do with this state of affairs. If there is one thing that the psychical research of the past eighty years has demonstrated over and over again—in fact, this is practically the only thing it can demonstrate upon demand—it is that the ordinary canons of scientific demonstration break down where evidence in this field is concerned. On the purely logical side (I shall get to the emotional side of things in a later chapter) we seem to be trapped in what might be termed the fallacy of the ever-receding horizon, which, in a nutshell, amounts more or less to always winding up where you were before, no matter how much evidence is adduced or what its quality. The way the thing works is that what is termed the antecedent (or just on-the-face-of-things) improbability of anything like psi phenomena is held to be so great that no evidence, as far as official science goes, ever succeeds in racking up the required number of points to balance it out. Thus after a given piece of evidence is put on trial and ruled against on this basis, the antecedent improbability of psi phenomena remains exactly what it was before, and the next go-around starts from—and, as one can see, arrives at—exactly the same place.

The gimmick that plays the major role in this Alice-in-Wonderland swindle is a variant of the one used by David Hume in his well-known argument against miracles. Is it more likely, asked this eighteenth-century British philosopher, that nature moves out of its course or that human testimony is fallible? When put this way no person pretending to any degree of rationality would do other than rule in favor of the latter alternative. But despite the fact that no sophisticated person would put things this way today—even the man in the street knows that it is not nature that is involved but merely our picture of nature, and that this, unlike what obtained in Hume's comparatively placid times, changes almost daily—this venerable chestnut is brought out when everything else fails and becomes thus the final hurdle that no piece of evidence has ever succeeded in taking. The only really modern advance in this argument has been the stripping off of the velvet glove implied in such courtly eighteenth-century terms as 'fallibility' and the getting right down to the brass knuckles of terms like mendacity, fraud, and collusion. Thus two of the strongest pieces of experimental work produced in recent years were attacked not on ordinary methodological or statistical grounds but, on the contrary, on the grounds that since these aspects of the work involved seemed unassailable, the only plausible conclusion left, and the one preferred hands down by each of the two critics concerned (each representing what may be more than a modest segment of orthodox scientific opinion today), was that some of the personnel involved in these investigations—in one case something like sixteen independent witnesses and checkers, several of them of high academic standing and not all of them by any means benevolently inclined toward the psi hypothesis—were collusively conspiring to produce gigantic frauds.[1]

On a lower level of discourse—to diverge for a moment from the main point—one runs into somewhat similar arguments, where the logic involved is likely to be more informal but no less effective because it is not explicit. One comes across it not in scientific journals, as in the case of the Humean argument, but in small scientific groups and societies, and it is not so much expressed as attitudinal. It is a variant of 'the man who speaks with angels' argument. In a well-known story, the pupils of one famous rabbi in the old country, in extolling the virtues of their leader, make the point to a rival faction that their rabbi speaks with angels. How do you know? the rival group asks. Because he says so. But how do you know he is telling the truth? Because, comes the answer, a man who talks with angels doesn't tell lies. The version of this argument that is used in reverse against people who give testimony or adduce evidence in parapsychology (and I have seen this many times) is: How can you credit anything that a person seriously interested in parapsychology says?

In the case of the collusive-fraud hypothesis, at any rate, I am again, as in the case of the trance hypothesis, forced to plead *nolo contendere.* I am not going to attempt to deny its cogency on its own grounds. In its own terms it is categorically unarguable and un-outflankable. In the first place, there is no such thing as a

[1] See Hansel, Price.

witness of unimpeachable integrity, be he the Bishop of Burpington (I hope there is no Burpington) or the Director of Advanced
Studies at the University of Astralvania, if for no other reason
than that, when the stakes are high, there will always be someone
to impugn it, always someone to lower the cloud (if it can possibly be done) that suspicious characters are proverbially supposed
to labor under. But quite apart from this, the eminence of people
has not in actual fact proved an infallible index to their integrity.
One has only to think of defecting physicists, the Thomas Wise
literary hoax, or the Piltdown-man fraud (to name only the
better-known ones) to realize that men in positions of highest trust,
or enjoying enviable reputations for competence and integrity, can
sometimes act, in relation to a given set of expectations, completely falsely. The question of motive is largely irrelevant because we are rarely in a position to adduce the really significant
facts of the matter, which may, indeed, be locked in someone's
unconscious. Secondly, we are only too well aware of behavior in
everyday life which runs counter to the dictates of common sense
and a naïvely conceived pleasure-pain balance.

However, the reason I am not going to attempt to refute the
collusive-fraud hypothesis, as others on occasion have (to my mind)
been unwise enough to try to do, is not just because it happens
to be logically impregnable (if one insists, all of a sudden, on being
that logical) but because I seriously doubt that it would do the
slightest good even if it could be refuted. The mind would tend
to close over the evidence anyway. If we may judge from everything that has ever happened in this field, the force of the data
presented in this book will soon enough become attenuated to
the point of extinction unless specific consequences follow from
their publication. Two almost indispensable ones, in my opinion,
are: one, that others besides Ted turn out to possess 'thoughtographic' abilities and be capable, perhaps through training, of
demonstrating them (Ted himself has complete confidence that
this will be so); two, that the presentation of these data will induce
scientists of good will and integrity to form a national or international committee of acknowledged authority to carry out tests
on Ted and finally to spell out publicly a verdict and the inferences from the data obtained. I might say in passing, however,
that such tests, if their purpose is sincerely to investigate and

not simply to debunk, should be carried out in a spirit which is prepared to recognize that if the phenomenon exists it has its own laws and does not necessarily appear on command or conform to completely arbitrary conditions. The tests, therefore, should be spaced over a sufficient period of time and should take sufficient account of the delicate psychological nature of the postulated phenomenon, to encourage rather than to discourage its appearance. (By the same token it would be neither feasible nor prudent for Ted to respond to any and every 'put up or shut up' challenge by individuals, groups, or organizations—*e.g.*, newspapers—whose purpose is open to some question. We have already had some experience with the unfortunate consequences of this sort of thing, and I must inform the reader that such requests will have to be ignored as scientifically pointless.)

Thus all we can hope for is for Ted or someone with similar abilities to come through in more or less official tests, and for this to happen often enough so that the collusive-fraud hypothesis becomes not logically inapplicable, as it plainly never will become no matter how many pillars of the scientific community are involved, but practically of little moment, like the arguments against inductive reasoning. (Perhaps there will some day be more people capable of being put under the shadow of the collusion hypothesis than there will be those who will care to raise the issue.)

Without a train of consequences of this sort, at any rate, I can guarantee that the data presented in this book will soon enough lose whatever effectiveness they may initially have had as far as being able to stir up an eddy in the mainstream of science goes. No known piece of evidence in the history of psychical research has failed in this way to lose its overall effectiveness, even after numbers of people became privately convinced, collusion hypothesis or no, Hume or no Hume, that the data involved, for their money, were unassailable. They were unassailable and absolutely dead, bypassed, effectively erased from the minds of thinking, acting men as if they had never existed.

In psychoanalysis we have a term for the process that goes on here: It is called 'isolation,' the stripping of a raw fact from its affect or emotional significance. It is a special form of the denial of reality which characterizes the mental life of most people some of the time (*e.g.*, the denial of the fact of their own inevitable

death; of the fact that ten thousand people a day starve to death
on this bountiful earth of ours) and of some people, who have certain well-known morbid tendencies, a good deal of the time. It
is almost always the result of some emotionally disturbing or
threatening aspects of having to face certain facts full on, in all
their implications, and is a defensive maneuver that allows business as usual to go on in the rest of one's life.

I won't go into this side of things here, but will simply state
again that there is little point in my attempting specifically to
defend anyone or the group involved in the securing of these data
against the charge of fraud and collusion since such a maneuver,
in the absence of consequences such as I have outlined, will turn
out to be of nit-picking significance anyway and the data involved—isolated, robbed of their affect and effectiveness in the
broader contexts of science—will, even if sworn to on a thousand
Bibles, stand only like spectral headstones in a dimly lit graveyard
of the mind.

May I, however, before leaving this subject, point out once
more that, from a purely formal standpoint, any hypothesis applied to any person or group of persons involved in observing,
securing, and validating a group of data should, by rights, be
applied to *all* such persons? I might mention, to come down to
cases, that while the only instance of possible fraud in Ted's case
that I personally observed is the one I have already reported, the
behavior of several hostile witnesses to Ted's trials, witnesses of
high standing whom I shall not, of course, name and whom I have
left entirely out of this account, came as close to what amounts to
downright scientific dishonesty as anything I can imagine. Where
psi phenomena are concerned, some people, apparently, proceed
on the principle that if fraud doesn't exist, it is necessary to invent it.

Now that this issue as I see it has been dealt with, perhaps we
may proceed to a type of datum which, granting provisional im-
munity, for working purposes, from the un-outflankable types of
hypotheses just discussed, ought to have considerable significance
from evidential as well as other viewpoints. These are data secured
in connection with attempts on Ted's part to hit targets chosen
by him and for him in various ways.

CHAPTER IX

The Target Situation

IT might seem that if Ted were repeatedly able to produce on film images corresponding to target structures more or less randomly selected for him, and that one could be sure he had had no prior means of knowing about, no hypothesis based upon normal means of image production would survive. But things are actually not as simple as this, at least not for everyone. The problem is: what constitutes a correspondence?

When Ted came up at Dr. Paley's with something that looked like, but actually was not, the Arch of Triumph in Paris, there arose the question of how we could best classify this. The image, as I say, was not the same as that of the target, unknown to Ted and me, that had officially been announced as such on the occasion of our formal auditorium experiment of two evenings before. It was close but, as in the instance of the image that emerged on the evening of our first experiment with the lensless camera, it was not identical. Second, and just as important from the standpoint of the formalities of conventional experimental evaluative procedures, and thus from the standpoint of objections that not a few scientifically trained persons would be bound to raise, no target had officially been set for Ted on this occasion. Since he

had not been explicitly directed to try for a particular image,
would it not be evaluating the situation a bit broadly to consider
the correspondence between the two representations, such as it
was, as definitely other than possibly that of chance? And if the
correspondence could be construed as conceivably the result of
chance, would it not then be open to any or all of the hypotheses
regarding normal means of image production that would otherwise apply?

On the following evening we were at the home of Dr. Robert A.
Bradley, where we had heard of strange goings-on suggestive of
poltergeist activity. Present, besides Dr. and Mrs. Bradley and my
wife and me, were Mr. Karl Vogel and Drs. Siegwalt O. Palleske
and Mario Iona of the University of Denver. Dr. Palleske supplied both camera and film. Ted wanted to start right out to catch
the ghost on film, but we asked him if he would mind first giving
us a close-up of the poorly visualized statue to the left of the left
pillar on top of the arch that he had gotten at Dr. Paley's (fig. 16).
Somewhat indifferently he agreed to try, though he would much
have preferred the ghost hunt. ("Don't they all wear sheets and
have pumpkins for heads?" he asked when the issue was raised as
to how he would identify the picture of a ghost.) He began with
one or two normals of his face, which soon faded out as blackies of
increasing depth took over. On shot number 8 the first image of the
evening appeared, a faint suggestion of columns, the base of
one and the top of another, broadly in the architectural vein of
the arch of the preceding evening but plainly not the same structure (fig. 60). On number 4 of the second roll, Dr. Iona triggering,
what appeared indeed to be a statue emerged on the top of the
column that had been vacant in the earlier print, as if in response
to our renewed requests for a close-up of the dimly seen statue we
had gotten the evening before. In this second print, fig. 61, the
placement of the image had undergone about a ninety-degree
rotation, the left-hand column came out slightly larger, and all
but the very top of the column on which the statue rested remained out of the picture. But the image was pretty clearly not
the close-up we had asked for, that is, of the statue produced at
Dr. Paley's.

Here too, thus, the problem arose of how to evaluate what had
taken place. In this instance, a more or less specific target had

(Fig. 60)

(Fig. 61)

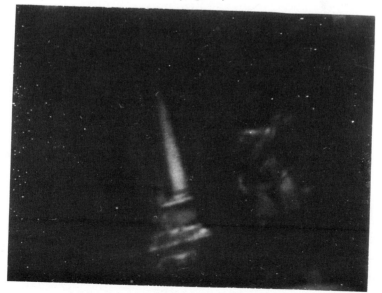

been set up for Ted to aim for, even though the way it had been
done was rather informal. It might appear to be ridiculous to
consider Ted's effort a total miss; but unless we can somehow
arrive at a kind of workable modification of the rules of the game
that everybody will agree upon, Ted's result could be officially
considered just as much of a miss, preposterous as this might
seem, as if he had come up with a camel or a canary. In fact,
several people to whom these data were shown, not overfond of
the psi hypothesis to start with, took this position and stuck to it.
It may be all very well for artists, who are completely at home
with their intuitively based evaluations, to consider this a bit on
the stuffy side, but scientific investigators, whatever their private
leanings—and we have only to recall Professor X and his rejection
of Ted's efforts because he came up with the wrong building—can
be very touchy in their official capacities about putting their seal
of approval on any evaluation that doesn't conform to conventional canons of procedure in this regard.

When we ask Ted to try for a target, what in effect we are doing
is employing one of the standard methods of testing a specific
hypothesis. The implied proposition, in formal terms, is: given
certain conditions, if the result of a particular set of operations
on the part of the experimental subject can be ascertained to fall
within a prespecified range of values, the hypothesis that the result
is due to either chance or to known means of production (outside
of collusion, of course) must be rejected. What is wrong in our
cases is that the data, however impressive they may be to some and
however suggestive and provocative to others, are just too ambiguous as they stand to give everyone a feeling of confidence that,
if they are rated as positive, grave errors are not being committed.
Here, of course, we are back to the old ever-receding-horizon
business. The errors wouldn't be considered so terrible if we were
playing the game of Twenty Questions at a party and someone had
got as close to the category requested as Ted had to the conceivably implicit or explicit targets. But where a great deal appears
to hinge on whether or not we evaluate a given experiment positively or negatively—some individuals imagine (erroneously, of
course) that all science stands or falls with the strength of the
bulwark against what has been called "the black tide of occult
mud"—and where any possibility of error is regarded by some as

potentially disastrous, the slightest departure from a strictly veridical one-to-one correspondence between target and result may be considered a very risky thing to allow.

However, other systems of evaluation are sometimes used. Had we said in advance, in the first instance cited (neglecting, of course, the fact that we weren't deliberately shooting for anything to start with), that we would accept anything that looked like a Roman-style arch and, in the second, that we would rate as a positive result anything that looked like a statue, we might be in a different position.

Something like this was actually tried on one occasion and the results, as luck would have it, were rather interesting. Dr. H. Marie Wormington, Curator of Archeology at the Denver Museum of Natural History, wanted to pick a specific target structure from a book on the pre-Columbian period in America; however, I suggested picking not one specific target but rather a general period or culture. This, I thought, would allow the degree of latitude that might make the difference between a hit and a miss in a tighter and more formal system of evaluation. Dr. Wormington agreed to this and named the Olmec period in Central America, from 800 to 400 B.C., as the target area. Ted was not told this choice, which I hardly think would have informed him much anyway. Shot number 7 (on film supplied by me) produced something that drew an excited exclamation from Dr. Wormington because, even though the image in it was obscured by some kind of white structure or cloud (fig. 62), it corresponded closely, even if not exactly, to part of one of the best-known Olmec artifacts in existence. A picture of one of these from Dr. Wormington's collection is shown in fig. 63. Shots numbers 8 and 14, however, seemed to impress Dr. Wormington even more. These were two slightly different versions (one of which is shown in fig. 64) of what appeared to her to be stelae that, so far as she knew, had not yet been described but were nevertheless consistent with the type of sculpted figuration seen in other well-known Olmec stelae, one of which she showed me in a photograph. (If these were not entirely from Ted's unconscious imagination, conceivably they may still be languishing in some Central American rain forest.) Had anyone asked me, by the way, what target Dr. Wormington would most likely have chosen, I would probably have said some-

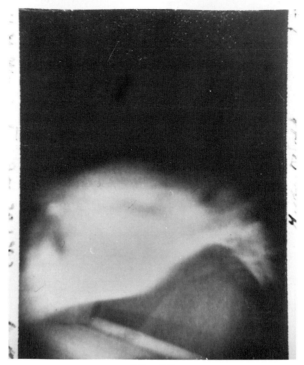

(Fig. 62)

(Fig. 63)

(Fig. 64)

thing from the 5,000 to 10,000 B.C. period in America, since this, so far as I knew, and not the Olmec culture, was her major interest.

Now here we have what might appear to be a successful payoff to our having made our evaluative framework somewhat more elastic. But even if such a procedure were acceptable to the old-guard methodologists of science—which is a big *if,* and probably wouldn't get us very far anyway; it would be like devaluating the currency but then having to work just as hard as before to pay for goods— it would hardly provide the answer to all the problems we would be faced with as soon as we stopped having the lucky breaks we had with Dr. Wormington. Suppose we had, in the first instance cited earlier, magnanimously agreed in advance to consider any arch at all—Moorish, Byzantine, Gothic—as a positive result, and Ted had come up not with an arch but with Joan of Arc, whose associative connection with the Arc de Triomphe is not too diffi-

cult to establish, or even a Triumph automobile (which Ted had
set his heart on). And suppose, in the second instance, we had
agreed to accept anything that looked even vaguely like a statue,
even a chess piece, whether in close-up or not, and Ted had come
up not with a statue but with a tailor's dummy or the Washington
Monument? And let us imagine that instead of coming up with
something like an Olmec artifact for Dr. Wormington, Ted had
produced a page right out of the *Farmer's Almanac,* which some
might construe as a relevant response because of the purely verbal
association between *Olmec* and *almanac.* How would we rate *these*
data? We can see at once that, to the very extent that we broaden
our boundaries to include a great many categories of data within
the range of what we will consider positive results, we lose that
fine power of discrimination between competing alternatives that
a good test for a specific hypothesis is supposed to provide.

The fact is, at any rate, that in no instance in which Ted was
given a target, revealed or concealed, to aim for did he come up
with an undistorted veridical response, that is, an image that bore
a point-for-point correspondence to the target as set out. (We will
recall that the Westminster Abbey target was really chosen by Ted
himself, even though it was accepted by the witnesses.) But now
comes a puzzling and highly significant fact: he repeatedly demonstrated his ability to cognize a hidden target, either specifically or
in terms of essential content, if, to beg a question, he had a mind
to, and even if he didn't manage to get his responses on film.

At the close of our officially somewhat-less-than-successful session before the local branch of the American Psychiatric Association, for instance, Dr. Merrill, one of the committee members
supervising the shoot, held a sealed envelope up to Ted and asked
what was in it. Ted's immediate response, the Eiffel Tower, was
quite correct. On another occasion Dr. Paley, another of the committee members, picked as a target an Indian tower dedicated to
the Hindu god Shiva. When Dr. Paley emerged from the room in
which this had been done, Ted immediately began to describe
the tower. "It's a pyramid, or a triangle, with a lot of circles on
it above one another." This was correct. On still another occasion
I picked as a target a full-page advertisement in a magazine. Its
two main features were a typewriter in the foreground and a
several-span suspension bridge in the background. As soon as I

came out of the room in which I had made my choice Ted said, "It's a bunch of little circles; no, it's the Brooklyn Bridge." His first choice I had to rate very high since that was exactly what the keys of the typewriter looked like from the angle they were shown in the ad, and his second, of course, I rated close to a bull's-eye.

Ted could be so good at this sort of thing, when he was in the groove, that it was sometimes hard to restrain him from trying to read the contents of people's minds and wallets indiscriminately, and I had repeatedly to point out to him that dozens, if not hundreds, of people could do this better than he but that the witnesses had come to see the thing that he was the champ at. When it came to getting these things down on film, however, Ted frequently missed, often to his own bafflement and despair. Nothing he got during the session following his correct calling of the target chosen by Dr. Paley bore the slightest resemblance to this target; and when he went on to picture shooting following his near bull's-eye with the target I had chosen on the other occasion, he wound up just about as far away from circles and bridges as one could get.

Now if we assume that it was not just from lack of ability correctly to cognize his targets that Ted was coming up with only near hits or wide misses, the problem arises of how to approach an understanding of what he was doing. If he could give us one Roman arch, why not the one implicitly asked for (and why not, while we are at it, at the time it was officially the target)? If he could give us a close-up of some statue in the ancient mode, why not the one requested? Were his substitutions, if they were substitutions, on a random basis? Was he being playful, or perverse? Or was he conceivably following deeper laws, lines of determination that were destined to remain for the most part hidden from us?

Let us put aside for the moment the methodological difficulties in trying to arrive at something more suitable than a simple hit-or-miss rating scale for Ted's responses and just continue to observe the sort of thing he does in a target situation. We can begin at a simple level, such as the near correspondences we have already seen, and proceed to more complex levels at which, using all the intuitive powers at our command, we can still make out,

(Fig. 65)

or at least imagine that we can, a connection of some sort between a given target and Ted's response.

One of the simplest examples of the distortion of a target picture in Ted's response occurred in a session at the home of Dr. James Galvin. It was here, it may be remembered, that Ted had felt impelled to do a bit of straying although, as one can see from the results about to be described, which occurred earlier in the session, there was no lack of the genuinely remarkable that evening. Near the start Dr. Galvin asked Ted if he could get on film a copy of an etching of the medieval town of Rothenburg (fig. 65) which was hanging on the wall of the room in which we were working. No sweat, said Ted; but would we mind if he didn't come up with exactly what was in the etching but with some of the buildings *around* those shown, which, he claimed, were pressing forward in his mind. He immediately came up with the image shown in fig. 66, which might not be of Rothenburg but appears at least to fit the image of buildings in the medieval mode and in fact can be seen to bear a certain correspondence to the target image. He then asked if we would mind if he went on to try again

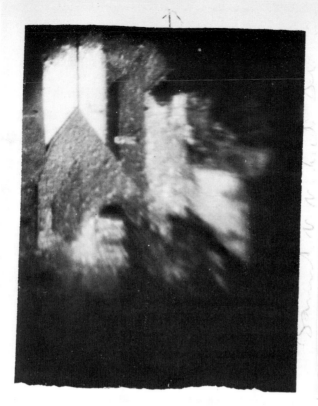

(Fig. 66)

for some shots of Central City, Colorado, buildings, which had started to come in two evenings earlier during the course of electro-encephalography. When these began to appear in the next few shots—at first they were a bit murky and indistinct and, as it turned out, were quite different from the Central City Opera House pictures he had got during electroencephalography—Ted asked how we would like it if he were to get two targets at once, one of Rothenburg and the other of whatever was coming in from Central City. He then asked Dr. Galvin to hold and trigger one camera, and his son, James junior, thirteen, to hold and trigger the other. While they knelt side by side in this way in front of Ted sitting on a sofa, Ted held gismos up to, but not quite touch-ing, both cameras and gave the signal to shoot. Dr. Galvin's print was a slightly altered version of the image shown in fig. 66. James junior's print is shown in fig. 67. It matches Williams' Livery Stable, across the street from the Opera House in Central City, with a few significant distortions, notably the size and somewhat elongated shape of the windows, and the fact that they appear to have been bricked in, which can be seen from a comparison with a picture of the livery stable (with Ted standing in front) taken several days later (fig. 68).[1] One of the most interesting distortions, however, is in the character of the masonry, which in the actual livery stable is old pressed brick (fig. 68, insert) and in Ted's picture is a kind of imbedded rock, which also characterized his image of the buildings in the medieval town. It might seem, in other words, that the livery stable had become endowed with this kind of masonry by a kind of perseveration, a carryover on a purely structural basis, as if an artist had had a certain amount of pigment left over after finishing one picture and had decided that he might as well use it for the next. (In a series of somewhat similar images of the same building that came in several days later, with Dr. Harold Elrick holding and triggering the camera as well as officiating with the gismo, the character of the masonry was not distinguishable.)

An interesting split-level near correspondence to a hidden target turned up in a session witnessed by Mrs. Marie Coleman Nelson, a psychologist. In this instance Ted presented us with a very revealing cutaway, as it were, into certain aspects of the 'perceptual' processes involved in his responses. (Ted not infrequently provided examples to suit the specific skills of the particular observer on hand.) Mrs. Nelson chose as a target the Hall of Mirrors at Versailles (fig. 69, upper left).[2] She made this selection in a room some thirty feet from where Ted and I were, and left it in the closed book lying on a table there. As far as Ted knew, she had chosen a building of some sort, but from a completely unknown source. I was aware only that she had tried to make her selection from a couple of vacation guidebooks, each containing close to a hundred pictures, that she had singled out

[1] In the control picture can be seen a patch on the wall where a playbill, shown to the left of a window in Ted's shot, had once been posted. The top four lines of the playbill in Ted's picture conform to the usual format—"Central City Opera House Association Presents"—but the lines below cannot be made out and to date have not been matched with any of the still-extant playbills of past years. A search through available sources by me and by Mr. James Davis of the Western History Division of the Denver Public Library, moreover, has failed to reveal evidence of the windows of Williams' Livery Stable ever having been bricked in.

[2] Photo in *France* (Cornerstone Library, 1963), supplied by French Government Tourist Office.

(Fig. 67)

(Fig. 68)

for this task. When Mrs. Nelson rejoined Ted and me after making her choice, Ted at first said that he was confused because two
kinds of images were coming up to him. He asked for a pencil
and paper and rapidly sketched the pillared and domed structure
shown in the lower portion of fig. 69; but he said he also "saw"
or somehow got the impression of "sails," which he proceeded
also to sketch (lower right) before taking up the camera. Then,
after one normal and several blackies, the image shown in the
upper right-hand portion of fig. 69 came in. This, with some
variation of angle of presentation, provided one of the two themes
of the evening, during which seventeen images were obtained.
(The second theme showed, rather unclearly but still recognizably,
what appeared to be a skiff, with sails down, on a river with the
kind of arched bridge and buildings along the far bank that can
be seen along the Seine River as it flows through Paris.)

What concerns us here is not only the two distinct types of
perceptual response which seemed to confuse Ted—the 'sails'
(which he served up in his drawing as a sort of hieroglyph) might
seem to have been based on something like a visual type awareness of the name Ver*sailles*—but the kind of presumptive process
which it makes sense to assume went into his distortion of the
target image into something structurally similar to but yet not
identical with it. He had been led to expect that a building would
be chosen as a target—the exterior of a building, that is, and not
its interior. If he did now somehow 'perceive' what appeared to
be columns and dome, which are the outstanding features of the
target picture, we can understand why he might have been led to
construct an image which would justify such an expectation,
namely a building with columns and dome as its principal *exterior*
features. Here distortion might be said to have occurred in the
service of the normalization of a perception that, in terms of a
prior set, would have to be judged as somewhat anomalous.

An instance in which we were able to observe the process of
perceptual and representational distortion taking place in two
stages, as it were, occurred during a session at the home of Dr.
David Starrett. At the beginning of the session, I noticed on Dr.
Starrett's bookshelf a book entitled, *Around the World in Two
Thousand Pictures* [3] and remarked that that would be a good title

---

[3] Milton A. Runyon and Vilma F. Bergane, eds. (Garden City: Doubleday, 1959).

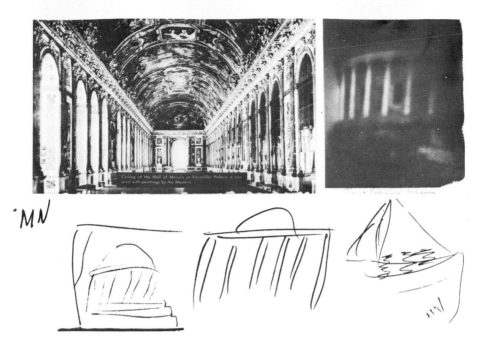

(Fig. 69)

(Fig. 70)

for Ted's specialty. Ted asked for the book and, without glancing
through it, started quickly flipping pages while holding it upside
down. "Say when," he commanded. Midway through, Dr. Starrett
said "when." We had landed on a page with pictures from Thai-
land on it, and after the building shown in fig. 70 had been
chosen as target, Ted hardly having looked at it, the book was
closed and put back on the shelf. After a couple of alternating
blackies and whities, Ted grew impatient. He asked for a pen and
rapidly sketched on an empty spot of newspaper next to an ad his
impressions of what the building looked like. In fig. 71 we see
how Ted had perceived it—a series of lines and planes, bearing an
easily discernible resemblance to the original but with some
transposition of the horizontal lines and the roof spikes. In the
next ten shots, interspersed with blackies and whities, Ted got
four only slightly differing versions of the image shown in fig. 72
which were, of course, impossible to duplicate on control shots.
The significant thing to note is that although both Ted's sketch
and his film images appear to be impressionistic renderings of the
target original, the film images seem to be a structural condensation of the latter—one can make out the crenelated effect in the
horizontal lines that can be seen in the original in the vertical
ones—and of the sketches.

In the examples just given, as in the earlier ones cited, Ted's
responses bear fairly obvious relationships to the target originals.
The next example of a presumptively distorted result in Ted's
target shooting is somewhat more complex, however, and leads
inevitably to the question of how far this sort of thing can go
before it becomes, so far as any scheme of evaluation goes, a clean
miss. Of the thirteen versions of a windmill that Ted produced at
Dr. Barbato's, several could be related to a target that had been
chosen by Dr. Barbato, but in a way that was neither expected
nor obvious. The target, selected from a book in a room about
twenty feet from where we were working, and not shown to Ted
or me until after the session, was a picture of the Piazza San Marco
in Venice (fig. 73). The two pictures which provide the best key
to the possible relationship between Ted's windmills and the
target are shown in figs. 24 and 74. In the latter we can see small
windows on the left-hand side of the tower corresponding to those
on the left-hand side of the tall tower, the campanile, in the target

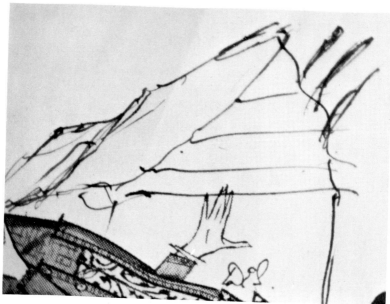

(Fig. 71)

(Fig. 72)

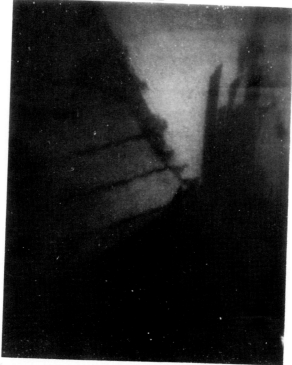

(Fig. 73)

(Fig. 74)

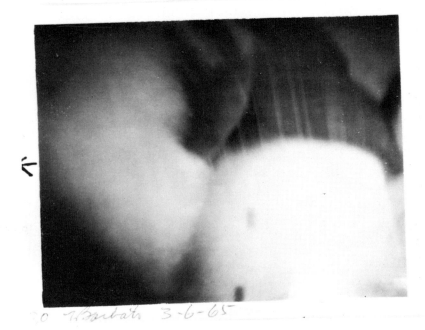

picture, a close-up of which is shown in the insert in fig. 73. In
the former, fig. 24, we can see the similarity between what we
referred to earlier as the toothbrushy looking windmill blades and
the striated structure to the right of the tower in the target picture,
the three floors of the building seen in receding perspective. It
is as if Ted had disassembled the target picture and had re-
assembled some of its component parts into a structure of entirely
different meaning and use and as if, once this transformation had
been accomplished, he then allowed the new structure to take off
on its own, resulting in images (fig. 25) which then bore little
discernible connection with the original idea. (In a session more
than a year later, incidentally, the Piazza San Marco target was
again presented to Ted, this time visually. His response once more
appeared to be a transformation, this time along quite different
lines.)

What gives the possibility of these distortions pertinence as far
as our present concern goes is that similar processes may be seen
to operate in a number of areas in which remembered or perceived images derived originally from the external world are
visually represented. Numerous experimental studies have eluci-
dated the role of various emotional, associational, and structural
factors in this kind of perceptual distortion, which has now become a commonplace of psychology. One of Fisher's subjects, who
had been tachistoscopically exposed (*i.e.*, for a fleeting instant) to
the image of a six-pointed star, and had been asked to draw the
image that came into her mind immediately afterward, drew the
stick figure shown at the left in fig. 75. At the right is the star
showing the presumptive derivation of the figure. Another subject
who was exposed similarly to the star, but who had recently heard
a joke about Sitting Bull, drew the image shown in fig. 76, also
presumably derived from the star. Similar results have been observed in dreams and hallucinations and in experiments with
people with so-called eidetic imagery, that is, with the capacity to
shut their eyes after looking briefly at a scene or a picture or a
printed page and still retain a vivid visual image of what they
have seen. Sometimes these images transform themselves, very
much in the manner of movie cartoons, television commercials,
and purposely contrived cinematic effects, so that what is actually
perceived a few seconds after exposure may bear only a tenuous

(Fig. 75)

(Fig. 76)

La tache devient lumineuse et rayonne comme un phare.

(Fig. 77)

structural relationship to the original. We may hypothesize some such process to have been the case with Ted and the target chosen by Dr. Barbato.

Not at all surprisingly, when we realize that all perception is subject to the processes of distortion and what Freud called secondary elaboration, we find that the sort of thing we may hypothesize Ted to have done in relation to the target chosen by Dr. Barbato shows up in the results of telepathic drawing experiments. Unfortunately, this is precisely what has provided critics with the loophole they need for rejecting just about all of this work and turning to the more controlled statistical type of experiment (to which, however, they have then never failed to find other grounds for objection, as I have already pointed out). In an experiment done by Warcollier, the target given was the letter Y, as seen in fig. 77. In the response drawn by the experimental subject the *Y* may be seen (or hypothesized, depending on one's point of view) to have become the lighthouse sending forth its luminous beams. (The result is oddly like Ted's windmill.) In another experiment, the target of a pyramid with the ball on top was transformed into a carafe with a triangularly perceived glass (fig. 78). In similar fashion, in a telepathic drawing experiment done several years ago by none other than my young cousin Jonathan, my assistant at the Palmer House session with Ted in Chicago, and his younger brother James, the target, an envelope, was transformed into the hourglass seen on the right in fig. 79.

Granting the possibility of similar distortions and transformations in what Ted may produce in a target situation, we can see how inappropriate it might be to try to evaluate his responses in terms of simple hits or misses. In fact, while hits might be intuitively recognizable within a somewhat expanded framework of evaluation, it becomes risky, by the same token, to affirm with any degree of reliability that a given response is a clear and total miss. All we can say is that we have failed to find a key to a possible correspondence. At the start of a session, for example, for which I picked as a hidden target a magazine advertisement showing an airplane in the clouds (fig. 80), Ted's immediate verbal response was "A giraffe," which struck me, of course, as quite wide of the mark. However, if we can conceive of the tail section of the plane (on which *United* is seen printed) as being the long neck of a creature like a giraffe, and the tail wing as providing a crude outline of its head, we can begin to divine a conceivable structural nucleus for Ted's response. If we now put this together with the name Air France, whose advertisement on the same page thrust itself out at one, and which may conceivably have provided the *AF* for "gir*AF*Fe," we may imagine possible lines of connection between Ted's miss and the target. We often unconsciously do rebuses and picture puzzles of this sort; our dreams are full of them.

A somewhat similar combination of structurally related factors deriving from different modes may be construed as having possibly played a role in a response to a hidden target picked by Dr. Paley during a session at my home at which Dr. Johann R. Marx was also present. (Camera as well as film were supplied by Dr. Paley.) The target chosen was a French château known as

4

1. Bonnet   4

Une carafe et un
verre sur un plateau
puis en gros cristal

.

Je remarque que le verre
reproduit une facette de —

(Fig. 78)

(Fig. 79)

6:00 P.M.
3/5/60

ENVELOPE

SUB: "SAW apple"

Maintenon (fig. 81).[4] Ted, in a room about thirty feet away, said
he didn't know exactly what it was but only that it was "something
somewhere in France." He was less interested in whatever the target
was, however, than in the imminent arrival of Mariner IV in the
vicinity of Mars. He was sure he could get there first if he could
possibly loft his mind into space. What he came up with, when
the images started coming in, was several versions of the configuration shown in fig. 82, which struck everyone immediately
as condensing the black background and the rocketlike turrets of
the picture of Maintenon with the idea of a spacecraft (and conceivably even a 'fifth'—of Cognac, no doubt) in orbit. However, it
was not until an artist's conception of the Air Force Manned
Orbiting Laboratory (fig. 83) was revealed at a White House press
conference several weeks afterward that a fuller appreciation of
the conceivable cogency of Ted's response became possible. In
addition to the manifest structural correspondence was the fact
that the *maint* of Maintenon is pronounced like "manned," providing a nucleus for a response based on a 'heard' rather than
'seen' type of perception from which the 'sails' of 'Versailles' was
conceivably derived. Here, thus, we would hypothesize an auditory
association to have been condensed with a purely graphic element
to form the final configuration. The whole thing, of course, would
have had to be done on a purely unconscious basis, exactly as in
dreams, in this case as in a telepathic dream. (We would not
strictly hypothesize this to be precognitive since the design and
artist's conception of the Manned Orbiting Laboratory was already in existence and thus accessible to the roving mind at the
time of Ted's picture.)

Unfortunately, when evaluation of what is or is not a target hit
depends on arbitrarily specified rules of correspondence, it may
be difficult to arrive at any sort of consensus of agreement in a
particular instance. (It was for this reason that Ted, on my advice,
declined the conditions set forth by a committee of the British
Society for Psychical Research in connection with a prize offered
for the production of 'physical phenomena.' When target hits were
insisted upon as the minimal criterion of success, it was easy to see
that endless controversy might have ensued over what might be

4 From *Merveilles des châteaux de l'Ile-de-France* (Paris: Librairie Hachette,
1963). Photo: BONNEFOY—*Réalités*.

(Fig. 80)

(Fig. 81)

(Fig. 82)

(Fig. 83)

construed to be a 'hit.') A panel of judges is sometimes used to rate correspondences, but this is obviously no substitute for informed insight.

At any rate, if, when Ted appears to miss a target, we make the assumption that he is not just missing in random fashion but possibly substituting an image of his own choosing, we can sometimes see that, exactly as in the mechanics of dream elaboration from an unconsciously selected nucleus, which might be regarded in this sense as a 'target' of sorts, he preserves something of the original target after all. However, it may be a matter of the purest happenstance that a hidden connection comes to light. A curious series of this kind began with a session in which Dr. Johann Marx chose for a hidden target a picture showing the stones of one of

(Fig. 84)

the great pyramids (fig. 84).[5] Ted asked if the target wasn't cobblestones of some sort, which was not too bad, but he got little that evening suggesting cobblestones and came up instead with a couple of pictures of structures that he had casually glanced at in a book less than an hour before our session started and which, for undetermined reasons, had apparently become Ted's actual 'target for tonight.' Figs. 85 and 86 show what he got, and fig. 87 shows the same structures, Trajan's Column in Rome and the dome of the Church of Santa Maria di Loreto across the square from it, in a book, which I had just brought home that evening,[6] that Ted had leafed through rapidly as he was literally standing on the doorstep before our departure for Dr. Marx's home. Several weeks later, at Dr. Chapin's, the hidden target was picked from a picture book on Charleston, which neither Ted nor I saw—it was kept in another room—or knew the title of. Ted asked if the picture chosen were not on page 89. A check revealed that the book had no page numbers. "That's funny," said Ted. "I seem to see 89 or something like that." Nothing he got during the evening bore much resemblance to Charleston (unless the two walking people seen earlier in fig. 22 could possibly be in that city) but one thing he got several versions of was a pyramid (fig. 88) that looked very much like the pyramid of Dahchour on page 189 of the target book used by Dr. Marx (fig. 89). The picture constituting the end papers of the Charleston book [7] was of cobblestones and entitled "The Cobblestones of Chalmers Street." Conceivably the telepathically perceived idea of cobblestones might have evoked a latent memory of Dr. Marx's target, with CHARleston triggering the choice of dahCHOUR as the common link response. This is, of course, only a speculation, but it is a hard one to ignore when it is so consistent with so much of what we know of the magpie tendencies of the unconscious. The picture in fig. 88, incidentally, was shot with the lensless camera. Curiously, one of the other images that came in that evening was of a group of buildings around St. Peter's Square in Rome (fig. 90; see also 23) that was also pictured in the book on Italy from

[5] Samivel, *Trésor de l'Égypte* (Paris: Arthaud, 1945). Photos by Michel Audrain.
[6] Patrice Molinard, Georges Pillement, and Felicien Marceau, *The Rome I Love* (New York: Tudor Publishing Company).
[7] *Charleston.* Photographic Studies by F. S. Lincoln (New York: Corinthian Publications, Inc., 1946).

(Fig. 85)

(Fig. 86)

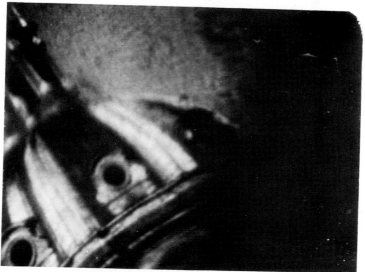

(Fig. 87)

(Fig. 88)

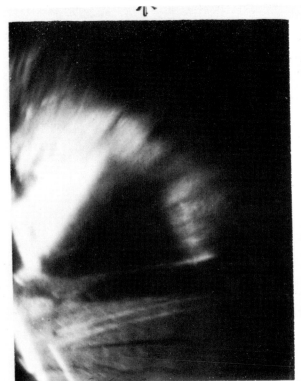

(Fig. 89)

which Dr. Barbato, three evenings earlier, had chosen his target. A portion of this picture is shown in fig. 91. Still another of Ted's images that evening (fig. 92) appeared to be a fusion of the shadows in his St. Peter's Square picture and the planes of the pyramid, as if Ted were out to demonstrate his virtuosity at unconscious condensation of structure, as well as, perhaps, his reluctance to be held down to any one simple target chosen by others.

Another example of Ted's apparent rejection of one target only to substitute something darkly derived from other elements lying about in the same source occurred at a session at Dr. Lehrburger's. The target chosen was a seascape from a group of pictures carried on two facing pages in the *World Book* volume in which the article on painting is found. When the fact that a target had been picked in another room was announced, Ted said immediately that he saw "dancing figures, like dancing clowns," and proceeded to get the image shown in fig. 93, on which figures that appear to be mumming or dancing may be seen. (When we asked for a

close-up, the better to identify the source of this image, we got
only the image shown in fig. 94, on which no figures can be seen.
This again was done with the lensless camera.) Although this bore
no relationship to the seascape, it bore an obvious ideological
relationship to a picture of the well-known Dégas painting of the
dancing ballerinas carried on the same page. But a closer structural correspondence was found a few pages away in a picture of
early Roman wall painting, shown in fig. 95.[8] Ted's figures are just
about the same size and seem almost to be cut out of the same
mold.

Still another example of a target response that seems to have
been altered by Ted according to a scheme—let us assume that
what happens is not purely random—that is just not revealed to us
but that again we are lucky enough to be able to trace from
certain bits and pieces that just happen to be lying around, occurred at the already mentioned session at the home of Dr. Hall.
Here too Ted appears to have rejected the hidden target set out
for him, but in a curiously ambivalent way. The target chosen
was from a book of photographs.[9] Ted got only one image that
could possibly have corresponded to it, and this was too blurry
and embryonic to be properly reproduced here. The bicycle that
came in several times during the evening, however, I had jokingly
predicted as the theme for the evening just before we had left my
home for Dr. Hall's, apropos its role in a ribald story that had
just been told. "Don't say that," pleaded Ted when I hazarded
that perhaps all we would get would be bicycles. "I'm just likely
to get one." However, Ted may not have totally rejected the
chosen target, as it turned out. The wavy spirochetal theme which
can be seen decorating what appears to be a wicker chair in the
bicycle pictures, one version of which is given here in fig. 96, bears
a striking resemblance to a decorative theme in a picture of a
cluttered-up museum of curiosa appearing on another page of the
book from which the target was selected. A relevant portion of this
is shown in fig. 97. In still another part of this busy picture may be
seen the struts of a roof beam (fig. 98) from which the V angle on
the frame of the bicycle may have been derived. One wonders

---

8 "Ulysses in the Land of the Lestrygonians." Courtesy Vatican Apostolic Library.
9 *Scotland*. Photographed by Edwin Smith. Text by G. S. Fraser. (London:
Thames and Hudson, 1955).

(Fig. 90)

(Fig. 91)

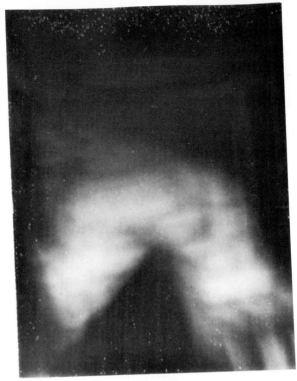

(Fig. 92)

(Fig. 93)

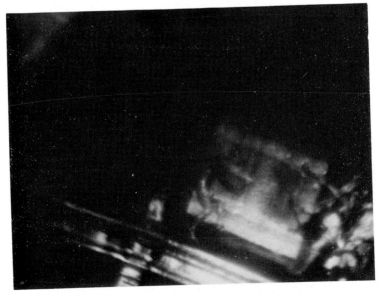

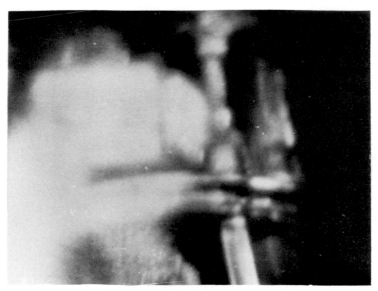

(Fig. 94)

(Fig. 95)

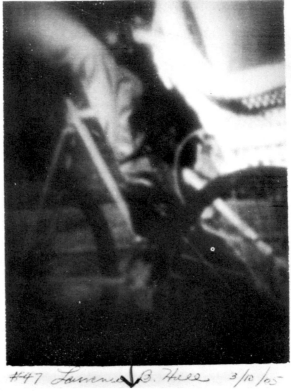

#47 Lawrence B. Hill 3/10/05

(Fig. 96)

(Fig. 97)   (Fig. 98)

whether Ted wasn't again picking and choosing to suit himself rather than others, but still offering a sort of cryptic compromise, a rather typical kind of response seen in children and grown-ups of a certain type of character structure when confronted with a demand to perform or produce according to someone else's stated or implied dictates. We shall see later that this happens to be one of Ted's most notable personality traits.

Difficult as it is to arrive at a reliable evaluation of responses in a target situation when the key to the offbeat correspondences involved may be comparatively simple in the structural sense, we are for all intents and purposes lost, without an almost miraculously lucky interpretative hit, when the associative pathways twist and turn along the intricate lines of strongly emotionally toned complexes of ideas and call upon the vast storehouse of symbolic connections that reside in the deep unconscious. Yet it is precisely in this that the richness and variety of all human creative responses are to be found; and it is for this reason, by the same token, that it is inherently unlikely that we can begin to appreciate and gain some comprehension of the full range of Ted's productions, in or out of the formal target situation, without calling upon every bit of help that the psychoanalyst, the anthropologist, and perhaps even the linguist can offer. It is just here, however—especially when we embark upon the perilously makeshift raft of psychoanalytic insight—that the tried and true man of science, who has nothing more difficult to do than measure the stars or play around with computers, may feel that we are drifting helplessly downstream toward the certain brink of perdition. For it is fundamentally because of lack of agreement on what constitutes a correspondence that many of the propositions of psychoanalysis have been logically rejected by several generations of rigorously trained scientists, ever since, in fact, Freud grandly ignored the sticky methodological aspects of the problem in his *The Interpretation of Dreams,* a work of genius if ever one was, and just proceeded to set his egg—and the world—on end anyway.

We owe much in our understanding of symbolic displacements, substitutions, and associative transformations that can be seen in man's expressive efforts, from some of his earliest-known artifacts right up to the latest poetic metaphors and surrealist creations, to Freud's brilliant analyses of such processes in dreams, witticisms, and psychopathological symptom formation. The range of such associative pathways is enormous, and depends partly on our individual experience and to a great extent on inborn connections that seem to have existed as far back as we have any records of man's mental processes at all. The following is one of Ted's target responses that may be presumed to have called upon symbolic associations that Ted in his conscious, waking state would—as he in fact did—disclaim not only any knowledge but even intuitive appreciation of (as I am afraid many readers will). Yet the connections involved may be seen all through the realm of the unconscious as expressed in dreams, art, folklore, ecclesiastic and pagan ritual.

Near the very beginning of a session at the home of Dr. John L. Lightburn, Ted asked, after a few warm-up shots, if anyone would care to suggest a target. Dr. Lightburn turned to his sixteen-year-old daughter, Linda. She immediately suggested the University of Rome, at which she was planning to take summer courses. Ted thought that was just fine, and asked for a camera. (At this part of the session film brought by me was being used, as we were saving the film supplied by Dr. Lightburn for later use.) When Dr. Lightburn said he thought that there were too many buildings involved for this to provide a very good target, Linda went into her bedroom and brought out a folder of the Foreign Language League School in which, among several pictures, two were of buildings at the University of Rome. She placed the folder on her lap and covered it with her hands. Ted said it didn't matter what building she picked—one was already in his mind, and he was going to shoot for it. On his first shot he came up with the picture shown in fig. 99. It was not one of the buildings of the University of Rome (we never found out what sort of building Ted had had in his mind) but bore a fairly obvious resemblance, even though shot from a different angle, to another Roman building pictured in the folder, the church, shown in fig. 100, called Trinita dei Monti. As far as could be determined, Ted, who had not moved from his chair about eight feet from the settee on which Linda had been sitting and to which she returned after getting her folder, had not been in a position to see either the picture of the church or, as will be shown later to be of some importance, its name printed next to it on the folder.

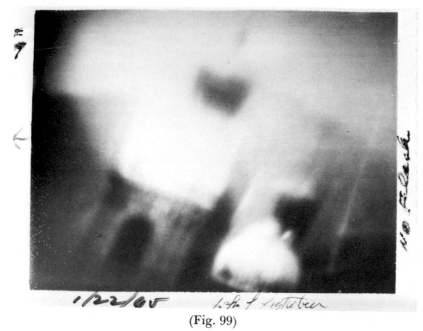

(Fig. 99)

(Fig. 100)

Now this is clearly an instance of a near hit that could be rated positively only within the broadened frame of evaluation mentioned earlier. The building Ted came up with was very much of the same style as the one in the folder held by Linda—it had at least two arched towers topped by cupolas—but it was not, as inspection will verify, a representation of the Trinita dei Monti itself, to say nothing of the fact that it was not one of the buildings within the officially designated target area, the University of Rome. (To indicate what kind of divergence is possible in this kind of intuitive rating, I can report that one brand new Ph.D. in one of the social sciences refused to acknowledge any resemblance at all between Ted's picture and the one in the folder.) What Ted came up with several shots later on, however, would certainly be considered outside the target area as structurally defined, and yet, from certain points of view, its high-order relevance would have to be granted. After a couple of weak passes at an image that at first was unidentifiable, Ted came up with the version shown in fig. 101. It shows a phallic-looking structure against a background which appears to be of high mountains, and what or where the scene depicted actually is—if, indeed, it has any

(Fig. 101)

existence outside of Ted's imagination—remains to this day unknown to me. But any psychoanalyst will recognize immediately
that the scene represents a profane version of the Trinita dei
Monti, or Trinity of the Mountains, by virtue of the universal
symbolic equivalence of the male generative organs and the notion
of a trinity, on the one hand, and of these organs and the supreme
power in nature and the cosmos on the other. This symbolic
equivalence, which may extend to certain darker aspects of the
mystery of the Holy Trinity, is not, as it happens, something
thought up by atheistic or nihilistic psychoanalysts with nothing
better to do, but may be glimpsed from prehistoric times on as
one of the major roots in the complex development of the universal idea of the Godhead. "The study of phallicism," says George
Ryley Scott in the opening words of his *Phallic Worship*, "is the
study of religion." Long before the sun, from its side, meta-
morphosed into various editions of the Godhead, from Apollo and
his chariot and Jupiter with his thunderbolts (the latter via an
easily traced transformation from the earlier phallic horned god)
to the variously nimbused versions of more highly developed
Eastern and Western theologies, the primordial religious *unio
mystica* which men sought and found in solar worship was concurrently expressed, primitively and directly (as if men feared to
get too far away from what could be immediately grasped), in a
joyous phallic worship, traces of which may be seen even today in
various ritualistic elements of complexly developed religions (not
to mention the Black Mass, said to be still practiced in certain
parts of the Christian world). Similarly the universally seen connection between the sun and the phallus as the 'first causes' and
givers of life and power that rise again after 'death' (in the latter
case a detumescent one) has been memorialized in countless primitive funerary and other monuments, from the subarctic fringes of
Scandinavia to the history-laden valleys of Italy, from the outer-
most reaches of Siberia to the Nile and New Guinea, that bear
witness to the primitive origins of the resurrection concept. The
thinness of the veneer, moreover, which for only a couple of
thousand years has obscured the connection between the highly
sublimated concept of the Trinity and the crude representation
of the genitalia as objects of religious veneration and adoration
may be seen in the ease with which heretical splinter groups in

the history of all Christian sects have slipped back into a more direct type of worship.[10]

To return now to the point at issue, the image of a phallic structure against a background of mountains that Ted produced would certainly have been bypassed as irrelevant to the target set out, however much the still extraordinary fact of any image at all might have impressed itself upon witnesses, had not observers

(Fig. 102)

[10] These connections do not fade away; they persist in the human unconscious as what Jung, to whose massive scholarship we owe much of what we know of phallic symbology and its transformations, has called archetypes, and may be seen at some time in some form in most people's expressive behavior, from the cryptic but still decipherable elaborations of dreams and symptom formation (*e.g.*, an obsessional need to touch things three times before going to bed) to the more overt productions of certain psychotics. A lovely example of the persistence of these archetypes in the comparatively sophisticated Western mind was demonstrated in the so-called automatic drawing of a lady patient of mine with a highly developed streak of mystic religiosity. In a hypnoid state of semitrance this woman's pencil traced out the drawing shown in fig. 102 which she characterized, after being restored to normal consciousness, as that of an ancient priestess worshiping the sun. And so it may certainly be; but one of the strong roots of this woman's particular mystic bent, as revealed in a good deal of independent clinical evidence, happened to be a difficultly sublimated fascination with the male genitalia (tragically denied her in life) which may be plainly seen to be more or less overtly hidden, so to speak, in the figure she drew.

been present who were capable of interpreting Ted's imagery, just as they would a graphically or verbally expressed fantasy, in terms of a kind of unconscious translation, known as primary process thinking, occurring regularly in dreams and art. It seems likely, however, that the significance of what Ted did in relation to a broadened target category would have been completely overlooked had he not first come up with an image that drew our attention in the first place to the Trinita dei Monti, that is, to a target that he had selected from among several which in actual fact, as over against merely formal design (and I do not believe that we are begging too much of a question here), had been set before him.

In our next example we return, as I promised we would, to the very first picture that Ted produced for me at our Palmer House session in Chicago, and to what it was about it that impressed me immediately when I saw it. As it happens, we are going to be dealing with another possible root of the resurrection concept, or at least as I tried—more or less unsuccessfully, as I indicated in Chapter I—to develop a certain thesis in regard to it for an audience at a midwestern medical school, which for its part was doing its best to stare me off the platform. My lecture dealt with evidence from clinical psychoanalytic material, as well as from prehistoric to modern art and other sources, pointing to the crescent form as a breast symbol, specifically as a symbol of that precious source of early sustenance and security which, like the crescent moon, will never completely disappear but will return again and again to fullness in the eternal cycle of nature. This was a tremendously powerful and reassuring symbol for early man—who was perennially threatened with the disappearance of the roving and unpredictable herds of mammoth, caribou, and bison—and doubtlessly figured in many types of magical ceremony aimed at forestalling famine. But in time this symbol also came to be associated with all real or threatened object loss—the loss, by death or separation, of persons close to us (which is the way it can be seen in today's unconscious)—and in later cultural developments, such as in Egyptian and early Judaic and Greco-Roman times and afterward, it became, sometimes alongside but occasionally condensed with phallic elements expressing the notion of resurrection after what is only a temporary death, a frequently seen ornament

on funerary monuments, where it represented the hope of im-
mortality, of return to a full and satisfying afterlife. (This condensation or fusion of the phallic and mammary that may be seen
all through prehistoric art may be news to some archeologists but
was apparently taken for granted by primitive man, who, much
more in touch with the unconscious mainsprings of his life and
being than we are, was nothing if not economical with his magical
symbols.) At any rate, among the slides I showed in my lecture in
illustration of this thesis were the two shown in figs. 103 and 104,
and what struck me immediately when Ted's first image, the Water
Tower, magically materialized before my eyes, seemingly out of
nothing, was the curious correspondence between the rather
crescent-shaped street lamps in it (fig. 4) and both the crescentlike
horns of the figure in the first (fig. 103) [11] and the rather similar
configuration (of still obscure meaning, so far as I know) in what
looks like an inverted hatstand in the second (fig. 104).[12] I had
used these slides to illustrate an early and also a comparatively
late form of condensation of the phallic and crescent motifs. In
the first, from a Bronze Age Iberian cave painting in which what
is thought to be the figure of a demon (but what may well be one
of the originally phallically horned gods) is represented, we see
the crescent theme throughout, in the horns and in the crescent-
shaped scythes in the hands of what may also be an early precursor
of the Grim Reaper (although this figure too, the later Father
Time, has multiple roots), while the 'I shall return' resurrection
theme is plainly given in the idea of the progression from the
thin sliver of a crescent to a full moon. The second slide, of an
Etruscan piece of about 800 B.C., was shown merely to illustrate
the persistence of the condensation of the crescent and what must
originally have been phallic horns as a stylized motif that had
probably long since lost its primary magical utility.

    At all events, as I saw Ted's image with its crescentlike street
lamps bearing such an obvious (to me, anyway) correspondence to
the phallic crescents in both slides, I was intrigued with the fact
that the other motif emphasized in the phallic tower was what

    [11] From Herbert Kühn, *Rock Pictures of Europe* (London: Sidgwick and Jackson,
1956).
    [12] Reprinted by permission of the publisher, Vanguard Press, from *Art of the
Etruscans* by Massimo Pallottino. (Photograph by Martin Hürlimann.)

(Fig. 103)   (Fig. 104)

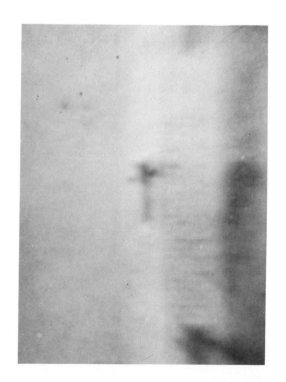

(Fig. 105)

appeared plainly to be figures of crosses (fig. 105) corresponding
to a comparatively late symbol incorporating the ideas of both
death and resurrection; and this conjunction is what my icily
received lecture of that afternoon, from whose failure I was still
smarting, was all about. I finally noticed, as I happened to look at
the picture upside down (fig. 106) that the crescentlike street
lamps had now become breasts with plainly represented nipples.
It occurred to me at once—the whole thing seemed so wildly improbable anyway (and one might as well get hung for a breast as
for a street lamp, I thought, as there is no greater magic to one
feat than to the other when one is conversant with the amazingly
clever symbolic elaborations and masterpieces of condensation that
even the most unimaginative people are able to toss off in their
dreams)—that Ted, in this picture-puzzle-like fashion, was unconsciously, and by pure telepathy of course, trying to give me a
kind of confirmation of my thesis and an appreciation that had
been so dismally lacking in my afternoon lecture, as if in this way
he could win my favor. This precise mechanism—a sort of echo in
agreement—might not have occurred to me had I not been thoroughly familiar with it from having seen it many times under
comparable circumstances in telepathic dreams of patients in
analysis, as if those in treatment with me were, at such times,
taking over the role of therapist and saying to me, in this psi-
conditioned language of the unconscious, "There, there, your
theses (doubts, suspicions, position, or whatever) are quite justified." Similar telepathically geared 'echo' dreams, that is, dreams
presumptively originating out of a similar kind of reassuring
activity, basically springing out of the patients' unconscious need
to gratify and thus secure in return the love and protection of the
therapist, have been reported by other psychoanalysts, even some
not particularly inclined toward the psi hypothesis.

Some weeks afterward I tried to produce a cross from the windows of the Chicago Water Tower by deliberately setting my
Polaroid camera (the same one Ted had used) out of focus. The
best I could do—the camera is apparently foolproof in this regard—
is shown in fig. 107. But the most curious part of the postscript to
the original event came several months still later as I was poring
over my notes on the first Palmer House session and trying to
make sense of the intriguing fact that Ted's first prediction, on

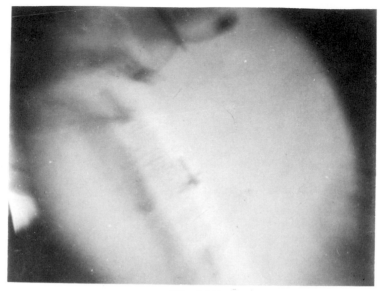

(Fig. 106)

(Fig. 107)

(Fig. 108)

(Fig. 109)

beginning to shoot that evening, was that he would get a long, tall structure "with a sign crosswise on it," which in a way could correspond to the tall Water Tower with the window which he had apparently distorted into a cross. I came across the two pictures of the Kremlin that I had used as targets for this session and which I had not bothered to look at since. What struck me now was that not only did the first picture (fig. 108) actually have in it a structure that corresponded in some measure to Ted's guess as to what it was, "a driveway, entrance, or a walkway"—a fact that I had failed to note at the time, as I had only a vague recollection of what I had put into this envelope and was in any case geared to looking for strictly veridical correspondences—but, more important, it incorporated in it both the crescent shape and the cross, which latter may be better seen topping the cupolas in the second picture (fig. 109). It looked now as if Ted may have done a magnificent job of distortion and condensation in reassembling the structural motifs of the original targets, which he insisted he would get but which I asked him to forget about in order to let his unconscious take over, and, allowing his unconscious really to take over, putting them together with the theme of my lecture to give me doubly what I wanted (and what my own unconscious was apparently quite hipped on at the time, as witness the target pictures I had chosen). It appeared as if Ted, in his graphic medium, may have done just what I some years ago described a patient as doing when, in a dream notable for its dazzlingly clever condensations and cross-references, she seemed to take over a controversy I was carrying on publicly respecting the validity of the telepathy hypothesis (1948). I have seen this sort of thing many times since, and I can confidently assure the reader that he probably does comparable things, even with the goodly spate of telepathy thrown in, repeatedly in his own dreams.

At this time I ascertained from a slide that Mrs. Oehler sent for my inspection that the Water Tower image that Ted had gotten on a former occasion, which I referred to earlier, was nothing like the one he had gotten for us at the Palmer House. It had been shot from a lower plane and a different angle and had neither crescents nor crosses anywhere in it.

I should like to say a word now about something I referred to earlier, the peculiar significance that the name *Stevens* had for me when it turned up in the second image that Ted got at our Palmer House session. I certainly cannot rank this incident on a level with that of the Water Tower image from the standpoint of the kind of unconscious mental activity we are discussing, but at the same time I hesitate completely to ignore it, as it does present certain points of interest. My last topic of conversation, lasting right up to the gate, with the colleague who, after my unsuccessful lecture, took me to the airport to enplane for Chicago and my first meeting with Ted, was a common acquaintance, Dr. James Stephens, Head of the Department of Neurology at the University of Colorado Medical School, who we both agreed was not only a first-rate clinician and teacher but a wonderful guy. I couldn't help saying something, however, about what an outspoken and implacable critic of the psi hypothesis he was, and cited his humorous but biting sallies at my expense at a recent meeting of a medical students' society where ESP had been the topic of the evening. I had often had the fantasy, when I ran up against people like him, of being able to stop them dead in their tracks by casually producing some dramatic and conclusive example of psi phenomena right on the spot instead of always having nothing better to offer than carefully compiled but unfortunately second-hand evidence, mostly on the dreary statistical side. Alas, no genie had ever popped out of a bottle to help me in these predicaments. How tempting to imagine that Ted had done this for me now in a peculiarly apt way, if only by proxy, as it were! But unfortunately for this supposition, I had always been firmly of the opinion that the unconscious, with its wide-ranging abilities and limitless facilities, does not make simple errors like mistaking *Stephens* for *Stevens,* and that if *Stephens* had actually been intended *Stephens* it would have been, as Ted's unconscious could easily have found a graphically expressed plot into which to weave it, even if an illuminated sign bearing it were not conveniently reposing in the files of memory. Thus I remained rather ambivalent toward this possible interpretation of the Stevens Hotel picture and, after my first flush of interest on seeing it turn up so soon after my discussion of Jim Stephens and his attitude toward psi phenomena, would probably have thrown it out had it not been for the fact that what it seemed to accomplish as a magical pick-me-up for my ego was, after all, definitely along the lines of what the Water Tower image had done for me. The odds in favor of chance always diminish when this type of consistency enters the picture, whatever other considerations are lacking. But some time later I happened to learn that Ted's unconscious was no better at spelling than his conscious mind and could be demonstrated to have made mistakes even less excusable, from the schoolmarm's point of view, than misspelling a name that I daresay many of its possessor's best friends might misspell in exactly the same way. Some months after our Palmer House session, Mr. Curtis Fuller, through whom, it will be recalled, I learned about Ted to begin with, sent for my inspection a picture (fig. 110) that Ted had gotten under his auspices some time earlier. It showed two stories of a building that looked like a warehouse on which, in somewhat out-of-focus but still more or less distinguishable letters, what appeared to be something like

(Fig. 110)

Air Division Canadian Moun—— was spelled out. The building was ultimately acknowledged by the Royal Canadian Mounted Police to be one of their Air Division hangars, but a close study of Ted's picture revealed that, in addition to a most interesting distortion of the original in the placement of the windows, the name Canadian was misspelled *Cainadain* (a fact also pointed out in a letter to me by the R.C.M.P. people). So, I don't know what to think about the *Stevens* thing after all.[13]

At any rate, we can see more than ever now that, granting the possible pertinence of some of these data, to insist on a scheme of evaluation of Ted's pictures hinging too tightly on the veridical correspondence in only explicitly stated target situations might be sacrificing, in favor of the bone-dry certainty of small things that a strait-laced conventional methodology allows, exactly what makes the human mind, with the richness and depth of its symbolic overtones (as well as its mistakes in spelling), such a unique thing. It has sometimes been claimed, however, that the psychoanalyst can make anything out of his material, especially when he himself is responsible for the extraction of the raw data. This, in all justice, is not entirely true, as a goodly percentage of the material that comes across the couch of the average analyst will resist the efforts of the most determined and double-jointed fantasy spinner to make any sense of at all, much less relate meaningfully, as should theoretically be the case with all communications, to the less hidden portions of the patient's life and conflicts. Nevertheless, there is something to the claim that an analyst left alone with his own material is far more dangerous than if he is simply let loose on data observed and annotated by others, if only for the reason that in the latter case his inevitable biases will have to wait until the primary data are out and on the table before they come into play and cannot, as they are sometimes said to do (and as witness our previous examples), occultly influence the very occurrence of these primary data themselves. I should like, therefore, to give an example of the application of psychoanalytic hypotheses to some of Ted's material that was observed elsewhere by others, not by way of showing that it takes more than a transparent device of this sort to foil a not-to-be-outwitted analyst, but to indicate that even under these circumstances the origin of Ted's

13 Dr. Stephens died on September 20, 1966, mourned by all who knew him.

(Fig. 111)

puzzling images may sometimes be rendered comprehensible when
we have the means of forging a key to the unconscious connections involved, and once more to underscore, reversely, the great
difficulty of adequately evaluating Ted's responses in a target
situation without such a key. And here, as circumstances would
have it, the theme of object loss and magical restitution, which
was discussed in connection with the previous example, and
which, as we shall see later, may be hypothesized to be somewhere
near the core of what Ted is accomplishing psychologically by
capturing on film—or resurrecting, as it were—an all-too-fleeting
external world, happened to be specifically implied in the very
nature of the target that Ted was asked to aim at.

On April 25, 1963, two weeks after the submarine *Thresher*

was lost at sea and presumably sunk, and while search crews were still on the hunt for clues to its disappearance, Ted was asked by Mrs. Pauline Oehler, the author of the earlier-mentioned article about him in *Fate* magazine, to try to locate it through his 'psychic photography.' What he came up with were several pictures of the submarine *Nautilus* which seemed to have been lifted detail for detail, except possibly for one or two slight distortions, from photographs in the *National Geographic* of January, 1959, which it was later ascertained that Ted's mother had had in her house. Results of this sort are sometimes seen in experiments in hypnosis, in which a subject, who for one reason or another is unable to carry out a request or command, comes up with a substitute offer or a fudging attempt at a compromise. The following now is from Mrs. Oehler's notes on a batch of pictures she sent me for study from a subsequent session: "Picture No. 19. Made here April 29, 1963. Ted was again trying to get a picture of the sunken *Thresher* when the Queen of England dropped in." Fig. 111 (picture number 19) shows the Queen of England wearing her crown of state.

Without question this would be judged, as in fact it was, a completely inappropiate response, a clear miss in relation to the target asked for. However, look now at the following anagram:

$$
\begin{array}{l}
\boxed{\text{E S T H E R}} \\
\boxed{\text{T H R E S} \quad \text{H E R}} \\
\text{e l i z a b e } \boxed{\text{T H R E}} \text{ g i n a}
\end{array}
$$

Esther happens to be the name of Ted's elderly mother, and Elizabeth Regina, of course, is the title borne by the queen of England in her official capacity, as she apparently was in the picture Ted 'caught' of her in her crown of state. Very interesting, the reader may remark, but just how can all this be tied together by any hypothesis that will endow the incident with meaning, as over against the, at first glance, very likely possibility that, apart from the extraordinary nature of the primary phenomenon itself, we are dealing with a curious but meaningless concatenation of elements thrown together purely by chance? Let me try to provide such an hypothesis.

A good deal of Ted's life, personality development, and

troubles, some of which I will touch upon in a later chapter, have been bound up with his ambivalent relationship to his mother. It may be hypothesized that the disappearance of the *Thresher* was unconsciously equated with the threatened possibility of the mother's 'disappearance,' in actuality a growing concern in view of her advancing age, not only because of the chance anagrammatic connection between Thresher and Esther but because of the symbolic equivalence of the sea and, in this case, the submarine itself with Mother. The sea is the primal mother from which all animal life was derived and is one of the most frequent symbols for mother, a seemingly universal archetype, seen in the variegated expressions of the unconscious. And although there is no real etymological connection between the two, despite such teasers as *mare* (sea) in Latin and *la mère* (mother) and *la mer* (sea) in French, the use of these roots as mother symbols occurs repeatedly in dreams in many languages in which, in fact, all *ma* syllables in names or objects (as in sub*ma*rine) may have this significance. The symbol 'Queen,' in the unconscious, is also 'mother.' Now comes the part that it is very unlikely that either Ted or Mrs. Oehler (since we are dotting all *i*'s and crossing all *t*'s in this examination of evidence) could consciously have come up with. If we hypothesize that the joining of the *TH* of Elizabeth with the *RE* of Regina was part of the unconscious scheme implied by bringing the queen in her official role into anagrammatic conjunction with the lost *Thresher*, this may be construed as an unconscious attempt at denial of the threatened loss and a magical restitution or resurrection of the mother, whose name also brings her into the anagram. First, the queen in her official role, like the crown, is in theory imperishable. This mother goes on forever; she can *not* disappear. Second, the means whereby this is accomplished, including the double insurance of tying together the end and the beginning in an abracadabrous knot, is as old as magic, presumably as old as unconscious symbolic thinking itself, and must have begun to appear in the history of mankind—long before the beginnings of written language, and long before the already sophisticated cave paintings of a presumably later stage in the development of magic and religion—as early as grunted syllables began to substitute for objects. Certain it is that the manipulation of words, the taking them

apart and putting them together again, is one of the oldest devices—as witness the already ancient word lore of the cabala—for
giving man fantasied control over the forces of life and death. It
is not only a common reparative and restitutive device in dreams
bearing death wishes against ambivalently loved objects and other
unconscious meanings (the great twelfth-century philosopher
Maimonides pointed out the anagrammatic devices hidden in the
dreams of the prophets) but may be seen in symptoms and personality dynamics (*e.g.*, many cases of addiction to crossword
puzzles) as an unconscious means of attempting to deal with feared
object loss in general. I have a whole file of anagrammatic dreams
illustrating these things.

Again, we must overrule the objection that Ted is not clever
enough to have thrown together such an ingenious thought device,
which might even be considered complicated enough to strain the
creative powers of a first-rank poet (or psychoanalyst). Ted happens to be, despite his lack of formal education, a very sharp
person, even outstandingly bright in certain respects; but the more
pertinent fact is that we are all geniuses in the unconscious—in
fact, a good part of genius consists in having access to and tapping
for use the ordinary unconscious, where every man is a Shake-
speare ("how infinite in faculty . . . in apprehension how like a
god!")—and, as I have said before, the average person would be
astounded (as he frequently is in analysis) if he could have demonstrated to him the amazingly ingenious constructions, both verbal
and graphic, which occasionally call upon information that he
never knew he remembered or even had, that he effortlessly
elaborates nightly while his wife imagines him to be merely snor-
ing like the unromantic clod that she sometimes thinks he is.
Thus if it were to be objected that a person who dropped out of
school after the fifth grade, as Ted did, would be highly unlikely
to make a production out of the significance of the queen as
Elizabeth Regina, I shall simply have to point out that Ted may
have dropped out of school but his unconscious did not and, in
fact, probably could have pulled the stunt off in the third or
fourth grade, a supposition which will perhaps receive some support when we come later to the immense epistemological implications of these data. In this instance, however, we have no need to
invoke hypotheses too far in advance of our present position,

which in any case might be considered as too tenuous to be taken seriously by those unacquainted with the powers of the human mind (to whom, in lieu of opportunity to learn about these things by first-hand investigation, I should like to recommend F. W. H. Myers' monumental survey in his *Human Personality*). We have only to apply the basic psi hypothesis to an event of a kind that takes place frequently in the lives of people, as demonstrated in countless dream analyses. Several months after I received from Mrs. Oehler Ted's picture of Queen Elizabeth, I had occasion to check an issue of the *National Geographic* for possible sources of pictures that Ted had gotten on other occasions. In the issue of January, 1961, on a page facing a picture of a room in the White House that corresponded—again with a slight change—to one of the pictures of a White House series that Ted had made some time earlier (he had been trying for President Kennedy, and had actually got him in a couple of shots), was a photograph of Queen Elizabeth and Prince Philip on the occasion of their visit of State to the White House. Below a full-length portrait of the royal pair in evening dress and appropriate decorations was the signature of the queen,

Thus what is termed in dream psychology a 'residue' that Ted could possibly have had psi contact with at some time may have been appropriately dredged up, like any other bit of associatively charged and meaningful material, when it was needed for the magical maneuvers of unconscious fantasy.

In this work, being in at all is being in up to the ears; there is no halfway; and it soon becomes apparent that one might just as well make thoroughgoing maximal assumptions as niggling ones. But psychoanalytic constructions in clinical situations are notoriously difficult to verify because they deal *post hoc* with unique historical events that do not lend themselves to experimental study or to a type of operation whose alternative outcomes include the possibility of their being definitely refuted. The reader, thus, has every right to reject most of the considerations I have brought to bear in connection with the last few of Ted's esoteric responses in target situations. If he does, however, he is of course still faced with the highly improbable fact of the pictures themselves, and, unless he can invent plausible hypotheses to account for these in normal terms (which, taking everything into consideration, he may find an unrewarding task—not one of the individuals who witnessed Ted at work was able to come up with a specific normal hypothesis), he may find himself as badly off as before. For his choice, when he comes to cash in his inferential chips, lies not between plausibility and implausibility in ordinary terms, but between discrete 'miracles,' so to speak, thrown up purely by chance and isolated from all lines of connection with anything else in the fabric of natural explanation, and 'miracles' which at least offer some points of explanatory consistency with other events in the still largely unexplored universe of man's mind. Either way he has a problem.

CHAPTER X

Who's in the Back of the Store, and Other Problems

I HAVE no illusions about the effect of the data presented thus far. Some people probably would have accepted a great deal less as sufficient virtually to rule out hypotheses based upon normal means of image production, and others, I am sure, are yet far from certain that every conceivable loophole has been plugged, every alternative possibility eliminated. Few parapsychologists will be in the former group; and few of the latter group, which will never lack for members, will ever get beyond the point of calling for tighter and tighter safeguards on this or that condition of trial (some dillies have been suggested) in an endless round of futile obsessional rituals. I see no point in playing this game, as it has never accomplished its professed purpose and, I am convinced, would produce no appreciable shift in the spectrum of effectual (versus idle) belief in the present instance.

For the present, thus, and pending further developments along lines indicated in Chapter VIII, I shall leave the data pretty much as they are and proceed as if the primary fact of their so-called paranormality were no longer in question. This being the case, certain aspects of their occurrence, their nature, and form demand consideration from both empirical and theoretical points of view.

Perhaps the first thing to consider, once we have decided to proceed as if normal hypotheses have been rendered highly implausible, is who or what is responsible for the images we have been studying, in the usual sense of immediate causation. Now this may seem a silly question, since it would offhand appear to be perfectly obvious that Ted is behind everything that goes on, even when others are handling the cameras at some distance from him. But matters are not quite as simple as this. Apart from the scientific unwisdom of anchoring ourselves to any rigid set of assumptions, stated or implied, when data of such extraordinary dimensions are involved, it so happens that there is a peculiarity in the manner in which this whole picture-taking business came about that will raise questions that might otherwise not have come into the picture, questions which will undoubtedly appear strange to many readers.

In 1955, when the story begins, Ted was holding the first steady job of his life, as an elevator operator and starter at the Conrad Hilton Hotel in Chicago, after a career marked by truancy, delinquency, and illness. A fellow employee, Mr. George Johannes, who dabbled in hypnosis, happened to discover that Ted was an excellent subject who complied easily with suggestions made along the usual lines. He conceived the idea of attempting with Ted something that had been reported from the very beginnings of modern-day hypnosis under Mesmer, the eighteenth-century physician who called the little-understood force he was experimenting with animal magnetism. From the time of Mesmer's first disciples, sporadic accounts appeared of people who appeared to be capable of being directed in hypnotic trance to go mentally to places at varying distances away and of reporting, sometimes in minutest detail, what they 'saw' at these places. In many reports, the kind of information obtained from the directed roamings of these so-called traveling clairvoyants was very little if at all different from the information obtained in sittings with good trance mediums. In both cases minutiae of certain scenes, including the description of furniture and pictures 'seen,' the doings of people at these scenes, the clothes worn, the visitors received, the letters, books, and newspapers read, would be reported on in verifiable detail.

The difference between the two lay in the staging. The traveling clairvoyant was made to feel, through suggestion, that he was actually moving through doors and corridors and behaving mentally as if he were virtually present at the site described, as if the center of his consciousness, his 'I,' were far away from his actual physical body. Such mechanisms are not usually suggested or invoked in the case of mediums, whose stage props are apt to involve concepts of a different order, frequently discarnate entities popularly known as 'spirits.' Curiously, experiments with traveling clairvoyance long ago went out of style even with psychical researchers, to say nothing of the modern-day statistically minded parapsychologist, and are of course never mentioned in standard textbooks on hypnosis from which, for all that today's student can learn about this subject, they have virtually been expunged. It is to Johannes' credit that he didn't take the opinion of present-day science on these matters but went boldly ahead on the basis of reports in the now largely forgotten literature on the subject.[1]

In many experiments with traveling clairvoyants, 'guides' were sometimes suggested to pilot the subjects to the scene about which information was desired. What more fitting, since hidden treasure was the object of Johannes' experiments with Ted—for that is what it soon became when Ted began to show promise along these lines—than that the guide suggested be Jean Laffite, the famous leader of a band of pirates and smugglers which preyed on shipping in southern waters. After fighting with the United States against the English in the Battle of New Orleans in 1815, Laffite was pardoned by President Madison, only finally to return to piracy and disappear into the Caribbean and legend when he could not restrain his men from attacking and plundering American ships. According to Ted, Laffite appeared to him for many months when he was under hypnosis (Johannes finally had to call

[1] In "Experiments in Clairvoyance," in the 1891-2 *Proceedings of the Society for Psychical Research*, Dr. Alfred Backman, a Swedish physician, reports on experiments with several traveling clairvoyant subjects in which several of his colleagues, whose signed statements are given, took part. (See also "Further Information as to Dr. Backman's Experiments in Clairvoyance," *ibid.*, July, 1892.) Another good account, that of Augustus de Morgan, the eminent nineteenth-century mathematician and logician, is given in Walter Franklin Prince's *Noted Witnesses for Psychic Occurrences.* The latter is well worth looking into for its collection of personal reports on a variety of types of psychical phenomena.

in a professional hypnotist to strengthen the 'illusion') and guided him to various spots where treasure was supposedly hidden. Unfortunately Laffite, who according to Ted took quite a shine to him and even took him on many gratuitous sightseeing excursions (Laffite wore the clothes of an early American seaman at these times, and often brought along his girl friend, who strangely talked in the same voice as he did), really never came clean about where his legendary booty was cached, and attempts to verify one or two hopeful leads in Florida came to nothing. (To this day, however, Ted feels that there is one cove on an island off the coast of South Africa that, from the strange way Laffite acted when showing him around the place, must be the real McCoy, and he fully intends to go there some day to find out). Gradually Laffite became harder and harder to summon up, and when he did put in what seemed to be a reluctant appearance he became, despite anything Johannes was able to do, increasingly transparent, so that Ted began to notice the background showing through him. He also became increasingly passive, and when Ted was at length directed by his mentor to try striking out for himself, the progressively fading Laffite came along a few times merely for the ride and then disappeared altogether (as all good pirates and generals should).

Ted began his treasure-hunting operations in and around Chicago. According to him, he was successful on several occasions in guiding Johannes and what seems now to have become a small syndicate of backers to various spots where digging uncovered 'treasure,' but this invariably turned out to be only token amounts—small change, in one case—that hardly paid for the cost of operations. Once a buried cache of several hundred dollars was scried, but by the time the syndicate got to the only vaguely marked spot, they found that another crew, which had undertaken digging operations in the vicinity for another reason, had already stumbled upon the loot. It was at this time that the idea occurred to Johannes that if Ted could perhaps get the details of what he claimed to be "seeing" on film, it might be a considerable aid in finding the exact spot where treasure was supposed to be hidden. One day he thrust a sealed camera at Ted and told him to go home and work on it. When the film, which was sent out for development (a Polaroid camera was not used at this time), came back with a couple of pictures on it, Ted was certain that Johannes had played a trick on him. He bought his own camera (still not a Polaroid) and began trying things on his own; and this, as he started going through the same process of doubt as everyone else did as to what was going on, is when his troubles began. When pictures came in, reason told him that this was impossible, and he wondered whether he was not stealing out and shooting them in his sleep. When someone claimed once to have seen him going downstairs with a camera in the dead of night, he became convinced that the mystery was solved; but this hypothesis had to be abandoned when one night he had himself locked in and the door to his room taped on the outside but he still somehow wound up with pictures.

He finally got hold of a Polaroid camera and started working in earnest to get pictures of possible treasure sites. His method at first was to point the camera at a wall about a foot away. Because the ratio of hits to misses was very low, he would go at it sometimes day after day, until he would virtually drop from exhaustion.

After many months of this, with no return in treasure—quite the opposite: nervousness and ill-health forced him to leave his job, and his attempts to explain to others what he was doing brought only ridicule—he was persuaded to see a psychiatrist, who, without bothering to ask for a demonstration, quickly put him on the right track. "I hypnotized Mr. Serios," this doctor wrote in answer to my inquiry, "and told him that in my opinion all it was was a dream which was making him nervous . . . and that all the pictures he had taken were something cock-eyed and to forget all about them." The therapy was brilliantly successful. Ted gave up his dream, destroyed about three hundred pictures in his possession, apologized to friends and family for his wild stories and weird behavior, and became himself thoroughly convinced that he had been the victim of a strange delusion. (According to Ted, Johannes himself somehow came to share this view.) For eighteen months after his visit to the psychiatrist, he didn't touch a camera and at length even went back to his old job. But as so often happens with hypnotic therapy, the beneficial results began to wear off and his old sense of unreality returned; only this time he began to wonder if there weren't something to the old picture-taking fantasy after all, and if the 'dream' he had been in hadn't started *after* his seeing the psychiatrist.

To resolve his confusion he went to a professional hypnotist, whom he picked out of the phone book, and laid the whole story before him. And this, says Ted, is where fate stepped in since he had no doubt that this man too would have tried to handle matters in the same way the psychiatrist had, had not an urgent phone call interrupted the interview. Ted was asked to step out into the secretary's outer office while the hypnotist took his call. When the hypnotist buzzed for him to be ushered in again, Ted presented him with six shots of scenes of India that he had gotten when he started playing around with a loaded Polaroid in the secretary's office while waiting. The secretary swore that Ted had done nothing except point the camera at the wall and shoot. When the hypnotist got over his own slight case of unreality, he asked Ted to come back the following day, and then began a series of sessions (at the hypnotist's regular fee, recalls Ted ruefully) that resulted in numerous pictures that this time the hypnotist took charge of to make sure that Ted would not do away with them in case he happened to slip a cog and go back to the idea that he was a fake. It was at this man's suggestion that Ted started pointing the camera at himself; but surprisingly, at this time, hypnosis lost its effect, and no more pictures were obtained except in the waking state.

Now there are aspects of this story—not only the strange role played at the beginning by the induced hallucinatory visions of Laffite but, instead of a strengthening inward acceptance of a privately experienced phenomenon that should gradually have fused with other aspects of selfhood, the development of a sense of unreality about it culminating in the somewhat too facile acceptance of the bizarre delusion of the whole thing's being a fraudulent concoction—that could conceivably reflect dark doings in the little understood (because much neglected) depths of the personality where the 'I' and a vast, thinly boundaried gallery of ghostly not-I forms seem to merge. Indeed, many people familiar with the extensive many-faceted data on phenomena ranging from multiple personality to what is frequently, although perhaps not always too helpfully, referred to as 'spirit possession' may feel that the data of Ted's case might well warrant consideration being given to the possibility of some organized psychic entity and intelligence other than Ted's ostensible own being responsible for the pictures. Even Ted himself, I think, would at times have been inclined to admit the legitimacy of the issue on introspective grounds. First, the sudden comings and goings of the 'fluence' would sometimes drive him crazy with bafflement. The power to get anything at all on film has at times deserted him with dramatic suddenness; when this has happened, "It's as if a curtain comes down, *ker-boom!* and that's all, brother," Ted has said, shaking his head at the awesomeness of this eclipse. (This alone is susceptible to psychoanalytic 'potty' hypotheses which, I think, have a definite plausibility in Ted's case, and might provide at least a partial explanation.) In addition to this was the complete foreignness of most of his images (more so than in dreams, where the perceiving and experiencing self is usually on the scene) and the seemingly complete independence of his film-image production from his widely varying moods. (Ted has, incidentally, never come up with 'filthy' pictures; but so far as I know, no clairvoyant, traveling or other, ever has.) Moreover, Ted does not, strange as this may appear, check out as a particularly good visualizer under ordinary circumstances. "Whatever the visualizing phenomenon is that he has," wrote Dr. Margaret Thaler Singer of Berkeley, California, who examined and scored a battery of psychological tests administered by Dr. Harl Young of Denver, "it comes from something other than his own 'vivid memory.'" (I had told Dr. Singer only that Ted was a psychically gifted person whose specialty had something to do with visualization.) "He gives no evidence of being skillful at drawing or of having vivid images of things he sees," Dr. Singer's report continued. "In fact just the opposite: if he is able to 'visualize' scenes, this must come from outside, and is not a demonstrable part of any special visual skills [he has]."

Now despite these considerations, which I feel it important to continue to keep in mind, and without prejudice to the great mass of important data on the subject of 'possession,' or to the philosophic complexities of the involved questions centering around identity and selfhood and what we now perhaps naïvely refer to (as if we were not begging certain questions in our basic concepts of this) as *the unconscious,* I see little point in not referring to

the perceiving, cognizing, organizing, and film-affecting agency
behind the pictures we are investigating as Ted in the same sense
as we would refer to anyone else as his ostensible self, that is, Ted
in some comparatively simple phase of his own being—more or
less the Ted who was observably in the front of the store—and
nobody or nothing else. This is not, to repeat, because I feel that
other hypotheses are, on a priori or other grounds, inherently
implausible—indeed I wish to emphasize that I consider the ill-
founded and thoroughly unscientific presuppositions and prejudices of the average scientist in this regard to be a mistake of the
first magnitude—but simply because I have come across no really
positive evidence, in all my dealings with Ted, of any other
consciousness, any other 'I,' lurking somewhere in the shadows
and using Ted and perhaps me as cat's-paws for its designs.
Neither anyone calling himself Jean Laffite nor anyone else declared himself when, in a standard approach to suspected nether
personalities that sometimes evokes the most astonishing results,
I repeatedly put the question "Who are you?" to Ted under
hypnosis, and tried other techniques of probing.[2]

It must be obvious to the reader, however, that bypassing such
hypotheses is hardly going to get us off the hook of the far-reaching
implications of the data once we begin to take a closer look at
them, and it may be that by the time we are much further along

2 I am well aware, however—indeed, I have seen this sort of thing clinically in
multiple personality and other forms of dissociation, some of it with a self-avowed
independent 'spirit' existence—that sometimes these so-called *soi-disant*, or self-
professing, entities hide for years behind the business-as-usual (or *almost* as usual,
as it frequently turns out when a careful history is later taken) façade of what may
appear to be only a somewhat unbalanced personality; and that it is not unusual—
I have records and tapes of this too—for some of these entities to become violently
angry at being flushed out and exposed. One sometimes gets the impression of
them holding their breath just behind the door of the manifest personality, waiting until your footsteps have died away and they can slip out unobserved. One
also gets the impression, when studying a good deal of data of this sort, however,
that the 'output' is dependent on the 'input' in a manner somewhat analogous
to what occurs when physicists get waves or particles depending on the particular
type of experimental arrangements they make with their light beam. In this realm
of 'the unconscious,' which seems to have as many internal (question: What exactly
do we mean by 'internal'?) planes as a diamond, with reflections of reflections
flashing about in every which way, what one gets when the parent personality mass
is split appears in some as yet little understood way to be dependent on where and
how the investigative 'blow' is struck, and not just on interpretative bias once the
cleavage has occurred. The observer, moreover, appears to be a creator in the truest
sense, and not just a passive spectator and annotator of what happens, as he is apt
to be led to believe.

he may be scrounging around for hypotheses that are scarcely less far out than the ones we have just decided to jettison.

Next to consider, at any rate, are certain aspects of the manner in which the images Ted is somehow instrumental in getting paranormally onto film get there. It is at once apparent, to begin with, that the physical laws of optics do not have much, if anything, to do with how this happens. (Blindfolding Ted, incidentally, is no bar to the production of clear images.) The camera does not register what it 'sees' but what it could not possibly take in were it behaving as a camera should in the physical world. It could just as well be a dummy stage prop for all that its physical characteristics seem to determine what happens on the film. If we ask why, however, if this is the case, Ted cannot get images on nonexposed film pack or, for that matter, on a ground-glass screen or other systems for registering images—in thin air, if it comes down to that—the answer is simply that our program so far has not made it feasible to spend much time in the development of such new techniques, although a promising start has been made on nonexposed film pack, with which Ted has gotten whities and what appear to be the beginnings of structurally definable imagery (supporting, at least, the hypothesis that light is not necessary for Ted's phenomena to occur). With each new technique, Ted is like a child going off a diving board for the first time, and what he is and is not able to accomplish may not make sense logically. Even after he had been successful in getting images with the camera manned by others behind partitions some distance away, or with someone's hand totally blocking out all light, he still was unable to get anything with a thin layer of masking tape over the lens. The fact that he is still largely dependent on a camera, although there is no demonstrable physical reason for this, may thus be of no greater significance than a pianist's being unable to perform in public without the stool he lugs around with him, an athlete's being dependent on a particular racket, bat, or club, or actors' being unable to perform except under the most exacting conditions demanded by purely personal psychological requirements.

If we ask, then, what *is* the source of the images Ted gets on film, if it is not physical in the usual sense, all we can say is that these images appear to derive mainly from objects at varying distances from him in the real world that he somehow gets information about. (I am, of course, excepting an indeterminate number of images whose real-world counterparts may never be identified because, as may possibly be the case in certain instances, they may not in fact exist, or because there are good grounds for presuming, as in the case of some fanciful Martian landscapes that Ted got during the period when he was trying to beat Mariner IV to the draw—and we need hardly await an actual landing for confirmation—that they are entirely imaginary in origin [fig. 112].) But although we do not know *how* Ted gets the specific information that he translates into images, the simple fact of information-getting through unknown means is, as I have several times already indicated, hardly without precedent, since countless persons besides Ted have also appeared capable of obtaining information about events which they can be presumed or demonstrated to have no way of normally knowing about.[3] The chief medium in which the information Ted gets is manifested, however, is largely peculiar to him, so let us take a closer look at some of his images in order to see what kind of problems arise in this connection.

The first is 'spatial.' Ted's pictures vary from those giving the appearance of being on-the-spot snapshots taken by an inexperienced (and perhaps not always sober) amateur to images which possibly owe whatever photographic quality they possess—these might perhaps best be called pseudo-photographic—to the fact that they are after all produced by some sort of imprinting on film. However, it is difficult to make assumptions, in any exact or

3 For various kinds of evidence of this, from well-documented and carefully worked-over compilations of spontaneous cases, which still constitute the backbone of our knowledge of these phenomena, to the statistical experiments which have dominated the field for the last few decades, I refer the reader to appropriate sources. As good a one as any for the study of spontaneous occurrences is the collection somewhat eerily entitled *Phantasms of the Living*, by Gurney and others (see the bibliography for fuller data on this and other sources mentioned in this footnote). An excellent up-to-date discussion of this kind of evidence may be found in L. E. Rhine's *Hidden Channels of the Mind*. Summaries and discussions of statistical experiments in the field have been provided in several books by J. B. Rhine and his associates, and by Soal and Bateman. I should advise the interested reader not to neglect to dip into the voluminous literature on mediumistic data as, from certain points of view, these are highly relevant to the problems of information-getting that arise in connection with Ted's pictures. Two excellent starters, which I highly recommend, are Tyrrell's *Science and Psychical Phenomena* (and any other books by this author that are available) and Smith's *The Mediumship of Mrs. Leonard*.

(Fig. 112)

physically meaningful sense, about the relationship between Ted's images and the structures in the external world they appear to correspond to, even when the identity and location of these structures may be known. Only in special instances, in fact, can we arrive at any kind of basis for narrowing somewhat our field of speculation in this regard, and these instances fall at the ends of a spectrum which includes all sorts of indeterminate intermediate cases.

At one end are examples such as Mrs. Oehler has shown me from her own and other collections (I have no proved examples of my own), in which images Ted got corresponded point for point, shadow for shadow, highlight for highlight with pictures in magazines or books. When people happened to be in the pictures, one would almost have to assume that what Ted was imaging *was* these pictures, or an exact counterpart of them in someone's mind at some time or other (there would, of course, be

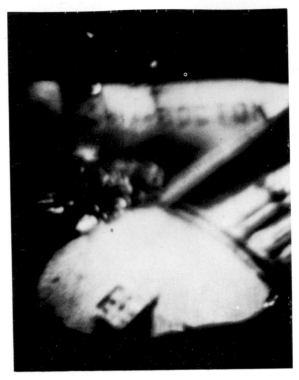

(Fig. 113)

no way of determining which) and not, in any easily imaginable sense, the same scene 'shot' by himself from an identical angle and under identical lighting conditions. Thus when Ted produced portions of pictures of the *Nautilus* and her crew that corresponded to pictures in the *National Geographic* there was no need to look farther for the external physical source of this highly relevant target response.

At the other end of the spectrum would be instances such as images of one of the Russian Vostok rockets, apparently in space, that Ted got on his own (figs. 113, 114). A diligent search in the worldwide literature failed to reveal, as one might expect, any photographic counterpart of these. Here one might also justifiably assume that the pictures do not represent images, in some form, in someone's mind or memory.

Between these two limiting types of cases are all sorts of instances where it would be difficult, because of the impossibility of

(Fig. 114)

ruling out certain conceivable alternatives, to arrive at any secure presumption as to the point in space (in so far as we can talk in spatial terms at all) from which Ted's images might have been derived. An example would be one of a series of phallic images that Ted got in the days following his having started a trend with his profane version of the Trinita dei Monti (fig. 101). The towers shown in fig. 115 (which Ted got with Dr. Frey and me witnessing, Dr. Frey supplying the film) were at first thought to be some Byzantine counterpart of the two towers of Ted's first Trinita dei Monti target response (fig. 99). Months later they were identified as the towers of Munich's Frauenkirche (or Ladies' Church). In the picture from which the identification was made (fig. 116),[4] the angle from which the towers were shot is so close to the angle from which they are seen in Ted's image as to lead

4 Eric Marcus, *Wir Reisen Nach Deutschland* (New York: Holt, Rinehart and Winston, 1964. Courtesy Monkmeyer Press, New York).

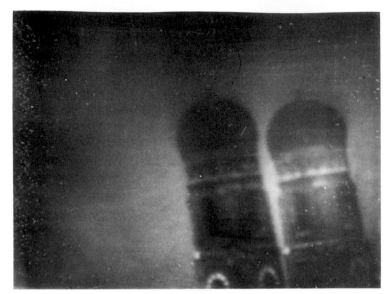

(Fig. 115)

(Fig. 116)

one to presume a vantage point to exist, on some building or hill in the neighborhood, from which many such pictures may have been taken. In this instance, thus, one cannot rule out the possibility of the actual source of Ted's image being a picture identical to it reposing in some book or tourist's album, even though one doesn't have on hand the actual photo that fills the bill. However, not all instances in between the two types of limiting cases cited present this degree of difficulty in ruling out certain possibilities as to source, as several to be given later will show.

One wonders, however, what there is to be gained from trying to pinpoint in physical terms the exact source in the external world of Ted's images when all source hypotheses involve transcending the ordinary barriers of communication in one way or another and the only difference between them would appear to be in respect to parameters that Ted himself seems to find not too relevant. It would appear as if the photo-simulating part of Ted's mind couldn't care less about factors such as distance when it passes up sources lying close at hand and ready to mind, such as the Westminster Abbey, Trajan's Column, and other official and unofficial target pictures, in order to come up with views which look as if they could very well have been registered by some apparatus close to the pictured objects themselves, however unlikely the angle of 'shooting' might have had to be (figs. 10, 85, 86).

It is precisely the fact, however, that nothing appears to be of less moment to whatever part of Ted's mind is responsible for the images he gets than considerations of distance in ordinary physical space that provides one of the most difficult hurdles for many people to take. It is somehow easier for some people to envisage a means of extrasensory communication, if extrasensory it has to be, that nevertheless respects the inverse square law of known types of radiation within the electromagnetic spectrum, and even many parapsychologists are loathe to give up without a fight on this issue.[5] However, quite apart from the formidable difficulties not only of quantifying the kinds of information involved but of identifying, isolating, tracking, and measuring the role of various factors conceivably involved in their 'transmission,' some investigators are dubious on general theoretical grounds

[5] Hoffman; Robertson.

that present-type physical hypotheses are at all applicable to psi phenomena.[6] Dr. Rush, who was one of the witnesses of the Westminster Abbey shot, wrote in 1943 that "no known process of energy-transfer has suggested even a plausible explanation of [psi] phenomena;" and Pascual Jordan, Professor of Theoretical Physics at the University of Hamburg, after surveying the field, concluded that there are no types of radiations now known or that could ever be known to physics that could account for the phenomena in their variety and entirety. The latter has declared flatly (1947) that psychical research "has to give up physics as a basic means of clarification." [7]

If we accept the fact for the time being, then, that psi events appear to occur in a way so far different from our present notions

[6] Some of the difficulties in the way of compiling quantifiable data on the experimental level of this problem, where hits and misses can be evaluated statistically in relation to varying distances, have been discussed by Osis, whose survey of the data of several statistical distance experiments (up to two thousand miles), and whose own experimental data (with Fahler), appear not to support the hypothesis of the independence of ESP from distance factors. However, the considerable mass of spontaneous material where information appears to come through (in dreams, visions, etc.) as clearly and in as much specific detail over maximum terrestrial distances as from the next room is quite impressive. Obviously, too, the relationship of any 'power' factor to the accuracy and intelligibility of the message in the types of information dealt with here has yet to be worked out. In my opinion, moreover, only if we had a space program far enough advanced so that the presence of intervening minds or relay systems existing in all sorts of animal life (and functioning en route like Telstar in relation to the communication of radio waves) could be experimentally ruled out could we even begin to deal with the complications introduced into the problem by the possibility of intermediate resonance and amplification systems. There is little doubt that the Russians, who have carried out successful distance experiments up to seventeen hundred kilometers (from Leningrad to Sevastopol) and who appear to be working full tilt on psi communication, will soon have some data on this problem.

[7] It might be noted, parenthetically, that physics itself has had to 'give up physics'—or at least physical-type radiation hypotheses—as a basic means of clarification in certain problem areas. One of these is the domain of all events, large and small, where attractive, or gravitational, 'forces' are held to apply, and the other is the mystery of how light gets across empty space. The former 'action at a distance' problem remained a basis of lively and at times acrimonious controversy from the time of Newton, who throughout the eighteenth century was indicted in many quarters as being 'occult,' until Einstein simply outflanked it by replacing 'force' assumptions with geometrical ones dealing with masses in a curved time-space manifold. In the other problem area, physicists have had to content themselves with the position expressed by Einstein when he wrote (with Infeld in *The Evolution of Physics*), "Our only way out seems to be to take for granted the fact that space has the physical property of transmitting electromagnetic waves, and not to bother too much about the meaning of this statement." (See also Bridgman on this problem.)

of how the world is put together as to present no particularly helpful clues in terms of these notions, we may as well adopt a purely phenomenological approach to the problem of the actual external source of Ted's images and, where a spatial assumption of one kind or another appears called for, fall back upon the postulate of indifference, which states, in effect, that when one does not have the means of deciding between two alternative assumptions, either one may be adopted. Thus, since there is ordinarily no advantage in thinking in terms of photographs in a book or album as the possible source of Ted's images, and certainly no advantage in substituting one obscurity for another by postulating images in someone's mind or memory as the source, there is no reason why one should not think of things, if this is at all helpful, *as if* the perceiving and registering part of Ted's mind were just where the images themselves would indicate it to be.

One advantage of provisionally adopting this 'things are just what they seem' approach is that this aspect of Ted's imaging could then be conveniently viewed in connection with a type of psychic and quasi-psychic experience so universally reported as to have achieved widespread representation in folklore and in one of our most familiar myths, that of the witch's broomstick ride. Apparently a higher percentage of the general population than is ordinarily thought—25 per cent, according to some authorities—have at one time or another experienced the sensation of leaving their bodies and, briefly or at greater length, seeing themselves or other things from a distance, almost invariably from a higher position in space, as if their point of perception were in a floating position or in a balloon. So-called out-of-the-body experiences have been reported in fevers, in states such as migraine and epilepsy, in delirium, under anesthesia, after shock, and in moribund conditions, especially the latter. Many such reports have been given by people who have briefly experienced clinical death and who have later been revived. But some people have experienced this seeming separation of the self from the body lying in bed between sleeping and waking, and it appears not uncommon with the new wave of LSD experiences, where Sydney Cohen has described subjects who "floated around the room yet could look down and see themselves sprawled on the bed." (At the time of this writing a substantial percentage of the population is said to be 'floating' on LSD.[8])

A significant aspect of these experiences is the unanimity of agreement among those who report them—a unanimity all the more striking in that the great majority of the subjects had never heard of the phenomenon before having experienced it—as to the complete qualitative difference between the experience of being out of the body and states of dreaming or reverie. (This is borne out in the several cases I have investigated.) And although many of these out-of-the-body experiences take place under conditions, such as traumatic concussion or terminal coma, in which awareness of any conscious kind, even dreaming, is supposed not to occur, some organized aspect of the person involved seems to perceive itself and its environment with perfect, sometimes preternatural clarity. (One cannot help thinking the clear pictures Ted got while in various states of clouded consciousness.) This part of the individual, moreover, seems to have a firm sense of continuity with his prior self, and has the experience of moving about in space on its own volition.

The following account, which was sent to the Research Officer of the Society for Psychical Research, is qualitatively typical of the group:

"The incident took place on August 3rd, 1944, near Saint Charles de Percy in Normandy. I was an armoured car officer engaged in medium and long range reconnaissance work with the 21st Army Group. At about 2:30 P.M. on the above-named day I was in a small armoured scout car which received a direct hit from a German anti-tank gun. Our car, which was full of various explosives, grenades, phosphorus bombs, etc., blew up. I might mention that it was stationary at the time, having just halted. The force of the explosion threw me about twenty feet away from the car and over a five-foot hedge. My clothes, etc., were on fire, and there were various pieces of phosphorus sticking to me which were also burning. Now my immediate reaction to the explosion, which appeared to me from the middle of it like a great white cold sheet, with a strong smell of cordite, was (naturally enough) fear. I

8 Several hundred cases of out-of-the-body experiences, of varying degrees of authentication, have been collected by Crookall (1964) and classified according to the state of the individual at the time of the experience—normal health, exhaustion, illness, shock, or moribundity. (See also Eastman; Stratton; Whiteman.)

imagined for a split second that I had gone to hell, and I quickly tried to recollect some particular vice which might have been my qualification. It is interesting to notice that I did not see any rapid 'trailer' of my past life as, I believe, drowning persons report. All this took a fraction of a second, and the next experience was definitely unusual. I was conscious of being two persons—one, lying on the ground in a field where I had fallen from the blast, my clothes, etc., on fire, and waving my limbs about wildly, at the same time uttering moans and gibbering with fear—I was quite conscious of both making these sounds, and at the same time hearing them as though coming from another person. The other 'me' was floating up in the air, about twenty feet from the ground, from which position I could see not only my other self on the ground, but also the hedge, the road, and the car which was surrounded by smoke and burning fiercely. I remember quite distinctly telling myself: 'It's no use gibbering like that—roll over and over to put the flames out.' This my ground body eventually did, rolling over into a ditch under the hedge where there was a slight amount of water. The flames went out, and at this stage I suddenly became one person again.

"Of course, the aerial viewpoint can be explained up to a point as a 'photograph' taken subconsciously as I was passing over the hedge as a result of the blast. This, however, does not explain the fact that I saw 'myself' on the ground quite clearly and for what seemed a long time, though it could not have been more than a minute or so." [9]

As I have indicated, many of the persons reporting these experiences describe what they see as if they were looking down from a floating position. This is true even when the experience appears to be very much akin to what is reported in directed traveling clairvoyance, as a number of them are, and normally unknowable veridical information is secured.[10] Now many of Ted's pictures, as may have been noticed, appear to have been shot from positions of this sort, and in certain instances where the 'looking down' aspect is not immediately apparent, attempts to duplicate the angles from which they seem to have been shot (quite apart from the fact that many of them seem to have been shot with a

[9] *Jour. Soc. Psych. Res.,* Vol. 34, 1948, p. 207.
[10] An interesting personal account of one such experience is given by Dr. Andrija Puharich in *The Sacred Mushroom.*

different focal-length lens than that in the Polaroid cameras and could not be duplicated even with close-up attachments) have led to the presumption that this could be done only from a helicopter or balloon or a physically difficult cantilevered position on some structure in the neighborhood. One such instance is cited by Mrs. Oehler in her paper. Another is Ted's Westminster Abbey image (fig. 10) where, it will be recalled, a difference was immediately noticed between it and the target picture. Mr. Simeon Edmunds, a London editor with some photographic experience, was unable to duplicate certain geometric features in Ted's picture (mainly the parallactic relationship of the top of the arched windows in the transept to the knobby-looking decorative features on the left-hand pilaster of the clock tower) in a number of ways tried, including from the top of a bus, and finally concluded that the picture would have had to be taken from a balloon. Still another is a color picture of the Denver Hilton Hotel (fig. 117, opposite

(Fig. 117)

the title page) that Ted got while trying for the Chicago Hilton ("I missed, damn it."). I held and triggered the model 100 camera for this one. As best I have been able to determine, this would have had to be shot with a different lens and from a position between the tops of the trees shown and a low park structure across the street, a position not achievable with an ordinary seven-foot stepladder but only with some special contrivance for getting the cameraman well into the air.

The subjective experience of seeing things from a floating position in space seems to occur on a continuum from instances at one end, when the person 'sees' things this way only in the mind's eye, and when there is no suggestion of his feeling as if he were out of his body (I have had analytic patients report memories of childhood scenes 'seen' in this way—when the experience was nevertheless extraordinary enough to be remarked on), to instances such as the out-of-the-body experiences cited above. Somewhere in between would be instances such as those not infrequently reported by psychics who do not claim the experience of leaving their bodies but who sometimes receive the impressions of what they are 'seeing' with hallucinatory vividness and as if "like a bird." Dutch parapsychologist, Professor W. H. C. Tenhaeff, has written of some psychics he has studied that "they feel as if they are somewhere in space (in the sky) and are looking down." [11] And when Ted began his 'seeing' experiences as a traveling clairvoyant in the company of Jean Laffite, although he had no visual experience of crossing space, as he recalls these journeys, his arrivals at destination were invariably from a position somewhere above treetop or building level, from which he would swoop in gracefully. "All of a sudden you were there, and you'd come in like a bird." [12]

[11] *Proceedings of the Parapsychological Institute of the State University of Utrecht.* No. 3, Jan., 1965.

[12] One cannot help conjecturing whether this kind of experience might not provide a possible explanation of an aspect of certain prehistoric earthenworks found in this country (for those in Ohio, see Morgan) which has continued to fascinate and baffle investigators, namely that their geometric patterns, sometimes hundreds of yards in extent individually and up to over a hundred acres in groups, can be visually appreciated (if they *were* meant to be so appreciated) only from heights that could not possibly have been physically achieved at the times they were laid out. These mounds, connected with passageways, were presumably used for burial and other social functions; but it is conceivable that out-of-the-body experiences

In the case of out-of-the-body experiences which, like Ted's images, appear to have a veridical component, it is again a matter of pure election, a tossup, whether we think of a part of the mind as having freed itself from the body and as having gone elsewhere, dressing itself out imaginatively in a self-image of sorts—something like a phantom limb with the power of auto-perception, let us say—or whether we think of it as staying where it is while simply exercising ESP (even when unconscious) but creating, at the same time, an appropriate hallucinatory role for itself in an effort somehow to normalize what is occurring.[13]

Now ordinarily one has to be careful in mixing up subjective experience with what one is commonly used to terming 'objective' experience in the world of physical reality. But one should be just as careful to avoid mistaking pure assumptions for fundamental limiting aspects of some kind of reality. The issue is not one of the separability of the mind from the brain—everyone grants some sort of empirical relationship between the two (although of exactly what sort is open to exploration of logical possibilities not generally taken into account) [14]—but of the spatial dependence of

---

might have played a magical ceremonial role in connection with what is for many peoples the prototype of all out-of-the-body experiences, death. Techniques for producing out-of-the-body experiences by fasting, prayer, drugs, and dancing till exhausted have been claimed by primitive peoples all over the world, and may have been used for ritualistic experiences that are lost to us except for what can be gleaned from birdman myths, which are universal. The cabalists were well aquainted with this phenomenon, and the 'great flight' across space of the Eskimo shaman is well known. Unfortunately Eliade, who in his book on shamanism cites many sources for universal belief in out-of-the-body experiences (pp. 477 ff.), assumes that 'seeing' with the mind in this way is a purely metaphorical manner of speaking.

13 One should, however, make special note of instances, like the one described by Professor Tenhaeff in the case of one of his clairvoyants (and which can be matched in the reports of traveling clairvoyants and not a few mediumistic descriptions), when the persons involved appear to be subject to a kind of optical illusion that might be experienced normally in the physical act of seeing. "During an experiment in Freiburg i. Br.," writes Tenhaeff (op. cit.), "Croiset described a wall with battlements. The lady who took part in the experiment denied that the wall which had been described had battlements. The paragnost [a term used by Tenhaeff for a sensitive or clairvoyant] maintained that they had to be there. He had 'seen' them so clearly. When, on the next day, we went to the building to verify the correctness of certain data in person, we found that we had to do with a case of optical illusion. Seen from a certain point, the windows of the building fell together with the upper side of the wall in such a way that one got the impression of the wall having been provided with battlements."

14 The fact that the brain has a perfectly evident role in perception, feeling, thinking, and volition is commonly cited as the clinching argument for the inseparability thesis, as if the undeniable fact of an empirical relationship of some

certain aspects of the behavior of the individual upon the where-abouts of the brain. Unfortunately it is difficult to begin to clarify this thickety subject, and to arrive at more adequate and more sophisticated definitions of some of the terms involved (like 'apart-ness' and 'mind') when we are given to an automatic circularity of reasoning—a special case of the ever-receding-horizon fallacy—which inevitably leads to a denial of any kind or degree of inde-pendence of the two, every time the matter comes into question, precisely *because* such independence is held to be categorically impossible.

Much of the difficulty with questions such as *where* the mind (or the self) is, in occurrences such as Ted's pictures and some of the more authentic out-of-the-body experiences reported, arises be-cause we try to use terms like 'where' and 'mind' in situations where they have little actual relevance. Our familiar notions about these terms stand up pretty well so long as we remain within a highly circumscribed circle of thinking activities, and play the game of observing and collecting facts and making myths by way of linking these facts together according to certain arbitrary rules. But these rules are not necessarily valid in all situations to which the term 'reality' can be applied. In certain situations—not only in connection with psi phenomena but in physics as well—these rules are simply bad habits that it would be well to get rid of. Thus we have got used to thinking of the mind in terms of space—it is 'in' the body, 'in' the brain, and moves from place to place only with the body and the brain—and seem to have lost sight of the fact that what we may actually do is quite the reverse, that is, experience space in terms of the properties of the mind. We come to regard space as a thing, as something that is characterized by a quality called extension and which 'contains' things like people and tables and continents and planets because we are used to measuring it with our eyes and our legs and extensions of these organs (tele-scopes, automobiles) and with our psychologically conditioned ideas of sequence and duration. But where space does not *neces-*

---

sort were all there was to the matter. Exactly *what* it is that is empirically demon-strable, however, remains to be clarified. It may be that the brain, as Henri Bergson long ago suspected, acts in certain respects like a selective filtering apparatus, such as a radio sender or receiver without which one obviously cannot communicate or receive information but which, while necessary, may not be sufficient and may not give the whole picture.

sarily figure in our ways of describing certain events, there is no sense retaining it at all in our thinking about these events. Thus, Kant, the first modern philosopher to investigate the character of space as a construct of the human mind, had little difficulty in accepting the irrelevance of the yardstick method of connecting (or rather, separating) events when writing to a friend of Swedenborg's accurate description of a fire in Stockholm, three hundred miles from where he had been staying.[15] He was, in consequence, as little disturbed by the strangeness of the occurrence as primitive peoples who accept this kind of 'knowing' as an everyday affair. Many primitives are less bothered by the 'mind' (or the 'self,' which they do not differentiate too clearly from what we call the mind) being in two places at once than they are by a concept of causality that restricts effects to the consequences of motions or perturbations in media that can be seen and excludes such manifestly powerful forces as thoughts and desires.

Close to the core of our difficulty here are problems that have never ceased to bother the philosophers: How do we come to know about the external world? How do we know that there *is* an external world? How do we know anything? Philosophers have made a great to-do out of the fact that the primary data of experience are not 'objects in themselves' but our own sense data, which we cannot eliminate even when we use the most refined laboratory instrumentation to put us in touch (note how our very language cannot escape our sensory modalities) with the ultimate constituents of matter and motion. But they are nevertheless satisfied to ascribe a kind of reality to the publicly sharable consistency and regularity which sense data provide, so that if they have never quite overcome the limitations pointed out by Plato in his well-known simile to the effect that we are all dwellers in caves condemned to live with our backs to the fire and capable of seeing only the shadows of things on the wall, they at least have the reassuring belief that they can for the most part tell the genuine shadows from the illusory ones that we sometimes see in dreams and hallucinations.

But psychologists have never been too comfortable with this easygoing acceptance of sense data as gilt-edged security in a world of appearances. There are certain aspects of how sense data get put

15 Prince, *op. cit.*

together into 'perceptions' and 'knowings' that have always bothered them and which, despite the contributions of at least a dozen different current theories of perception—theories based on models ranging from the purely psychological to the neurophysiological and mathematical—continue to remain just beyond our grasp (here again note the language with which we connote the activity of the mind).[16] One such problem is that of how the perception of the constancy of size, shape, position, or color of an object is maintained, to take a visual example, when our sense data provide us only an ever moving, shifting, changing group of lines, hues, and shadows. The same with other modalities. Our sensory apparatuses are constantly in states of variable excitation from the world around us, which is never still (any more than the forest, which every nature lover knows is whirringly, buzzingly, beepingly, and crawlingly alive) yet behaves, so far as our auditory, tactile, olfactory, and kinesthetic perceptions are concerned, with a similar constancy. (It is questionable whether the mathematical models which have been proposed by Wiener and others for the problem of visual constancy have much applicability in the case of these other modalities.) A second problem is that of wholes, and how we come to know a thing as a thing and not just a bunch of discretely perceived sensory qualities. A connected problem is how we know, purely in terms of the information supplied by our sense data, where a thing leaves off and the other things around it, the objects in depth in its background, begin. The apperception of this aspect of things appears paradoxically to involve some kind of prior comprehension of relationships that is not given in the primary data of the senses themselves, or in anything that can be psychologically, neurophysiologically or mathematically extrapolated from them. Still another connected problem is that of how we come to know the *meaning* of a thing so that we can separate it not just visually or auditorily or tactually but in what William James called the big bloomin' buzzin' confusion of lived experience from all the things around that it is not. Everybody seems to know what meaning means (everybody, that is, except philosophers who make careers out of trying to define it) but no one is quite sure how it gets attached to things before learning has had a chance to take place. The problem here is that learning

16 See Allport.

cannot take place, nor is there a basis on which anything can get organized and crystallized out from a sensorially competing background, *until* what our senses show us has some kind of meaning. And finally, nobody has even the slightest semblance of a theory as to how the big leap occurs, the utterly inexplicable transformation from the physical fact of waves of various kinds impinging on sense organs of various kinds to the mental facts which exist in an entirely new domain of experience, the domain of red and warmth and smooth and E flat. These are 'qualities' of an utterly new kind that are not given in the physics of the sense data but are somehow connected with that enigma of enigmas, consciousness.

Now the gestalt psychologists tell us that all the prepackaging that occurs before things take on their form and meaning 'in' consciousness is accomplished by some synthesizing and organizing principle in something they call 'mind,' which, like consciousness itself, they accept as given but whose finer structure they look to the neurophysiologists for. But the neurophysiologists confess that this occult wonder, the key to the whole business, is beyond them and are tempted to pass the buck back to the philosophers, the more positivistic among whom, however, have serious doubts about the very existence of any such 'ghost in the machine' in the first place. We are confronted, thus, with a state of affairs in which philosophers, some of whom don't believe in a figment of the mind called a mind, tell us that our knowledge of the external world depends on sense data the lowliest of which, according to the psychologists, don't make sense apart from the mind's knowledge of the world; and in which all of them seem to agree not on *if* the mind is, much less *what* it is, but only, absurdly enough, on where it isn't.

No doubt the philosophers and psychologists would have come to somewhat different conclusions about the problem of knowledge had they based their investigations on the data provided by people like Ted instead of on the general run of cave dwellers. (The special cave within a cave that our savants inhabit is a story in itself.) Obviously Ted's kind of 'knowing,' to come back to the question of where his mind or mind's eye is when it gets the information about objects in the external world that it somehow puts on film, does not depend on what his senses tell him but, if anything, the reverse: his senses, if we view what he gets on film as in some way an analogue of sensation, depend on what he knows, what he has gotten information about in some other way entirely. (This is clearly a complete turnabout of the venerable doctrine, *Nihil in intellectu est quod non prius in sensu fuerat*—nothing is in the mind that was not first present in the senses.) Moreover, if we study the testimony of hosts of other psychically gifted individuals of various stripes—sensitives of one kind or another, clairvoyants, mediums—we find that in their experience sensation bears a relationship to knowing that is more like that of language to thought than that of cause to effect. Sometimes, it is true, language seems to dictate or entail thought, especially where it is privately habitual or culturally set (and no better examples could probably be found than our use of terms like 'matter' and 'mind,' or such an anomaly as 'life after death') but at higher levels language *expresses* thought, is a means chiefly of dressing out and putting on public display that which originates in other modes entirely and which, in its deeper reaches, its 'sweet silent sessions,' is truly ineffable (instrumentalist theories about the origin of language notwithstanding). In this sense, so far as the 'knowing' involved in psychic experience goes, we may correctly speak of the 'language of imagery' in so far as imagery dresses out and conveys in a conveniently organized way, to the limited part of the self that is consciously aware, that information which has already been secured. In this kind of knowing, the knowing that somehow goes on before imagery or any other sensory experience enters the picture, one almost gets the impression, from the testimony of mediumistically gifted persons, that 'meaning' is the first thing that is apperceived (if we can conceive of the Cheshire smile without the cat) and that everything else follows from that, in much the same way that certain ideas seem to exist formlessly in the unconscious, as only potentialities as it were, before they enter upon a phase of particular conscious actuality.

Sometimes mediums and other psychically gifted persons—clairvoyant, telepaths—are at a loss to explain how their knowledge of the persons or events they report on comes to them, but they are often as certain of this newly and mysteriously acquired knowledge, which later may turn out to be perfectly correct, as they are of anything in the sphere of their own memories or sensorially based consciousness. It seems to be like knowledge in dreams, in which we know without knowing *how* we know that we are proceeding in a northerly direction, or that it is thirteen minutes past four, or that a given action is going to take place. Sometimes mediums or clairvoyants have difficulty finding the right words into which to translate their certain but formless knowledge so long as it remains raw and undifferentiated; but if it should pass over into a 'seeing,' a 'hearing,' or a 'feeling,' as it sometimes does quite easily and automatically, then this difficulty is obviated.[17] Frequently, however, knowledge comes directly in the form of sensory experience of hallucinatory vividness where the sensory modalities that come into play—visual, auditory, tactile, olfactory— appear to depend on what sensations *ought* to be involved if the person or the event is to present itself in a characteristic way. Sometimes the sensory modality chosen seems to bear only a symbolic connection with the type of information involved, like the strong smell of roses to represent an alleged communicator to whom this was especially meaningful in life, or the smell of smoke to convey the idea of fire (one of the most frequent types of mediumistic and clairvoyant types of 'translation,' suggesting the persistence of an archaic way of functioning that might have had enormous survival value in primitive times). At other times the knowledge arrives by a process that would appear to be closely allied to what the psychoanalysts call identification, so that the medium or sensitive is aware only of being overcome by a peculiar kind of pain or feeling (of depression, hopelessness) that is sharply differentiable from his own experience. Perhaps the most common sensory modality in which knowledge is dressed out, however, is the visual, and this, as is the case with other modalities, can come directly, either as some attenuated, perhaps quasi-visual 'mind's eye' experience (such as the half-seeing, half-knowing that takes place in memory 'images') or with such hallucinatory force as to take precedence over, and blot out, all normal visual experience. One sensitive in the group studied by Professor Tenhaeff reported an image he saw to be so sharp "I could see the blades of grass between the bricks of the pavement." Others spoke of a film passing at great speed before them and of being able to retain only fragments of what they saw. Another investigator reported on a

17 Tyrrell, *op. cit.*, chap. XIX.

clairvoyant whose 'pictures' came to him so strongly that he felt they could be photographed.

Coming back to the problems with which the philosophers and the psychologists deal, if, for a moment, we were to imagine that the type of experience demonstrated by psychically 'gifted' people were the rule and ordinary sensorially mediated knowing the exception (as if individuals limited to this were like people marooned on an island, perfectly able to be in touch with all local goings-on but cut off from communication with the rest of the world), we would no doubt have arrived at a theory of knowledge that would not have depended on perception, and on a theory of perception in which the problems of constancy, meaning, prior knowledge, and all the rest might not arise, or at least would not present some of the seemingly insurmountable difficulties they now do. 'Knowing' might then have to be taken for granted (as we have to take so many things for granted in our universe) as occurring by some kind of direct process which, as far as the external world goes, we ordinarily ascribe only to God and for ourselves can analogize only to the knowing of oneself and one's body with which we are all familiar and take for granted. Prototypal knowing (not to be confused with Plato's remembrance of a past life) would then precede sensation and not depend upon it. Sensorially mediated knowing might then turn out to be regarded only as a special 'fine tuning' device for concentrating probabilities—funneling them together in areas where space *is* a relevant parameter, as it were—and for maintaining stability within certain biological and social contexts. And if we could, then, hypothecate this as a model of how information is communicated between all event systems in the universe, the relation of the individual event to the aggregate—now described but hardly accounted for by the theory of probability—might become clearer and we might begin to see our way out of the enigma of why anything at all should work in what ought, according to our present concepts, to be a perfectly chaotic mess.

But one major factor would still be missing, the 'motor' in all this, the kinetic or executive factor. Information must be acted on to be effectual, to keep things running. And this brings us back to Ted and the relation between his 'knowing' and the peculiar way he has of manifesting it.

For the most part Ted does not 'see' the images he is somehow instrumental in actualizing; the film is, as it were, his visual apparatus and his consciousness. His images on film appear to be equivalent to the mental images of other types of psychics. But while the others make one big leap, from 'knowing' to images in consciousness, he makes another, from knowing to patterns on film. One type of event is hardly more comprehensible, or less incomprehensible, than the other; and neither is more incomprehensible than the leap from physical sense data to sensation. All remain firm against reductionist hypotheses: they are just there, facts of existence. But there are facts about these facts of existence that might warrant further discussion, if only to show what difficulties we can get into when we try systematically to ignore them.

CHAPTER XI

A Tour de Force

1

A CHEMICALLY sensitized surface outside the skull may be an unusual place for the appearance of images more familiarly met with in waking consciousness, but, as I learned to my surprise when I began to look into the subject in preparation for this chapter, such a displacement (if we may so refer to it) was not unknown among early photographers, especially those with a confirmed spiritualist bias. In fact getting 'psychic' images on photographic plates has been reported almost since the beginning of photography and at certain periods—notably the 1860's and 1870's—seems to have been somewhat of a minor rage, like the Ouija board and table turning. Between 1919 and 1923 there flourished in Britain and on the Continent a Society for the Study of Supernormal Pictures, a group made up mostly of professional photographers, and with Sir Arthur Conan Doyle as one of its officers. However, outside the work of Tomokichi Fukurai, whose *Clairvoyance and Thought-ography* appeared in English in 1931 (but which most people, myself included, had never heard of until Ted appeared on the scene—Fukurai is not mentioned in a *Biographical Dictionary of*

Parapsychology which appeared in 1964), 'psychic photography,' as it was generally called, was so little known among today's parapsychologists that one could almost suppose it to have been carefully deleted from the record, like the unsavory past of a dictator. Indeed, the early work in the field was subjected to a critical review in 1891 by a spokesman for the then young British Society for Psychical Research and written off, without even a pretense of firsthand investigation (such as was then being carried out by that body on thought-transference, apparitions, unexplained rappings, and other occurrences that science disdained to deal with), as hardly warranting further consideration. "It appeared to me," wrote the reviewer, "that, after eliminating what might certainly or probably be attributed to trickery, the remaining evidence was hardly sufficient in amount to establish even a *prima facie* case for investigation, in vew of the immense theoretical difficulties involved." [1]

Nevertheless, when I glance over what I am able to get hold of or piece together of these early reports—including even some of those reviewed in 1891—it is difficult for me to avoid the impression that, despite what was in all likelihood the grossest knavery practiced by several 'spirit photographers,' there may well have been a core of genuinely unexplainable phenomena.[2] After one has discounted a number of cheeseclothy and seemingly doubly exposed 'spirit photographs' of departed relatives (and occasionally late lamented pooches) hovering alongside the solemn-faced dupes who were induced to sit for these photographic reunions, there still remain the spotty accounts of occurrences reported by both professionals and nonprofessionals which are suspiciously like the sort of thing that can be observed with Ted, such as the mirror image of a sitter's locket portrait of a dead son showing up on the plate with the sitter, along with the rim of the locket itself, and living people appearing when they shouldn't, and vice versa. Moreover, the testimony of well-known and seemingly reliable

1 Sidgwick.
2 See articles by John Beattie, *British Journal of Photography*, 1872-3; by "M. A. (Oxon.)," *Human Nature*, 1874-5; *Personal Experiences of William H. Mumler* (1875); and an article by J. Traill Taylor, ed., in *The British Journal of Photography*, March 17, 1893 (reprinted in Glendinning, *The Veil Lifted*). Also: James Coates, *Photographing the Invisible;* Arthur Conan Doyle, *The Case for Spirit Photography;* J. J. Morse, *A Brief History of Spirit Photography;* A. Russell Wallace, *Miracles and Modern Spiritualism.*

witnesses as to the conditions under which the images appeared—secretly earmarked plates supplied by incognito sitter-witnesses themselves, rigid control of the camera and all conditions in and outside the darkroom by other witnesses—would leave anyone who has worked with Ted wondering where, outside of sheer senseless collusion, the loopholes for fraud were in many instances. Curiously, too, several of the witnesses and commentators and even photographers themselves were highly embarrassed and puzzled by the only-too-plainly-fake looks of some of the 'spirit' photos whose production they had carefully supervised, and took pains to point out that better jobs could easily have been done with the clumsiest trickery. (Some were careful to point out, also, that the 'extras' appearing on these photos were not images of spirits at all but simply, in some inexplicable way, of no longer living people of whom, in some cases, no photographs were known to exist.) [3]

Of the later reports, as effectually buried in the archives as if they had never been written, the most interesting, outside of Fukurai's, is an account in 1914 by Professor (of philosophy at Columbia University) James H. Hyslop of a series of photographs made over a period of several years by a Mrs. Marguerite Du Pont Lee (one of the "powder people" Du Ponts and a wealthy, philanthropically inclined woman, Dr. Hyslop noted by way of hinting that at least a mercenary motive for fraud was not in the picture). Mrs. Lee began her 'psychic photography' because she was instructed to do so by a Dr. Bocock, an Episcopalian minister who

---

[3] This was, however, certainly not so in the case of the alleged 'spirit' photograph of Abraham Lincoln which is several times referred to in the early reports. W. H. Mumler, the earliest known 'spirit photographer,' who was later tried for obtaining money under false pretenses and, apparently on the strength of numerous witnesses, acquitted, gave this account of how Mrs. Lincoln visited his studio: "I had just finished taking a picture for a gentleman who resides in Canada, when the door-bell rang, and a lady dressed in black, wearing a crape veil, was ushered in. The veil was so thick it was impossible to distinguish a single feature of her face . . . I requested her to be seated; would be ready for her in a moment. I went into my dark room and coated a plate. When I came out I found her seated, with her veil still over her face. I asked if she intended having her picture taken with her veil. She replied, 'When you are ready, I will remove it.' I said I was ready, whereupon she removed the veil, and the picture was taken." The lady gave her name as 'Mrs. Lindall,' and was told to call for the pictures in three days. Only when he saw the print, according to Mumler, did he realize who his sitter had been. "The picture of Mr. Lincoln is an excellent one. He is seen standing behind her, with his hands resting on her shoulders, and looking down, with a pleasant smile." And entirely unperturbed, I might add from looking at a reproduction of the picture given in Coates (*op. cit.*), by the fact that all he seems to have had on was his long winter drawers.

had died in another city some ten years before but who allegedly took to sending her messages, in what was purported to be his own hand, through her own automatic writing. The conditions of observation and control of Mrs. Lee's image making were far from adequate; Dr. Hyslop himself, on the two occasions he made the overnight journey from New York to Washington to supervise some trials, failed to observe results of any interest. But quite a few of the hundreds of pictures produced by her show features similar to what can be observed under highly controlled conditions with Ted. (Dr. Hyslop merely presented and discussed the data, circumspectly avoiding a verdict.) Of the more down-to-earth photographs there were a number in which objects which should have shown up on the plates failed to appear and others in which objects which allegedly were not in the room showed up in a jumble that on close inspection appeared to be somewhat like the montage effects that Ted sometimes comes up with. One or two of these were quite extraordinary from a topological point of view, such as a pair of dowel-backed chairs woven together like interlocking rings. Dr. Hyslop, at any rate, was unable to duplicate selected examples of this group with multiple exposures. Most of Mrs. Lee's pictures, however, showed the late Reverend Bocock in a variety of improbable poses that one might think no self-respecting bona fide spirit would care to be caught alive in. But some were allegedly in poses that relatives of the late minister claimed did not exist in any extant photographs of him.

It might be remarked here, incidentally, that there is little difference in principle between Ted's images of people still living but shown in some pose or action other than what they happened to be in or doing at the time the image was produced and the hundreds of images of late relatives that were allegedly produced paranormally when 'spirit photography' was the vogue. Actually Ted has produced pictures of unidentified people in various poses, some with almost snapshot clarity, who might not have been living, for all anyone knows, at the time their pictures materialized. I hesitate to reproduce these (except for shots like those shown in fig. 22 and 118, where I feel I may safely chance it) [4] for

---

[4] Fig. 118: One of a series shot with Dr. Frey holding and snapping the camera, having loaded it with my film, inside a radiotherapy room. I was watching from outside, through a window. Time: night.

(Fig. 118)

fear of what happened to one or two of the early spirit photographers when some of the unidentified 'extras' who appeared in their ghostly galleries turned out to be not only living but litigious.

2

Fukurai's work, which was done mainly between 1910 and 1913, was a departure from the prevailing vogue of spirit photography (but not enough of a departure, unfortunately, to prevent his being forced to resign his professorship at the Imperial University of Tokyo). Working mostly with opaquely wrapped dry plates, he began by asking his several subjects, who were known psychics, to concentrate on simple forms, like squares or circles, and then went on to more complex forms like calligraphic figures, and finally to figures of living people like himself. He experimented boldly with distances up to three hundred miles and with the imprinting of a selected one of several plates held together. He succeeded also in getting part of one figure on one plate and the complementary part on another (fig. 119). But of special interest were the incidental target distortions and substitutions which occasionally showed up, and one feature which bore a striking resemblance to some of the things done by Ted and, as it turns out, also by others. One of Fukurai's subjects was a lady medium whose thoughtographic efforts were supposedly complemented on occasion by bizarre touches added by an impish secondary personality, calling itself the Goblin, which was always making trouble for the medium and for Fukurai.[5] The Goblin was not above pulling Fukurai's professional leg. One day when Fukurai was puzzled by a peculiar graininess which he described as "something like short feathers [which] appeared in a vortex all over the plate," (fig. 120) the Goblin informed him that these were its wing feathers, the results of *its* thoughtographic efforts. Now the same kind of feathery graininess may be seen in some of the pictures Ted gets without benefit of Goblin and on a film emulsion presumably of rather different molecular composition from what must have coated the plates that Fukurai used. Good examples of Ted's 'feathers' may be seen in figs. 25 and 121. (The latter, taken unsupervised, would have little interest except for the peculiar grain that showed up on it.) But this appears to be only a somewhat coarser version of what shows up in other instances—*e.g.*, figs. 48, 88, 122 [6]—as a sort of burst of light seeming to arise from the central figure of the picture, an effect apparently not unknown to other workers. Fig. 123 is reproduced from Carrington's *Mod-*

5 It is interesting to observe a Japanese secondary personality of fifty years ago conform to what appears to be a universal pattern for these entities. If there are several secondary personalities, as is sometimes the case, there is always one which is amoral, earthy, of lively intelligence and according to whom, whether in the case of a French peasant, a New England spinster, a young Southern housewife, or a Denver factory worker, the primary is a bore, a creep, and a square. They all delight in tormenting the primary personalities, just as Eve Black tormented Eve White in the fascinating *Three Faces of Eve* study reported by Drs. Thigpen and Cleckley. The Goblin would do things like sending the primary's temperature skyrocketing in order to gain concessions from Fukurai, and then bringing it down to normal within a minute or two after a deal had been agreed upon.

6 Fig. 122 emerged during the session for which Fig. 73 was the official target. Note the superficial similarity of the arched windows of the penthouse to those in the picture of the campanile. The question arose whether this unidentified building were not a compromise hit condensing the features of the official concealed target chosen by Dr. Barbato and those of a certain hotel, which it somewhat resembled, chosen mentally as a target by Mrs. Barbato from shots of it she had seen on television a little while before our session began.

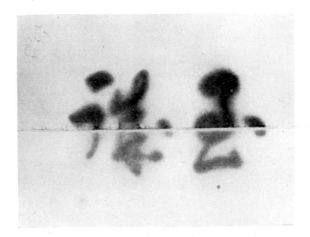

(Fig. 119)

(Fig. 120)

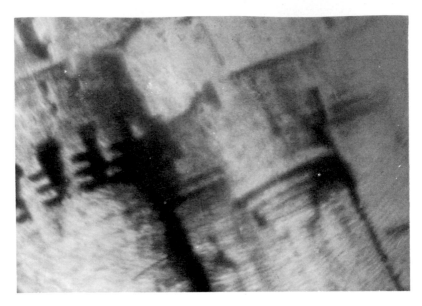

(Fig. 121)

(Fig. 122)

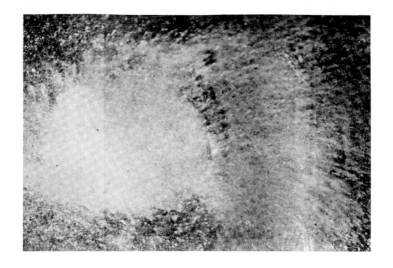

(Fig. 123)

ern Psychical Phenomena (1919) with the caption: " 'Vital radiations' issuing from the human body and impressing (directly) a photographic plate." (The provenance and circumstances of this picture are not given.)

3

We have not, of course, the slightest idea of what these striations might represent. If they do, as Carrington suggests—with his fingers crossed, apparently—represent 'radiations,' these are of a sort which have so far not been positively identified. Since the time of Mesmer alleged effluvia with various types of manifestations have been reported in association with persons of high psychic sensitivity, but repeatable objective evidences of these 'emanations' have not been demonstrated.[7] Nevertheless, and despite the earlier-mentioned conclusions of some physicists that no type of radiation now known could account for psi phenomena, the possibility of explanatory hypotheses in terms of occult radiations or fields of force of some sort has continued to challenge the imaginations of physical and mathematical theoreticians.[8]

[7] Fodor: "Emanations."
[8] Dobbs; Taetzsch.

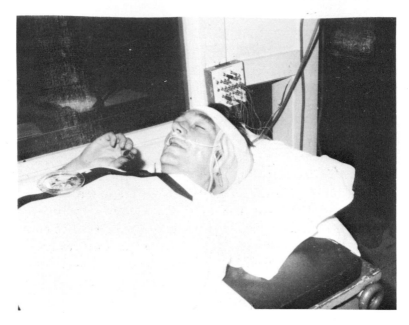

(Fig. 124)

So far Ted has lent himself to fairly well-controlled investigation of several radiation hypotheses, covering large portions of
the electromagnetic spectrum, and although certain anomalous
findings of as yet undetermined significance have turned up, no
definitely positive supporting data for any of these hypotheses
have been obtained. I shall present this work in as much detail as
seems pertinent, with some discussion of one or two of the unusual
methodological problems associated with investigations of this
sort.

One of the first things to be investigated was the possibility of
something showing up during electroencephalographic (brain
wave) tests. Nothing did on the two occasions Ted was studied.
On the first of these, during the initial phase of our work, Ted
was hooked up simultaneously (fig. 124) to an electroencephalo-
graph (EEG) and to a multiple-channel recorder designed to
register changes in respiration, blood pressure, heart function,
and so forth. Unfortunately the polygraph, as it is called, was not
working properly, and this latter aspect of our investigation has

yet to be repeated. Ted's only presumptive effect on film on this occasion, too, was too indefinite to draw any conclusions from. On the second occasion, about a year later, with just the EEG in use, Ted got several pictures, including those shown in figs. 125 and 126—impossible to duplicate close-ups of portions of the Opera House at Central City, Colorado, which he had just happened to see for a moment on television the evening before. (The picture in fig. 126 was shot, incidentally, with Dr. Metcalf holding and triggering the camera, Ted on the gismo. Dr. Metcalf supplied film and camera.) No effects on the EEG were noted that were in any way out of the ordinary—nothing, that is, beyond the undifferentiated effects normally expected with the type of attention Ted was giving to a mental task.[9] (Ted's baseline reading, incidentally, was quite within the normal range and was consistent with the diagnosis of a personality type characterized by the relative absence of inner conflict or stress.)

One of the next things to be investigated was the relation of Ted's thoughtographic phenomena to detectable changes in magnetic fields surrounding him and the film. This was a tempting line of investigation not only because of the suggestive similarity— if perhaps only superficial—of some of the 'feathery' striations seen on some of Ted's pictures and those of other 'thoughtographers' to the appearance obtained with iron filings and other granular metallic substances in magnetic fields, but also because the evidence of the biologic effects of magnetic fields is considerable.[10] Not the least interesting of these is the so-called magnetic-phosphene effect, a subjective sensation of light experienced when changing magnetic fields are applied to the human head. Since 1840, moreover, it had been claimed that certain persons were able visually to detect the make and break of magnetic currents, and in 1883 a committee of the British Society for Psychical Research, led by the physicist, W. F. Barrett, definitely confirmed the earlier work on this phenomenon.

Unfortunately this is an area where fully satisfactory investigations with Ted still remain to be carried out. On the one occasion

---

[9] Dr. Hans Berger, the discoverer of brain waves, granted the possible reality of telepathic phenomena but did not believe that whatever type of brain wave 'radiation' was measured by the EEG could account for them.

[10] Becker; Tromp.

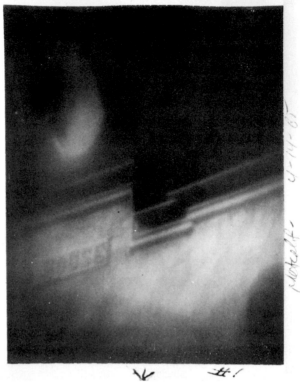

(Fig. 125)

(Fig. 126)

Ted attempted a number of trial shots within the immediate vicinity of the pickup of a magnetometer sensitive enough to detect small changes in body fields—an excellent recording seismograph in the area—the separation of possible thoughtographic events from the range of effects produced by the unavoidable movements of Ted's body and the camera was found too difficult. All Ted got on this occasion, in any case, were a few blackies, a not-too-surprising result considering that after the dead branch of a tree on the hillside on which the seismograph pickup was situated almost put his eye out, a chair collapsed under him, and various other unpleasantnesses occurred.

However, it is possible to report several findings conceivably relevant to the question of the relation of Ted's thoughtographic phenomena to induced or existing magnetic fields. First, paranormal images obtained by Ted while the camera was placed in magnetic fields ranging from 400 to 1200 gauss—enough to lift a one-pound monkey wrench two inches (the *gauss* is a unit of magnetic force named after the great nineteenth-century mathematician and physicist—the earth's magnetic field varies from about 0.2 to 0.6 gauss) did not differ significantly, on half a dozen trials, from similar images obtained with no such fields in force. (Shots taken by ordinary means with the camera in such fields also did not differ from shots of the same scenes taken in the absence of such fields.) Secondly, images Ted got in situations where the earth's magnetic field was considerably attenuated do not differ from images he gets under ordinary circumstances. These situations I shall now describe in connection with investigations primarily undertaken for other reasons.

The first was inside a so-called Faraday cage, a chamber shielded by copper-mesh screen designed primarily to provide the very high attenuation of radar and radio waves above the visible and infrared portion of the electromagnetic spectrum but which may also provide a high attenuation of the earth's magnetic field and electrostatic forces. The 6 by 9 by 7 foot high, doubly screened cage kindly put at our disposal by the Department of Research and Engineering of the Gates Rubber Company of Denver was designed to provide about 60 to 70 per cent (by actual measurement) attenuation of the earth's magnetic field at its center, along with virtually complete attenuation of electrostatic forces. The electromagnetic field attenuation measurements, made at a frequency of 27.025 megacycles, showed a very high attenuation (to about 0.3 decibels) with the transmitter in the cage (and with only a single screen door in use, as in our experiment) and the receiver sixty-five feet from it on the outside, and vice versa, and virtually complete attenuation for remote transmitters.

Ted produced images both inside the cage, holding the camera himself, and through the single screen door of the cage, with me holding and triggering the camera on the outside, a couple of feet away from Ted and some inches away from the screen door, Mr. James A. Hurry, Chief Physicist of the Research and Engineering Department of the Gates Rubber Company, holding the gismo. (Camera and film for validating shots were provided by Mr. Hurry.) An image obtained in this way, outside the cage, similar to several shot inside, is shown in fig. 127. The target, provided by Mr. Hurry, was a picture of isochromatic stress lines, which Ted saw, when it was turned the way it is shown in fig. 128, as "eyes looking at a line of people."

The other test situation which provided probably an equal or greater degree of attenuation of the earth's magnetic field, as indicated by the more or less completely random fluctuations of a compass at the point where Ted was stationed, was in the Whole Body Radiation Counting Chamber of the Colorado State Public Health Department, Denver (fig. 129). The purpose for which Ted was tested in this chamber, however, was not primarily in connection with magnetic fields but to determine if any increase in normally present amounts of radioactivity could be detected in Ted's presumptively paranormal camera activity. A sensitive crystal pickup inside this 7 by 7 by 7 foot chamber, whose 5-inch steel walls are lined with $\frac{1}{8}$-inch lead, is designed to detect just about any X-ray, gamma or high range beta radiation around.

Ted got a total of nine paranormal shots out of twenty-eight tries during three successive twenty-minute counting periods while stationed within eighteen inches (the normal testing distance) of the crystal pickup. In the third period he got four definite images and two blackies out of twelve tries. I was with Ted in the chamber, both of us in monkey suits. There was no increase in radiation over a control twenty-minute period.[11]

11 The pictures Ted got during the testing period inside the chamber are interest-

THRU Single Screen

J.A.HURRY Feb 22, 1966

Jim Dean 2-22-66

(Fig. 127)

As for the possibility that X-rays may in some way have been involved in Ted's thoughtographic phenomena, the negative results of the whole-body radiation test supported the results of tests conducted along other lines. On several earlier occasions Ted was successful in getting definite images on film with different strengths and thicknesses of lead-impregnated glass, of the type

---

ing from the standpoint of the peculiar type of correspondence to the target chosen. The target chosen by Mr. Albert J. Hazle, Radiological Health Specialist, after Ted and I were inside the chamber, was the drawing of the Colorado Public Service Nuclear Reactor Plant shown in fig. 130. When Mr. Hazle chose this he remarked to Mr. Wesley Anderson, his associate, that it was too bad he couldn't find a nuclear power plant with a reactor dome. Almost immediately, and before the fact that the target had been picked was announced over the intercom, Ted started shaking his head, as if puzzled. "Are you guys doin' something with a parts catalogue?" he yelled over the intercom. He then proceeded to get a series of images similar to the one shown in fig. 131, which he later also got outside the chamber with both Mr. Hazle and Mr. Anderson holding and triggering the camera. It is apparently the dome of a nuclear reactor plant, similar to the one shown in fig. 132, that Mr. Hazle found in the "1965-66 International Buyer's Guide and Reference Data Issue" of the magazine *Nucleonics* lying on his desk, which could correctly be described as a "parts catalogue."

(Fig. 128)

(Fig. 129)

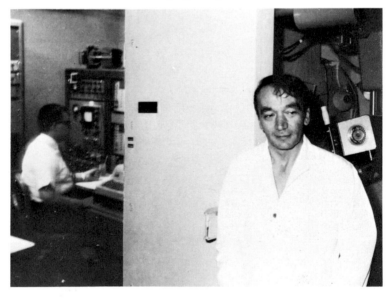

THE PUBLIC SERVICE COMPANY OF COLORADO
HTGR NUCLEAR POWER STATION

(Fig. 130)

(Fig. 131)

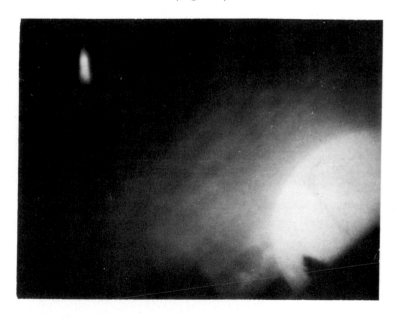

used in radiology laboratories to attenuate X-rays, between him and the camera at the time of shooting. In one informal session Ted got several shots while I held two ¼-inch slabs of this glass, each of more than sufficient strength to shield out the amount of X-ray ordinarily maximally used in lead-lined hospital radiology rooms, between his head and the camera, which he was holding in his lap. One shot, taken on the occasion when Ted got his other Hilton Hotel picture, among others, is shown in fig. 133. (On the graduated strip shown in fig. 134, the lightest portion was produced by five times the intensity of X-ray normally used to photograph the bones of the hand and wrist.) On another occasion, shooting through the ¼-inch lead-impregnated glass window of a radiology laboratory equivalent in shielding power to twice the ⅛-inch lead lining the walls of the room, with me holding the camera on the outside on the other side of the window, and with an extra slab of this glass placed over the window for good measure, Ted got (on color film) a weak but definite version of the picture shown in fig. 135. (Ted was hot at this point, but we had run out of film.) On a third occasion, inside another radiology laboratory lined with ¼-inch lead, Ted got three different types of images through a window made up of several panes of glass of equivalent shielding power. One of these images (fig. 136) shows what appears to be the corner and cornice of a building obscured by what may be reflections in the glass. I was on the outside holding a model 100 Polaroid camera up to the glass. Ted held his gismo up to the glass from the inside, and I shot at his signal, using a flash. Control shots showed nothing remotely like this image.

4

It may be thought that these tests with Ted, in addition to tests which the conditions of several experiments described earlier may incidentally have provided, might (subject of course to the limitations of data that have not been repeatedly verified) pretty well dispose of physical hypotheses based upon radiation within just about the entire nonvisible portion of the electromagnetic spectrum, from long radio waves to short gamma rays. (Infrared, or heat radiation rays, as well as ultraviolet rays, were probably covered by Ted's several times shooting through partitions and

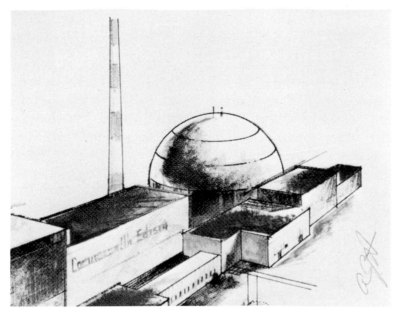

(Fig. 132)

(Fig. 133)

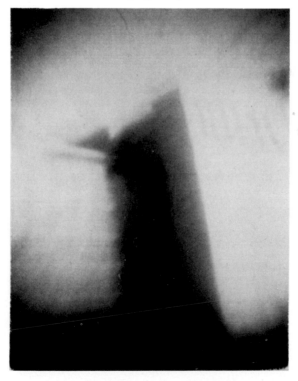

(Fig. 134)

(Fig. 135)

closed shutters and camera, if not through the total of ½-inch lead glass which was used on occasion. Ted, incidentally, produced two perfect whities out of eight tries on the only occasion a roll of Polaroid Land 413 infrared film was used in our tests. I might state here, incidentally, that ordinary photographic light-meters placed between Ted and the camera showed no response during shooting.) Unfortunately, however, our troubles on this score are far from over. I shall now have to introduce the reader to a set of rules of inference—or better, of noninference—that apply peculiarly in the Alice-through-the-looking-glass world that research in psi phenomena provides. These modifications of the rules of inference that ordinarily suffice in scientific experiments may now leave the reader a bit puzzled as to how much of the electromagnetic spectrum we actually have eliminated. Let us start by taking a closer look at the tests conducted through the lead-impregnated glass and, after attempting to weigh one or two considerations not touched upon in our initial report of the data, see what inferences are then left to us.

First, let us try to deal with a question no doubt already present

(Fig. 136)

in the minds of some alert readers. How can we be sure that Ted did not affect or imprint the film *before* he stepped into the lead-lined rooms or, in the more informal session, before the slabs of lead glass were placed between him and the camera? If it is supposed, by way of answer, that had this occurred there surely would have been signs of a double exposure on the print, let me assure the reader that it is not so simple as one might imagine to get definite signs of a double exposure under these circumstances. Reflections in the glass, highlights, and so forth tend to plague our control efforts. But even granting that some difference between a singly and doubly exposed film should normally be demonstrable under the circumstances in which the tests were done, we are confronted by a more fundamentally disturbing consideration.

Just when we think we have squarely in our sights an important aspect of the Sorcerer, or whoever or whatever is responsible for what is going on, we suddenly discover that we have no idea of where the Sorcerer's Apprentice is or what *he* is up to. I am referring to a perfectly conceivable motivational complex (if you will) in some stratum of Ted's unconscious (ditto) that we can never either quite pin down or eliminate as a hypothethical factor in all our doings. Let us suppose that Ted, all unknowingly, did imprint the film before stepping into the 'tank,' as we came to refer to the lead-lined radiology laboratories we used in our experiments. But let us further suppose that in another stratum of Ted's unconscious the Sorcerer's Apprentice has at the same time decided to so affect the film emulsion that no further molecular action can take place on it between the initial imprint and the developing process, which would normally occur immediately after the shutter of the camera, pointing at Ted through the lead-glass window after he has entered the tank, has been triggered. Have we the means of conclusively establishing that what we have hypothetically cooked up could not have taken place? Unfortunately not. Here we are up against one of the aspects of a fundamental indeterminacy which, by virtue of the range of possibilities involved in the very type of psi hypotheses we are testing, we cannot seem to get beyond. If we grant the possibility of Ted's being able to affect the molecular structure of the emulsion in one way—when various configurations result from his mental effort—how can we be sure that, for whatever reason (motive is here again irrelevant, just as it is in the case of conscious fraud), he is not in some way affecting this molecular substrate so that no further change can occur on it? To say that this would be very hard to do chemically is to forget that, by hypothesis, we are dealing not with a straight-line run-of-the-mill chemist but with one who has at his command all the tricks and powers of Merlin, Prospero, or even, for aught we are yet in a position to say definitely to the contrary, the Creator? The problem is: just how do you contrive a container for the universal solvent?

Now I am going to put the reader on the spot and ask him to try to arrive at a decision in terms of the following data. In order to narrow down the range of inferences that I felt could legitimately be made in the situation, I arranged to have film sent me in a 1/16-inch lead-lined container from Berkeley, California, twelve hundred and fifty miles away. I requested that it be ascertained that the batch of film purchased for this test had, to the best of anyone's knowledge, been on the shelves of the place where it was bought in Berkeley at least one month prior to the earliest date we began this series of experiments, so that we would have to assume that any paranormal inprint on any of this film (by Ted, anyway) would have had to be made prior to this time, either on the shelves of some shop or warehouse in Berkeley or as it was passing over or near Denver in a shipment to Berkeley by plane or train from the east. The plan was to open the lead-lined container in order to load a camera with a roll of film from it only after Ted had been safely installed in the tank, and then to ask Ted to shoot for a target preferably chosen after he was inside. If Ted were to get results within what might be adjudged a positive range under these conditions, the following alternatives would then be left us: either Ted imprinted the film 'precognitively' before the entire series of experiments along these lines had been formally decided upon, or similarly in respect to the target (I do not feel it warranted to enter at this time into the ins and outs of methodological problems in 'precognition' research itself) while the film was twelve hundred and fifty miles away—*or* the lead-impregnated glass was no bar to whatever went on during the process of 'thoughtographic' imprinting. (Strictly, this statement would of course hold up only to the equivalent of the shielding powers of the 1/16-inch lead container the film was shipped in.)

This is the narrowest channel into which we can corral the data in terms of which we can make reliable inferences; and to my mind there is no procedure which will enable us to decide firmly between these alternatives. We are faced thus with a kind of indeterminacy in certain respects not unlike that established in the principle which asserts that it is impossible precisely to determine at the same time the position *and* velocity of an elementary particle.

Now as to the actual outcome of this fine-print codicil to our tests. On six occasions when the tests were run under the more stringent conditions, four of these with other observers in attendance and three with observers sealed inside the tank with Ted, Ted failed to get anything through the glass that could definitely be stated to be a paranormal result. On four of these occasions it was established that he was hot and cooking in terms of images and blackies shot inside with independent observers holding and triggering the cameras, but even on these occasions all Ted got through the windows were blackies which, perfect as they may have been (and unreproduceable on control shots), left much to be desired as far as providing the foundation for inference we should have liked. (All observers pretty much agreed that only definite images would have been wholly satisfactory.)

Where, then, does this leave us? The reader may imagine that he can, in a pinch, always fall back upon the data provided by the tests in the Whole Body Radiation Counting Chamber as far as radiation in the X-ray band of the spectrum goes. He may reason that, whatever difficulties may arise over the interpretation of the lead-glass data, the results of the direct measurement of radiation were clearly and unambiguously negative.

Poor reader! I regret that it will now be necessary for me to undermine his confidence in just what he can infer from the tests in the Whole Body Radiation Counting Chamber, well executed as I believe they were. We are, as it turns out, subject in that situation to the same indeterminacy limitations which faced us in the lead-glass experiments, with a slightly different but no less troublesome twist. (However, I should like to advise the reader with no particular stomach for this sort of thing that he may safely skip to the end of this chapter.)

Between the radiation-sensitive crystal pickup in the counting chamber and the oscilloscope on the console outside, lie several multiplier and analyzer tubes any one of which may somehow be affected by the very sort of power we are testing. But how? Is not

Ted securely sealed inside the steel- and lead-lined chamber? He is indeed, and this is a very comforting bit of knowledge—so long as we are confident that the only assumptions worth entertaining in the situation are that Ted is the *only* agent behind everything that is going on, from start to finish, and that what he is doing can be subsumed under the heading of a single process. Unfortunately, there are other assumptions that must be entertained because of the very nature of the phenomena being investigated, and regardless of the degree of implausibility we may wish to assign them we can never quite eliminate them as logical possibilities.

The first counterassumption we must entertain is that whatever 'occult' powers Ted has may also be possessed by others, by the experimenters and observers, perhaps, and that these may exercise these latent powers in unobstrusive ways, possibly in the very act of measurement. Can we be certain that the observers are not exercising such hypothesized latent powers to inhibit or cancel out the effects on the 'action indicators' of whatever Ted is doing? Motive here again is utterly irrelevant. If we entertain the possibility that the observers may harbor their own Sorcerer's Apprentices, then all we can say is that Sorcerer's Apprentices will be Sorcerer's Apprentices—capricious, unpredictable, mischievous just for the hell of it, perhaps—and that we might as well give up trying to outguess them.

The second counterassumption we may as well consider (again it must be emphasized that one can't go into this kind of research halfway; if you are in at all, you are in up to your neck) is that Ted may be affecting the film by one process, let us say by something in the beta or gamma range of radiation, but using something else—God knows what, but something—to jam the electron beams in the analyzer tubes on the outside of the chamber and so scramble the data which emerge that no evidence of beta or gamma radiation is forthcoming. If it is objected that it is unlikely that the Sorcerer's Apprentice can get through the steel- and lead-lined chamber to carry out his mischievous canceling effect, we must of course immediately refer back to the fact that our raw indicator readings have revealed nothing that need be stopped by such a barrier in the first place. We find, in fact, that we are in a hall of mirrors, and that no matter how many monitors, each one of which may again involve an action indicator of some sort, we assign to the job of getting information about what is doing at any

given step of the way between Ted and the final record, the possibility of getting a 'false' positive or a 'false' negative—in fact of
getting really mixed up in trying to differentiate the one from the
other—cannot be eliminated. Our only hope of distinguishing the
'real' from the possibly false effect, it turns out, lies (subject of
course to the 'time-of-action' limitation discussed above) in the
crossing of a barrier of some sort, as Ted may well have done in
the case of the Faraday cage and the lead-glass tests. But by very
virtue of the fact that this is possible, the possibility cannot be
entirely eliminated of his having done something like this in the
radiation-counting chamber test to obscure some radiative effect
taking place inside.

An interesting and instructive example of what may have been
a 'false positive' in a test where the 'action indicator' was the
behavior of a pointer was provided by the results of a test
Ted claims he was given by a physicist some time before our work
began. I cannot vouch for the authenticity of any part of this story,
but no matter—it will illustrate as well as anything the important
principle involved. According to Ted, a Chicago physicist once
asked to see a demonstration of Ted's phenomena. No pictures
were produced, but apparently enough occurred to prompt the
physicist to activate a pointer-reading type radiation counter
somewhere in the vicinity of Ted's head or body. On the first pass,
according to the story, the pointer swung wildly up to its maximum reading in one range. The physicist, much taken aback,
gave Ted a suspicious look and warned him that he'd get sick if
he kept on "swallowing that stuff" (meaning, presumably, some
radioactive material). On the second and subsequent readings the
pointer settled down and the initial wild swing was never repeated.
When Ted assured the physicist that he had not ingested any
radioactive material (which, in any case, would have had to be
rapidly eliminated in order not to register on the second and
subsequent readings), the physicist, when pressed for an explanation, concluded that they had just witnessed a sudden and most
improbable burst of intense cosmic radiation at precisely the
moment the first reading was taken.

As I say, this story must be taken purely anecdotally. My inquiries to the physicist concerned produced a curt reply (some
weeks later) which indicated that the matter did not warrant
pushing further. The sole and entire content of the reply was,

"There was a misunderstanding about one reading. I found nothing on the detector about him." Let us suppose for the sake of illustration, however, that the details of the "misunderstanding" were as Ted gave them. In that case, what may we infer (neglecting for the moment the 'cosmic ray' explanation allegedly given by the physicist himself)? That there was possibly a sudden burst of some kind of high-energy radiation from Ted? Or that Ted (let us say) had in some equally improbable and unusual other manner affected the mechanism of the radiation counter, right up to the pointer itself? We simply do not know, and have no way of finding out.

In the case of the Whole Body Radiation Counter Test, thus, we are unable to rule out the possibility of a 'false' negative result. In the case of the physicist's application of the radiation counter to Ted, we are unable to rule out the possibility of a 'false' positive result. I put the term false in quotes precisely because, it would seem, we are totally unable to assign exact meanings to 'true' and 'false' in contexts such as those described. We are, in effect, faced with something very much like the famous logical dilemma of the traveler who is told by a Cretan he meets, "All Cretans are liars." The traveler can make no inference from this statement that is not plainly negated by a contradiction inherent in the very fact of the statement's being made by a person who is a member of the class of liars the statement is about.

There is, I believe, a practical approach that might for certain purposes be adopted in the face of this problem, even if there appears to be no definite logical way out of the dilemma it imposes. We shall come to this presently. Here I shall have to return for a moment to a distinction that was made a little while ago between the type of inference allowable to us from the crossing of a barrier of some sort, as in the case of the Faraday cage and the positive lead-glass experiments, and the affecting of an action indicator of some kind, as in the Whole Body Radiation Counting Chamber experiment. It was indicated that only in the former case, the crossing of a barrier, could we make a definite inference (subject, again, to the time-of-action restriction that was mentioned) as to the type of occurrence that had or had not taken place. Here, however, we are clearly limited in terms of the type of result: in the case of a positive result, we can say the barrier was crossed (and that, when the barrier is a shield with specific capacities to attenuate radiation within known limits of the spectrum, certain types of radiation were thereby virtually ruled out). In the negative case, however, we obviously cannot attribute the result to the effect of the barrier when we have no means of determining for certain that the test body—in our instances, Ted—was actively cooking. Here we may seek refuge in a statistical approach and come to some position based upon what we judge to be the probabilities of the situation. If we do a suitably randomized series of tests for 'hotness' we hope that some sort of an answer will be properly forthcoming. But it is just here, in dealing with the negative instance in psi research, that we may be faced with data of such contradictory import that generally acceptable rules for making a decision about what we should believe to have taken place may not be found. Let me show how this may be.

A series of experiments was undertaken in which perforated print-sized rectangles of twenty-eight-gauge lead (about 1/64-inch thick) were placed in the camera between the lens and the film, immediately in front of the film. The results were as follows. On one occasion a rectangular area about 1 by 2 inches was cut out of the lead shield. Out of sixteen trials, six whities (fig. 137) or partial whities eventuated, showing that Ted was at least 'beaming.' On another occasion, transverse slits were cut out of the lead. The results were not too different (fig. 138). On these occasions Ted was told at the outset what was being attempted; merely the form of the cutouts was kept from him, but this he of course inferred when the first clear whities showed through. On a third occasion I departed from my otherwise strictly adhered to policy of not trying deliberately to hoodwink Ted in situations of this sort (I assumed that unconsciously Ted could be aware of everything and that any deliberate deception on my part might confuse and irritate him) and used a lead shield with only a minute pinhole in the center. Out of sixteen tries about a half-dozen showed a pinhole-size speck of white on otherwise black prints, and the others were totally black. On all three occasions the randomization of shots taken with the lead-shielded cameras with those done with nonshielded cameras was sufficient to indicate that the results could not be attributed solely to chance (which would more or less take care of one witness's half-serious suggestion that on the last series perhaps all Ted was getting, except for the few on which the pinhole showed, were blackies, an idea that might pose

(Fig. 137)

(Fig. 138)

a neat avant garde 'black on black' epistemological riddle).

Here we are confronted with negative results which cannot be waived on the usual grounds that only positive results are meaningful in situations of this sort. Somewhere in the neighborhood of perhaps twenty to thirty presumptive 'beamings' (out of forty tries) with no signs of crossing the barrier placed in front of the film cannot so easily be considered as not necessarily significant. But significant of what? Let us, to advance the argument, imagine that our tests had been extended indefinitely, and that every time we tried to get past a barrier of twenty-eight-gauge lead placed in this position in a perfectly randomized series, the results were negative. Had we only these data to go on, might we not be tempted to consider the case closed? But we have the fact that a lead-glass shield of something on the order of thirty times (by density) the attenuating power for X-ray, arranged to be in a position which should have provided at least the same relative degree of effectiveness to practically all nonvisible radiation in the short-wave range, failed to act as a barrier to whatever was going on between Ted (let us presume) and the film emulsion. (We are, for argument's sake, neglecting the qualifying possibilities discussed earlier which, in any case, could have also been operative to give positive results in the present tests, which clearly was not the case.) What are we to do with two sets of contradictory data which apparently cannot be reconciled? (Let us recall that Ted similarly was stopped, as far as images went, by a thin layer of masking tape while he had no difficulty in getting through hands and other opacities in front of the lens.)

Obviously, the reader may reason, we must here be dealing with the fine black hand of our Sorcerer's Apprentice again; and if this troublemaker is going to insist on being so stubborn as to stick indefinitely to the same answer (for our procedure asked a question), so much the worse for him. We can arbitrarily rule him out of existence as a purely psychological figment of some kind and accept only the *really*, the *genuinely* positive data of the lead-glass tests. Alas for this ploy, not everyone is going to be satisfied with it, and if those readers who insist on adopting it will step to one side of the room, they may find that those readers who are not satisfied with it have decided to adopt a somewhat different ploy, that of arbitrarily ruling out of the game of judging and decision making, if not out of existence, those readers who *are* satisfied with it. And I must confess that the whole thing does, to my mind, begin to assume a faint but disturbing resemblance in certain features to the famous trial of the Knave of Hearts (to come back to Alice and the strange world both she and we are in) where it was precisely the fact that the letter was *unsigned* that, to the King, pointed unequivocally to the Knave of Hearts as the culprit because, it was argued, if the Knave *had* written such an incriminating document he obviously wouldn't have been fool enough to put his signature to it.

In attempting to fathom the 'true' information content of data like these, thus, are we thrust back upon the kind of double-reverse divination practiced by poker and ticktacktoe players— 'If he thinks I'm going to do this he'll do that, but if he thinks I'm thinking this . . .', and so forth? This would be most unfortunate, since the unconscious (our Sorcerer's Apprentice) of any decent psychic worth the designation could outplay any games-theorist indefinitely because only *it* would have the up-to-the-minute information which must remain forever just beyond the grasp of the data-interpreting opposition.

If, then, we are to take these different kinds of considerations seriously—and how should we not?—we must continue to remain somewhat uncertain as to the status of various radiation hypotheses, since even in the case of the Faraday-cage experiment, we neglected to use the film brought in a shielded container from afar to obviate the possibility of imprinting having occurred before Ted stepped into the cage. And even though this lack can in principle be corrected, we are at best then left, as we would be in the case of the lead-glass tank experiments if Ted were to succeed in getting through, with the choice of two alternative hypotheses, that of a successful passing of the barrier *or* that of the imprinting at a great distance of an image corresponding in a way to a target that had not been chosen until after Ted had been sealed in the tank—a feat which can be matched by a great deal of 'precognitive' psi data I shall not go into here but which must, I am afraid, be entertained as hypothetically possible.[12]

---

[12] However, Faraday-cage experiments done by Russian investigators on other types of psi phenomena appear not to be subject to the type of uncertainty involved here. The late L. L. Vasiliev, Professor of Physiology at the State University of Leningrad, described experiments in his recent book *Experiments in Mental Suggestion* in which the method used for testing telepathically transmitted information was the induction of hypnosis and the waking from hypnotic sleep of subjects in 1 to 3 millimeter iron- and lead-screened chambers produced by the nonverbal (*i.e.,*

Now as to what we can make of all these data as far as various radiation hypotheses go. As I have indicated, I do not believe it possible, in this no-holds-barred-all-bets-off kind of situation, logically to outwit or outflank a hypothetical Sorcerer's Apprentice giving 'false' information; but it may be worthwhile outsitting it. After a while, with no way of really distinguishing between true and false, consistency may win the day, like the suitor with only character and persistence to outbalance his otherwise only modest attainments. It may be that we shall have to carry on our tests and measurements indefinitely, and to note carefully, for what they are worth, the statements of as many Cretans as we may meet up with, in the hope that in the long run our data will show enough of a tendency to point in certain directions to warrant a higher degree of confidence in the plausibility of one hypothesis over another. But even so, we should never lose sight of the fact that the problem of measurement is unavoidably complicated by indeterminate influences on the parts of agents and measurers alike, and that if we do get trends which seem to stick, all we can say with certainty is that a bunch of ordinarily individualistic Sorcerer's Apprentices have, for reasons which we may never succeed in comprehending, decided to agree to allow just that to happen. But should this occur we would, of course, by this very token have left the domain of parapsychological events and be verging upon ordinary physical law. In any case, however, if we are going to play the game at all, we can do little else but follow the lead of

---

mental) suggestion of an agent outside the chamber and sometimes himself screened by metal. This method of inducing hypnosis was first extensively investigated by French workers in the 1880's over distances up to a quarter of a mile and has since been studied at greater distances by others (including me). In the experiments described by Vasiliev, in which the subjects were placed in Faraday cages allegedly capable of shielding out all but the "very improbable" kilometer-long waves or the very short ones beyond the soft X-rays, the means of testing for the onset and termination of hypnotic sleep was to instruct the subjects to compress a pneumatic bulb at regular several-second intervals while awake. This activity, recorded on a moving drum, ceased when the subject fell asleep and resumed when the subject woke up again. Summarizing the results of a series of experiments (including the long-distance experiments mentioned in Chapter X, in which a modification of the pneumatic-balloon method was used to start and stop the transmission in Sevastopol of radio waves which were picked up by a receiver in the Leningrad Laboratory of Brain Research and automatically recorded on a moving drum), Vasiliev wrote: "Contrary to all expectation screening by metal did not cause any even faintly perceptible weakening of telepathic transmission. Even under conditions of double screening mental suggestion continued to act with the same degree of effectiveness as without screening."

the philosophically resigned crap player who said, "The game may be rigged, but it's the only game in town."

5

Poor us! We started our investigation of radiation hypotheses with high hope only to find at the end that we are in the peculiar position of the husband in Molnar's celebrated play who will never know (as the audience never does) whether or not his wife was really onto the fact that the dashing guardsman she kept her secret tryst with was actually only her husband in disguise.

At this point, however, is it not time finally to ask just how much of Ted's phenomena any conceivable radiation hypothesis can fundamentally account for? Can we explain, in terms of any type of straight-line radiation, just how it is that Ted always manages to affect only one print-sized film rectangle at a time, and nothing from the adjoining film or (except rarely) the rest of the roll? Let us for the moment imagine that entities that are kin both to the particles now dealt with by physics and the viruses now being explored by biophysics—infinitely subtle 'viricles,' let us say—will some day be found to play a role in a kind of field peculiar to certain types of events now subsumed under psi phenomena that only some as yet undreamed-of offshoot of information theory will be able to explicate.[13] (With my rudimentary knowledge of these disciplines—somewhat more minuscule, I should judge, than the average educated layman's—it costs me nothing to write these blank checks.) The essential issue is how far we can go with such a field toward explaining not just the phenomenon of physicochemical changes in the film emulsion— this is no worse than the problem of the psychologists and the neurophysiologists in trying to account for sensation and consciousness in terms of the raw physics of vibrations—but the all-important fact of the *organization* of these changes into *meaningful* patterns of light and shade and line and mass. It would be like

[13] The Russians, as might be expected, have not completely abandoned the question of the energetic nature of psi phenomena as a futile problem. Vasiliev, noting the rapidly mushrooming discoveries of nuclear physics, is loathe to rule out the possibility that "sooner or later a new macro-field will be discovered which will go beyond the boundaries of atoms and engulf surrounding space." He lays great store in the future development of information theory, which may render obsolete some of the earlier energetic conceptions.

trying to account for Michelangelo's Medici pieces in terms solely of the chemical composition of the marble, or for Mozart's music in terms of the chromatic scale.

The fact is that physicists and biologists have also for some time been bumping into themselves around corners and are now beginning to suspect that they too are running low on purely physical-type hypotheses to account for what goes on in their interpenetrating realms. They may not go so far as the physicist Jordan who, in the work referred to earlier in which he denied for all time physics' capability of explaining psi phenomena in terms of radiations, has envisaged the day when physics might properly be viewed as a branch of psychology; but most of them are a long way from the crude, atomic billiard-ball materialism of Democritus and Rutherford. To Sir James Jeans, the more he contemplated the infinitesimally small world of the atom and the unimaginably extended yet somehow bound together cosmos of the great whirling bodies, the universe began to look more like a great thought than like a great machine. "Mind no longer appears like an accidental intruder into the realm of matter," he wrote. "We are beginning to suspect that we ought rather to hail it as the creator and governor of the realm of matter—not of course our individual minds, but the mind in which the atoms out of which our individual minds have grown exist as thoughts." Eddington was convinced that "the world-stuff behind our pointer readings is of nature continuous with the mind." Margenau was led to impute what almost amounts to a mind in miniature to the electron, and Schroedinger, who has been almost obsessionally preoccupied with the paradox of how mind came to leave itself out in elaborating its picture of the universe when it is all the while so obviously an integral part of everything, has come to feel that the motions of the atoms cannot be understood apart from what we understand as mind.

Thus, whatever the fundamental process, and however it may ultimately be integrated with process hypotheses we now term physical, the motions of the molecules that must go into the formation of Ted's film images can still be described more easily, if necessarily loosely, in terms of a thought-directed paint brush than of a computer-guided ray gun; and we might as well, lacking further data on the physical side for the present, turn back to this aspect of things for a few more looks at the problems involved.

CHAPTER XII

Back to Mind

THE way Ted's images appear to be built up on the film, quite apart from all the other 'mental' aspects of the whole business, closely resembles what glimpses we get (and they are, alas, only glimpses) of the formation of images in consciousness from data variously supplied. Closest of all, perhaps, is the resemblance to what has been described as the manner in which other psychics, who get their knowledge in visual terms, build up their 'impressions' piece by piece until the whole seems to spring to life from a number of at first separate parts. One psychic described by Tenhaeff illustrated this by making drawings of the separate elements of which his picture of what was inside a sealed envelope was formed. Another, in trying to convey how his impressions were built up, stated, "First you would for instance see two legs and then a tail and thus, gradually, the whole figure, a cow for instance, was formed." Unfortunately we have not yet been successful in getting Ted's image formation *in statu nascendi* on movie film, or under developing solution on print paper in the subdued filtered light of a photographic darkroom, although a beginning has been made in the latter. We have, thus, had to rely for our knowledge of the organizing and synthesizing processes at work on what can be pieced together from serial versions of images as they come up on the prints themselves.

There have been numerous instances when Ted's images seemed to have died a-borning, or rather to have been early-term miscarriages, in that often what appeared clearly to be parts of as yet unidentifiable structures never went on to coalesce with other elements into any recognizable final shape before the kaleidoscopic process moved on to other configurations or faded out entirely. In this passing show, images would float by like strange creatures of the deep, illuminated for a brief moment in the beam of a bathysphere, only to pass on and never be seen again. But on one occasion one such embryonic form was rescued from eternal oblivion by what appeared to be pure gambler's luck—the turn of a card, so to speak. On this evening Ted had gone through almost a dozen rolls of film without getting one clear image; in fact, more normals (of his face) had shown up than in any other session for many months, more, it seemed, than the cumulative total of such shots during this period. It began to look as if Ted's long, unbroken streak of productive sessions had finally come to an end. The witnesses present at my house on this occasion—Professor J. Allen Hynek of Northwestern University's Department of Astronomy, an ophthalmologist who prefers to remain anonymous, and Dr. Frey, who acted as notetaker in the debacle—were tantalized by a few *formes frustes* of what appeared to be two themes, but since these could not be definitely claimed as potential structures, let alone specifically identified, they were not counted as positive even though nothing like them could be duplicated on control shots.[1] Finally Ted, miffed, mystified, and near collapse (about seven quarts of beer had gone down the hatch during the session and, as I found out later, he had been drinking around the clock for several days), admitted he was licked. A few minutes later Professor Hynek, his camera packed and his coat on, was about to follow the ophthalmologist out when he paused, literally on the

[1] The ophthalmologist produced one perfect blackie on a control shot, unique among hundreds carried out over numerous sessions. Ted was standing alongside the doctor on this attempt, and watching with an amused grin. How to interpret this remains moot, because of the obvious methodological bind which attends all experiments of this sort. It is to be expected that sooner or later someone will come up with the Statue of Liberty or some such on a control shot and this, unfortunately, will almost automatically, although wrongly of course, be interpreted by some as inescapable proof of fraud.

threshold, and asked if Ted would consent to try one more roll. By the time Ted had got around to agreeing—he merely shrugged by way of indicating that he didn't have much hope but would go to bat again anyway (if he could have another drink)—the ophthalmologist had left; but Professor Hynek and Dr. Frey came back and settled down for another few shots. The film brought by Dr. Hynek had been all used up, but I loaded his camera, a model 800 and easily differentiable from mine, with one of my rolls. Almost immediately, as if grateful for this reprieve from a kind of banishment, Ted came up with the automobile image in fig. 139, which almost certainly would have remained in everlasting limbo had it not been for Professor Hynek's inspired last-minute gamble. (It should be noted that even though my film had been used for this, it was counted as a strictly controlled hit because of its obvious correspondence to some of the embryonic theme forms, one of which is shown in fig. 140, which had earlier come in on Professor Hynek's camera loaded with his own film.) A few shots

(Fig. 139)

Nov. 14   J. A. Hynek   1965

and no more than two or three minutes later, a second image, more or less the same, came in on another camera.

On other occasions successive shots have dredged up parts of images that were capable of being put together into a more or less complete pattern but which failed to unite before 'the process' shifted to some other theme. Fig. 141, for example, which appears to be a copy of a religious painting with a saint as the central figure, is a composite made by me of two shots, neither of which constituted a whole image. These shots occurred during the session in which Dr. Wormington suggested the Olmec target theme, to which they appear to bear no relationship. The fragments were ushered in by Ted saying, quite abruptly and emphatically, just before the appearance of the first one on shot number 4 (the 'helmet,' fig. 62, didn't appear until shot number 7 and the stelae, fig. 64, until number 8), "I see hands—hands are coming through." Here, unlike times when he seemed to have some control over what would come through, and other times

(Fig. 140)

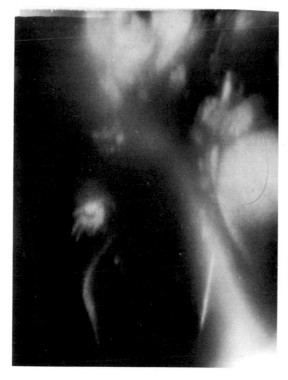

(Fig. 141)

when he would not only have no control but also no intimation in conscious imagery of what would show up, Ted appeared to act like a passive observer of unidentified floating objects for which his mind was merely a reflecting screen.

This brings us back for a moment to the curious point which I alluded to in a previous chapter, Ted's poor ability as a visualizer. This is the more strange in view not just of the clarity and correctness of essential detail of which he is capable in his film images, but of the fact that he sometimes does see his images more or less hallucinatorily before or as he gets them on film, as in the example just given. As I have already indicated, the kind of 'visualization' which goes into his film images is so different from what he is normally capable of as to lead one to wonder if two different processes, or processes on two different cognitive levels, are not involved. On most occasions what Ted gets on film appears to be as independent of what he is able to visualize consciously as dream images would be (which of course also points up how little we know of dream imagery). One might compare, for example, his Westminster Abbey film image (fig. 10) which, after all, is Westminster Abbey to the last and least detail, with his rather poor visualization of it in his drawing (fig. 7). Equally baffling, however, is the fact that on occasion his film imagery has appeared to conform to his rather poor conscious recall of an image rather than to the image itself. (We may remember the occasion when the film image Ted got, fig. 72, was a cross between his only-fair impression of the target chosen by Dr. Starrett and the target itself.) One is led to wonder if, in some way, conscious sensory experience inhibits or otherwise interferes with the kind of cognition that takes place on the levels from which Ted's film images ordinarily proceed. On the whole, Ted seems so far to have done at least as well getting correspondences to targets that have been completely hidden from him as with targets he has seen; and on one occasion when half the target was exposed (fig. 142, upper half [2]) and the other half covered with cardboard, one of the recurrent themes he got (fig. 143) offered a better correspondence to certain details in the lower, hidden half (fig. 144—unfortunately the stones in the wall in the lower half of the target are not too susceptible to enlargement for comparative purposes) than to anything in the exposed portion. (Dr. Carl Zimet provided the camera, film, and target choice for this experiment.) On other occasions when this experiment was tried, Ted was successful in condensing correspondences to both the exposed and hidden portions of the target, as if it didn't particularly matter which way it came to him.

In addition to the questions raised by the foregoing, the factors enabling Ted on some occasions to exercise some degree of conscious control over what he gets on film remain still as obscure as when our work began. Nor do we get any clues from studying the work of the thoughtographers of the past. The sensitives Fukurai worked with seemed to be able to exercise this control but most 'spirit photographers' never knew what, if anything, would show up on their plates. Attempts "to produce definite conscious thought-pictures, with the cooperation of a photographic medium," wrote an official of the Society for the Study of Super-

---

2 Courtesy of British Travel Association.

(Fig. 142)

(Fig. 143)

(Fig. 144)

normal Pictures in Conan Doyle's *The Case for Spirit Photography,* "have almost always proved abortive in our experiments in this country. Some of the continental members of the SSSP, however, have concentrated on this line of research and have succeeded in obtaining thoughtographs which, more or less, resemble the object on which the thoughts of the subject have been intensely concentrated."

Sometimes Ted doesn't know exactly the image that will materialize from his conscious effort to call something up from the vasty deep but, like all creative artists, he seems to have perfect faith that some unconscious sifting, selecting, and organizing process will take over and provide just the right configuration. On one occasion, when he had been shooting through the lead glass in a lead-lined room of one radiology laboratory, we kept getting a baffling series of striations (fig. 145) always more or less in the same place on the prints. When these were finally identified as a reflected artifact, Ted was exasperated. He stepped out of the tank and demanded a camera. "I'll show you I can get them lines away from the window," he muttered as he triggered a shot off the cuff and handed the camera back to me. The image he got (fig. 146) was not of the lines we had been getting but was never-

(Fig. 145)

(Fig. 146)

theless composed chiefly of striations, as if in an attempt to justify or legitimize the artifactual version. Ted had nothing particular in mind when he snapped.

When a battle ensues between images he might be consciously aiming for and images that crash the field despite his strongest efforts to keep them out, Ted sometimes acts like a slightly exasperated referee in a boxing match between two youngsters who can't quite keep to the rules. Something like this took place during one of the sessions preceding Mariner IV's arrival in the vicinity of Mars, when Ted announced that he was ready for another try at photographing the planet. Drs. Frey, Lehrburger, Merrill, and Wadsworth showed up for the big shoot, Drs. Lehrburger and Merrill with their own cameras and film. Ted wanted to get nothing less this time than the Martian landscape with signs saying "this way to the canals," but when informed that the closest shots Mariner would get (in case he wanted confirmation of his images) would show only segments of the Martian globe, he agreed to settle for something like this. His first clear shots then indeed began to show what appeared to be segments of a sphere. But then, despite anything Ted could do, something like a town in the distance started to come in on the sphere (fig. 147); and that was it, with minor variations (and switches to another theme that was rather like Ted's version of the canals—without sign), for the rest of the evening. Ted was bitterly disappointed. (Most of the more than forty pictures of this and other structures that came in this evening, incidentally, did so with Ted in no contact with the camera. Each of the witnesses took turns at holding and triggering.)

Of special interest are instances when the structures imaged appear to be almost plastically building up before one's eyes. Fig. 148, for instance (witnessed by Drs. Palleske and Bradley, besides myself and several others), shows a snub-nosed version of an unidentified structure—it is not the Washington Monument (or if it is, it is a distorted version of it)—whose perfect prismatic form came to full realization only five shots later (fig. 149). It was almost as if it were being molded out of clay. Such a building-up is a counterpart of the progressive dissolution of the features of Ted's face that not infrequently occurs before outside images take

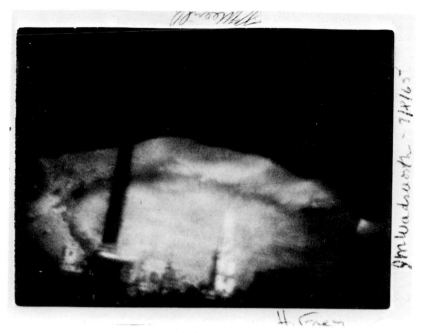

(Fig. 147)

(Fig. 148)

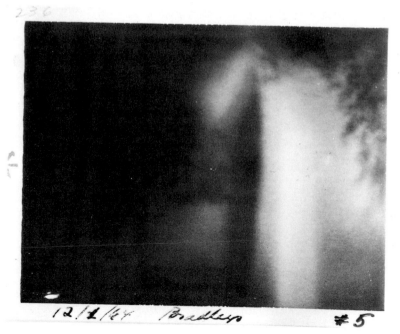

(Fig. 149)

over. (His face sometimes begins to run like a wax figure under heat.)

What takes place here bears a certain resemblance (although not of course in the truly genetic sense) to the building up of more or less complete forms from numerous varieties of partial and incomplete embryonic forms reported (and sometimes photographed) by observers of alleged materializations produced by certain types of mediums in trance. These forms too are described as often never progressing beyond their initial in-between stages before they recede and disappear, and forms closely resembling well-known embryological monsters (with fragments of skin, bits of hair, teeth, glandular tissue, all jumbled together) have been described.[3] This is, however, such a bitterly controversial and malodorous chapter in the history of psychical research—para-

[3] Hair-curling reports and reviews of these investigations, some of which date back to the mid-nineteenth century and which I warn the reader not to consult before he has seen everything, read everything, and rid his mind of all cant, may be found in Geley, Richet, and Schrenck-Notzing.

psychologists seem to vie with nonparapsychologists in discrediting the data and the principals involved, even those of the latter most eminent in their own scientific fields (physics, physiology, medicine)—that I hesitate even to bring it up. However, not only plain fairness but also scientific circumspection forces me to do so.[4]

The problem remains, however, of how Ted's effects on photographic film are accomplished. What other evidence, besides the highly controversial data just mentioned, do we have of what is commonly referred to as the effect of mind on matter? And *can* we account for this effect?

I will not undertake here a review of what I think is an impressive amount of positive evidence on the occurrence of what are referred to as physical psi phenomena, as it is too easy for the naturally skeptical reader to dismiss such second-hand accounts as in some way biased and spurious, whereas he will be far less able to escape the impact of firsthand reports which give the conditions under which the observations were made in specific detail. I shall therefore refer the interested reader to several excellent sources, among which will be found reports by physicists and biologists, among others, on the normally unexplainable movement of objects under test conditions in the presence of mediums, as well as under a variety of other circumstances.[5] Although in all

---

[4] One difficulty seems to be that, in the midst of suspicions and charges of the most unsavory kind, only two or at most three hypotheses are considered—fraud, non-fraud, or a simple combination of the two—whereas there may be almost as many conceivable alternatives applicable to the highly complex data involved as the number of disputed embryonic forms allegedly being observed. An interesting and highly informative, if somewhat rabidly partisan, record of this controversy may be found in Dr. Hans Gerloff's *The Crisis in Parapsychology*.

It is almost certain that we will never get anywhere in the field of psychical research with conventional hypotheses, and it may even be that our ideas have not been far out or crazy *enough*. After all, Ted's phenomena are themselves incredible at first encounter. These data, hardly more so from certain points of view, at least suggest a bridge between the kind of organizing processes observed in the formation of Ted's 'thoughtographic' images and certain still largely enigmatic aspects of cellular biology. I deeply feel that what is needed here is a group of earnest and courageous investigators each of whom will, like Ulysses, lash himself to the mast of true scientific impartiality and, with his eyes and ears open to the sirens of public opinion and his own deeply rooted prejudices, reopen this largely discredited area of research—provided, that is, that subjects for study can be found. I am inclined to believe, from personal communications that I am far from willing to discredit because they lack gilt-edged authentication, that this is possible, and I hope that this may turn out to be one offshoot of the presentation of these data on Ted.

[5] See Barrett, Crawford, Crookes, Feilding, Grad, Lodge, Owen, L. E. Rhine (1963),

but one of these reports (Grad) the level on which the observations were made was macroscopic, in contrast to the ostensibly molecular level on which Ted's phenomena occur, the problems involved are very much the same.[6] Here, as I think may also be said in the case of the data supplied by Ted, the question of chief relevance is not whether one finds the reports 'believable' in the common psychological sense but only whether, as Ducasse stated in his 1951 review of the evidence supplied by the physicist Crookes, "any person that owns allegiance to the recognized criteria of dependable evidence has any rational right *not* to believe" such reports. "If, as is indeed the case," Professor Ducasse continued, "I still find psychological difficulty in believing that the [phenomena] reported occurred, then there is for me only to confess that my psychological reluctance to follow where the evidence leads means that I am not as rational as I should be."[7]

The trouble is, as far as our inability to deal with uncommon

---

and Richet. For an able critical review of laboratory experiments on psychokinesis (PK) see Girden (whose Scotch verdict of "not proven," however, to my mind merely points up the futility of ever trying to catch up with the ever-receding horizon with a purely statistical approach).

[6] Crookes, a physicist, attempted to measure 'psychic force' exerted on an apparatus attached directly to a spring balance, which registered tracings on a moving drum, and Crawford, an engineer, found that during levitation of objects their weight appeared to be added to that of the medium. However, we encounter here a problem similar to those met with elsewhere in the field of experimental parapsychology and perhaps exemplified by Ted's differential response to lead plate and lead-impregnated glass: one can't tell whether or not, or to what degree, a subject is merely dishing up data to order, by way of unconsciously conforming to biases of his own or of the investigators; nor can one, when pointer readings happen to be involved, determine, again *ex hypothesi*, what the pointer readings involved mean— changes in the underlying quantity the reading is supposed to vary *with* or changes directly in the position of the pointer itself.

[7] Richet, a Nobel prizewinner in physiology and medicine, wrote of Crookes' reports, "These experiments made by a renowned experimentalist are so striking and so exact that it is amazing that they should not have been universally accepted. But I will make my confession: until I had seen Eusapia [Palladino] at Milan I was absolutely sure that Crookes must have fallen into some terrible error. And so was Ochorowicz; but he repented and said, as I do, smiting my breast, *'Pater peccavi.'*" (*Thirty Years of Psychical Research*).

One method of dealing with unpalatable data is, of course, to attempt to discredit the source. An effort has recently been made to incriminate Crookes as an outright fraud, and as the lover of one of the lady mediums he worked with. It seems that 'exposure' of one sort or another has invariably been the fate of investigators who have attempted to crack the barrier of scientific resistance where physical psi phenomena are concerned (Schrenck-Notzing, *op. cit.*). (Needless to say, I shall be unpleasantly affected but hardly surprised by such consequences in the present case.)

but verifiable data of this sort goes, that modern science, and each of us individually, has grown up in an ironbound dualistic tradition which had its first formal statement in Plato, was taken up and developed by the medieval schoolmen, largely because it fitted in well with prevailing religious doctrine, and came to fullest expression in the school of Descartes, whose adherents ground out volumes and volumes of sophistical argument attempting to show how matter, conceived of as a sort of irreducible x-axis of events, could interact with mind, an equally irreducible y-axis. The confusion that resulted laid the basis for all later philosophy, and attempts to resolve the matter-mind, or body-mind, dichotomy have, consequently, been its central preoccupation ever since. There has been no major philosopher who has not had a whack at it.

I won't go into the various devices and contortions utilized by philosophers in an attempt to resolve or outflank this problem. These have been ably reviewed in standard compendia on such matters.[8] Besides, as I have indicated, the subject has been treated by practically every professional philosopher from Descartes on.[9] The trend today is away from dualist, or interactionist, positions, and certainly from uncompromising idealist or materialist positions, and toward one or another version of what is termed neutral monism, according to which matter and mind are not two fundamentally different modes of being, and certainly not two different substances, but merely different ways of stating propositions about events which cannot be adequately described except in terms of both—two types of logically complementary abstractions, if you will, or two types of organization or coding of a single underlying informational process.[10]

[8] Chappell; Flew; Hook.

[9] See Beloff, Broad, Dewey, Ducasse (1951), Hawkins and Russell for a few representative modern approaches.

[10] This, however, does not sit too well with many neurophysiologists who have taken up the question. Sherrington, who conceives of mind as outside the measurable matter-energy system of physical events, inclines toward a dualist position, while Eccles, who also defends a dualist position, has gone so far in his *The Neurophysiological Basis of Mind* as to invoke psi phenomena as an 'explanation' of how the nonphysical mind affects the brain. He postulates that the mind modifies the spatiotemporal activity of the neuronal networks of the brain by exerting "fields of influence" which can be detected only by a special property of the cerebral

Nevertheless, one can hardly avoid the impression, when glancing through current literature on the problem, that the sophisticated logical and linguistic conventions that have been adopted amount to little more than a marriage of convenience, an uneasy truce between two main philosophical schools which still have little use for each other and each of which deep down feels that the two types of organization it is currently fashionable to speak of are *really* two types of organization of what is basically (whisper behind the hand, knowing wink) m-a-t-t-e-r or, as the case may be, m-i-n-d. It appears to be too difficult to unlearn a dualism that, though apparently not native, somehow gets into us with our mother's milk, or shortly thereafter. Nor do I think that matters are helped very much by contriving an updated kind of atomism whereby we no longer deal with matter and mind in the large but with curious individual half-material, half-mental hybrid entities which (notwithstanding my earlier 'viricle' fantasy) leave us with precisely the same problems in the small.[11] For those unconsoled by philosophical abstractions, the problem remains of how mind moves one simple little molecule. Explain that, and the rest is easy.

So we arrive at the peculiar state of affairs in which philosophers and scientists, in trying to get that one molecule to move, are desperately trying to find a way back to a universe that the primitive (and the child, according to the detailed studies of Piaget) has never left. The fact is that all theories, whether interactionist or monist, are helpful only by way of explaining and justifying what to a primitive is not a construct, a clever linguistic rapprochement, but a way of life. The primitive feels the relationship of his thoughts to the outer world to be pretty much of a piece with his relationship to his own body. He takes it for granted that his thoughts can do things. He would find no need for a special theory to account for the physically uncaused movement of objects in the presence of mediums. His medicine men and shamans do these things all the time—but only for serious ritual purposes, like

---

cortex that has a "sensitivity of a different kind and order from that of any physical instrument." Eccles, apparently, would find the problem of how Ted's mind affects photographic film little different in principle from how it affects his brain. Both would be accomplished by "fields of influence" too subtle to be detected by ordinary instruments. The gain is questionable.

11 Whately Carington, *Matter, Mind and Meaning.*

re-establishing a mutually beneficial harmony between the tribe and nature. Poltergeists? Every tribe has them; they are obviously the thoughts and feelings of disgruntled individuals who go on a tear in this way but succeed only in being a bit of a nuisance and ultimately bores since no one is seriously frightened by these puerile tricks. A primitive Galileo or Einstein, as a matter of fact, would probably ask entirely different questions from the ones we do. Squatting on his heels and thoughtfully pulling on the stick in his nose, he might, if confronted with a late Western visitor who gave a faithful account of how things are in the civilized world, wonder how it is that a large segment of the globe has elaborated theories that are so patently false, theories of something inside a person called a 'mind' that is supposed to be like an invisible container for his thoughts and feelings and which can affect his face and limbs directly but not things outside himself, like sticks and stones and the thoughts and desires of others. Taking the sometime direct connection of his will with the outer world to be as indubitable as his own self, he might ask how it is that everybody doesn't feel this way. But if he were especially brilliant, and could rise for a moment above his own culturally conditioned beliefs and ways of viewing things in a lived context, he might ask the sixty-four goat or pig (or wife) question: How is it that mountains, which everyone knows that faith can move, stay mostly in the same place; and how come, when it is obvious that everybody *can* do simple things like move objects by simply willing them to move, and be in two places at once, and so forth, that most people prefer (if we may put it this way) not to, just as most people in the world that his visitor described to him prefer not to steal and murder and cross red traffic lights, although they obviously could if they wanted to? Is there, he might finally ask himself, anything special about the people who make ostentatious use of the powers which everybody latently has?

CHAPTER XIII

The Importance of Being Serios

UNFORTUNATELY, if there is something special about people like Ted who break the rules in such uncommon ways, we are very far from being able to determine specifically what it is or to produce it on order. When it comes to major physical psychics, and not just the general run of people who may have (as we have reason to believe most do) telepathic experiences of one sort or another, we may find out a few things about *why* they may need to conduct their mind-matter transactions in such outrageous disregard of long solidifying and now practically built-in tribal custom; but when we try to find out *what* it is that enables them to do openly what theoretical considerations (which we shall have to put off for later discussion) lead us to suppose everyone has the power latently to do, we are apt to go around in circles, again like the psychologists when they confront the unbridgeable chasm between sense data and sensation, and the physicists when they wonder what it is that produces order out of chaos among the atoms. Even if there is nothing categorically and qualitatively different about the big-time physical psychics—something in their genes, for instance (and genetic studies of Ted, incidentally, have revealed nothing out of the ordinary, as have also hormonal studies)—that enables them to do openly and ostentatiously what others only fantasy and dream of doing; even if there is only something in the peculiar *organization* of their minds and personalities, and possibly something in the dialectic relationship between these people and their societies, we still are unable at present to define and isolate any crucially determinative factor in this organization or relationship which would enable us to separate with any great degree of success the haves from the have-nots in this regard.

Besides, there appears to be—superficially at least—rather a diversity of types among highly gifted psychics. Compare Ted, for example, with a somewhat pathetic and forlorn member of a circle of psychic photographers studied by the Society for the Study of Supernormal Pictures whom Conan Doyle describes as "a little, elderly charwoman, a humble white mouse of a person, with her sad face, her frayed gloves and her little handbag which excites the worst suspicions in the minds of her critics." [1]

At any rate, Ted happens to share with many people who have to create a world of their own, particularly artists and writers, the psychology of the abandoned child, the child who has lost all hope of being loved and cherished within a secure environment. He envisages the world as a bleak, hostile place where no basis for trust is to be found, where men have to be got along with somehow and where women, who are by nature unfaithful, are to be feared, placated, tricked into giving, seduced into loving, and never allowed to get the upper hand. According to his Rorschach and other psychological-test responses, his world, and what uncertain human relationships it provides, is deteriorating, decaying, crumbling, and falling apart.

But this is a fork in the road to which great numbers of people come soon after their infancy, to the signpost which points to art, to science, to religion, to an endless and futile war against society

[1] The originator of the Baker Street Irregulars became interested in this Mrs. Deane when, with true Holmesian thoroughness, he happened to examine under a magnifying glass one of her pictures and found (my dear Watson) "a small but correct representation of the Assyrian fish-God, Dagon, wearing the peculiar hat with which that deity is always associated." With "this freakish result . . . so removed from the normal powers of a charwoman," Doyle began an examination of Mrs. Deane's claims which ultimately led to a positive judgment— a position from which I have never been compelled to budge."

along criminal paths, or to the conformity of quiet desperation and the any number of ways in which the body takes up the burden and cries itself sick. There are a bewildering number of paths, from this fork on, with no guiding signs at all; and we have no way of predicting which one a person will take or, until he is well on his way, how far along it he will go. He may, having suffered in one way or another what is experienced as a loss of important figures in his life in infancy or childhood—and this need not be by such a major event as death—attempt to capture and cling to the eternal and the invariant in mathematics or religion, or to people his world with creatures of his imagination which he can manipulate, control, and dispose of as he sees fit; or he may, like Casanova, who wrote movingly about being deserted by his mother at an early age ("In this way did my [mother] get rid of me"), spend a lifetime recapturing her and proving over and over again that her loss was really nothing, that she could be replaced by hundreds of others. But who can say what makes an abandoned child into a Leonardo (who did all his recapturing and controlling on paper and canvas) and not just a hack dauber and inconsequential hobbyist; or even how it was that Casanova, when he became a melancholy old man to whom only the pen remained, and who had to write from morning to night to stave off the terrible depression which he had spent a lifetime trying to stay clear of, gave us one of the most fascinating and brilliant accounts we have of the manners and morals of his time, and not just drivel? Similarly, we cannot say what makes a Ted a Ted, what endows him with the highly unusual ability to capture and control a fugitive world by simply willing it to appear on film.

Take another strand in the looming of Ted's personality that, in hindsight, may be supposed to have somehow woven itself into his peculiar way of conjuring up his 'visions' out of darkness. In addition to his 'abandoned child' complex, Ted gives every evidence of the strong role played in his life by what is known in psychoanalytic parlance as the *primal scene*. He slept in the parental bedroom until the age of eight, when he ceded his place to twins, brother and sister, who were born at that time. He remembers frequently waking up with a feeling of terror because the house seemed to be shaking and, he feared, about to fall down. Only much later did the older boys in the neighborhood tell him what this was all about. He also suffered recurrent nightmares of earth-quakes, and of struggle with and sometimes pursuit by powerful male figures, one of whom he remembers having turned on and bludgeoned to death before he awoke screaming with terror. These kept up until he began his 'thoughtography,' when they were replaced by equally terrible nightmares, which he has to this day, of being pursued by a camera, shaking as if in anger, its malevolent eye glaring at him from a fully extended bellows. According to psychoanalysis, Ted's lifelong insomnia, which started in early childhood, and his need to turn night into day may very likely also be related to the special trauma of being privy to what went on in the parental bedroom, as may indeed, in a displacement of a guilty and ambivalent attitude toward 'looking,' have been his difficulties in taking in and absorbing what went on in school. (This latter might be seen as confluent with whatever difficulty during the nursing period, or whatever accident of weaning or early real or fantasied separation from his mother, might have con-tributed toward Ted's 'orally deprived' characteristics.)

But here again we come to the crossroads. A dominance of primal-scene material—and this even in frequent conjunction with early oral deprivation or separation from security figures—may be seen in many persons who take a variety of routes in development, some productive and consistent with advancement and apprecia-tion in our society, some leading only to illness and failure. Somer-set Maugham, who like Casanova had to write to avoid black despair, filled his stories and plays with perfidious women and with men whose fate it was to be agonized witnesses to their infidelities. A famous movie director, whose obvious and ac-knowledged 'orality' is part of his trademark, shows very much the same tendencies in his work. Why did these too not drop out of school at an early age, or become notorious Casanovas in the flesh? And would they have been able to do what Ted does had an accident of fortune opened the possibility up to them? It is doubt-ful.

We are thus, in trying to feel our way into what it is about Ted that is so special, left to make what shift we can with a kind of after-the-fact mythologizing, a crude 'bumps on the personality' approach that may leave us far short of ideal understanding; it may nevertheless reveal to a reader here or there (or allow such at

least to think so) glimpses of a kind of truth he might not otherwise come by and which is, taken all in all, at any rate at present,
uncodifiable.

Ted was born in Kansas City, Missouri, the first child of Esther
MacNeil and August Serios, a Greek café owner and cook who
gave up professional wrestling when the then-on-the-rise great Jim
Londos tossed him out of the ring with one of his later famous
airplane spins and broke several of his bones. (This was in the
great days of wrestling, says Ted proudly, when guys were thrown
out of the ring for real.)

Although Ted never had a chance to see his father in action,
some of his earliest memories are of listening to his father's old-
time cronies, some of whom are still around and still at it, telling
fabulous tales of Gus Serios' prowess—of the time he pinned Frank
Gotch with a hammerlock and toehold, or of the time he won two
out of three falls from World's Champion George Haken-
schmitchs, the Russian Lion. Ted, who likes to give imitations of
his father throwing hundred-pound sacks of potatoes like so many
feather pillows, claims his father was the strongest man he ever
knew—and the gentlest. Even when Ted started to truant at an
early age—he never got beyond the fifth grade, from which he was
finally let out at sixteen ("I was a whiz at school," Ted says, "but
I never went much.")—his father never lit into him when he
would search him out and discover him up to some mischief in a
lot or alley in the neighborhood, but would lead him quietly
home, gently admonishing him about the unwisdom and im-
propriety of staying out of school. At this time, the depression
having begun, there was little work to be had, and Serios *père*
was home tending house most of the time. Ted's mother was out
from morning to night earning depressed wages as a seamstress.

All his trouble, Ted says, started after his father's sudden death,
when he was twenty. Up to this time, after giving up on school,
he had done a certain amount of innocent bumming around or
had worked fitfully, usually with his lifelong buddy, Matt (who at
this stage was the terror of Chicago's North Side with a left hook
that could lift a piano mover), as a car wash or car shagger in
garages. The worst that ever happened before his father died,
according to Ted, was that he and Matt would occasionally take
off with one of the garage cars and sometimes neglect to return it.

This once or twice earned them spells in custody. (What made the cops maddest, Ted insists, was their sometimes leaving a car parked across the street from a police station and then phoning in to report it stolen.) Following his father's death, Ted left home for several hitches in the Merchant Marine, interspersed with stretches during which he remains, for the historian, as elusive as the Scarlet Pimpernel.

Exactly what went on during this period of several years is even less clear than during the more than usually murky other periods of Ted's uneven life, but he hints that there are several things in it that he would not care to have catch up with him. He admits to jumping ship several times, on impulse, and shacking up in some coastal town with a "broad" ("Dumb and dirty is the way I like 'em.") whose support of him—mainly beer and 'vittles'—he took as a matter of course, only to jump again when the need to take off came upon him and he would light out without so much as a broad-and-butter note. Somehow he wound up in the armed services, but this too didn't lead to glory for either him or the services, as his inability to stay put and fulfill any kind of routine or abide by any restrictions ("No goddamn sergeant was going to ride *me*.") again landed him in trouble. He left under some kind of cloud that he prefers not to talk about (but the army, he says, will never be awarded any posthumous Purple Heart by him either).

Following his discharge from the army, Ted's mother, in one of several attempts in later years to ease the struggle for existence for her wayward son (a struggle which Ted has never formally acknowledged), set him up as a cashier-manager, supposed also to double as water boy, in a small café in the little town of Harvard, sixty miles from Chicago. Ted soon found this peacetime situation also rather confining. One day he emptied the till, made the down payment on a cool-looking convertible, and took off for the open road. He insists that he had in mind transferring the assets of the café, which started to go downhill anyway when the patrons found themselves invited to get their own goddamn silverware and water, to a taxi company which he intended to start with a friend in the same town; but his story is somewhat unclear on this point. The sole rolling stock of the alleged corporation, at any rate, soon devolved back to the finance company, and Ted found himself, only a few weeks after the opening of the Little Chicago Cafe, again, in the parlance of actors and executives, at liberty. This status was soon altered when it was discovered that a lady whose premises Ted happened to have been sharing for a few months—a divorced war bride from Germany—was providing food and sundry articles useful to them and others from various stores without bothering to check at the cashier on the way out.

Aside from his erratic hitches in the Merchant Marine, and his stint at the Chicago Hilton (he is not sure whether he considers this the high or the low point of his career), Ted has never done anything that might be considered ordinary work. He agrees with Matt, whose boyhood aura of strength, toughness and invincibility has curiously never been marred by the reality of the something less than impressive figure he cuts today, and who is still, peculiarly enough, the philosophic spokesman of the pair, that if you have to work and stay poor, as most people do, you might as well not work and be good and poor. But Matt, whose situation is somewhat different, has occasionally had to take part-time work (the part of the time, shrugs Ted, when he is sober) as a janitor or handy man, which Ted would never stoop to. Feeling keenly his renegade position in the game of one-upmanship that continually goes on between him and Ted, however, Matt insists on referring to his status not as part-time worker but as "partially retired." Ted prefers to think of himself as totally retired.

Curiously enough, even today, after a life as sadly wanting in those worldly and otherworldly merits that generally pass for virtue, and despite the Church having (because of a matter that Ted prefers to say little about) washed up with him some years ago, Ted still considers himself a devout, if not in the usual sense 'good,' Catholic, and feels that he still stands a fair chance of winding up in heaven. His relationship with God, which has always sustained him in the rough spots, is both intensely intimate and rather original. "God," he says, "understands me; he knows I'm human." Atheism is absolutely incomprehensible to him. "What do them guys do when they're in a tight spot," he asks, "like when the cops are layin' for them?" He calls upon the Lord frequently, holds Him in reverent awe, but never falters in his belief that He is much more flexible in outlook than is generally considered to be the case. God is not only merciful and forgiving, but also capable of the most personal kind of identification in certain situations. For instance, broads. Ted, never one for staying put, used on occasion to slip out of his bed and ward during his stay in the tuberculosis sanitarium—in fact he would sometimes go AWOL for days at a time, his final discharge occurring on a more or less *ex post facto* basis—and go wandering around in the subterranean corridors between the different buildings, occasionally managing to keep a tryst and even make time in some dark alcove or storeroom he would commandeer for the purpose. (He didn't have to import girl friends, he claims, as many of the personnel, especially in the commissary department, were romantically inclined.) One day, in one of these basement corridors, he cornered and wooed a patient from the women's ward, a perfect doll, he recalls with a tinge of regret because of the way it turned out, but called a retreat when the fact that the place they found themselves in was the chapel suddenly impressed itself upon him. The lady seized the change of venue that followed as an excuse to cool off, or at least to say she had, and the affair was never consummated, as she was soon afterward discharged and Ted never did find out what her name was. He says of this fiasco, "Jesus will never forgive me," (for not going ahead, that is) "and I don't know whether I'll ever forgive Him." He feels very strongly that the misinterpretation, or at least misapplication, of the Pauline doctrine, that it is better to marry than to burn, is responsible for many of the ills in the world, and he is sure that Jesus would see things his way were he alive today. "When it comes down to that," says Ted forcefully, and with the solemnity of a bishop, "I beg to differ with the priests."

Despite his divergences in respect to this and one or two other fine points of moral theology, Ted's faith in and reliance on prayer, which is the rock on which all higher spiritual transactions rest, is absolute, and he never fails to include in his prayers other sinners like himself, heathens, who abound in his circle of acquaintances, and even, judging from various remarks he has let drop on occasion, animals, toward whom he experiences an almost mystic and apparently reciprocated feeling of kinship. Similarly his reverence for and faith in the comforting and therapeutic powers of even the material symbols of the Lord border on the absolute. Once he pressed upon me his rosary, which he is rarely without, after one particularly wearing session that ended about two-thirty in the morning (his peak hour) when I complained of being absolutely done in. He was deeply moved when I accepted it gratefully, and was later convinced that it was this and nothing else that had staved off imminent collapse on my part. The fact that a crucifix's aura of holiness could be questioned by others, as when the investigating committee of the District Branch of the American Psychiatric Association requested to appropriate his for a couple of days in order to look into the possibility of unsuspected *natural* emanations from it, was deeply shocking to him. "The sin is on their heads," he proclaimed, washing his hands of any responsibility for consequences very likely to ensue from such obvious sacrilege.

The degree of feeling and responsibility Ted shows for animals is largely a measure of his lack of basic trust in humans. He maintains a thriving flock of pigeons in a dovecot on premises he maintains (his official residence) in a small garret over a garage looking onto an alley a few doors down from his mother's nursing home, where he also maintains several cats and two dogs. (The psychoanalyst might link Ted's pigeon 'taming' with such ostensibly disparate tendencies as his propensity for letting his queen be taken in chess and his 'love 'em and leave 'em' behavior toward women and others as part of the 'abandoned child' complex.) He claims a proprietary interest, moveover, in cats, totaling an even dozen, farmed out to Matt (who looks out for the occupants of Ted's loft when he is away), to his mother, and to several ex-girl friends, and he refers to each one (the cats, that is) by name. Strays of every kind find sanctuary with him, even though they ultimately wind up with someone else taking care of them and footing the bills. "You don't know what happens to cats when them dogcatcher bastards get hold of them," he says gloomily.

But people who poison pigeons are the lowest in Ted's book. Not long ago he was sure that a neighbor up the alley had caught and poisoned several of his pigeons. Revenge was swift. He and Matt waited until the evildoer's car was parked for the night and then quickly and expeditiously slashed all its tires and smashed a few windows. The perfection of the speedy withdrawal that had been planned to follow was marred only by Matt's losing his glasses in the snow (one earpiece was gone to start with, and the bit of string he had in its place must have slipped off in the heat of the action) and in his haste, after time lost in futile searching, throwing the getaway car into reverse, causing it to lurch backward into a parked truck.

Ted's feeling for animals sometimes contrasts dramatically with an apparent lack of consideration for humans. One day, driving downtown, he spotted a dog running dangerously along the curb and looking hesitantly for a place to cross the busy thoroughfare. Ted groaned and remarked that it killed him every time he saw an animal in a similar plight, and insisted on stopping so that he could get out and pilot the dog to safety. Unappreciatively, the dog ran off before he could get to it. "The worst of it is that you can't teach them dumb mutts nothin'," he said as he got back into the car. No more than two minutes later, traffic seemed to slow down and bow outward ahead of us. When we came abreast of the origin of the bottleneck we saw that it was a legless man propelling himself along the street in a wheelchair. "What the hell," exploded Ted in irritation, "if this stupid bastard thinks he's in trouble now, wait . . . !"

The seeming callousness that Ted can sometimes exhibit in situations like this is not based on a primary lack of feeling but, if anything, the reverse, a too-strong identification leading to the evocation of painful feelings with which he cannot cope except by a crude or jocular remark, or a show of toughness that may seem out of place. Actually, his tendency toward empathy and identification in all sorts of human situations is quite remarkable and showed up clearly in his psychological tests. His empathically grounded perceptions of people, moreover, can be amazingly accurate. On one of his first days in Denver he noticed a woman walking around one of the hospital buildings with a vacant and unvarying schizophrenic smile. What was she always smiling about? Ted asked, puzzled; but before I had had a chance to frame an answer he launched into an off-the-cuff description of what he thought must be the emptiness, fearfulness, and confusion of the woman's inner world that could have done very well as a Rorschach report.

But Ted never allows his intuitive judgments to interfere with his everyday ratings of people. These depend almost exclusively on what he thinks people think of *him,* and consist of two main categories, bums and bastards, and regular guys. Cops and other people he thinks do not like or approve of him are automatically bums and bastards. People who he feels like him are regular guys, or great guys, without reference to any other criteria. (This system, simplicity itself, is of course widely in use in all walks of life.)

On the purely cognitive side, and when he is unencumbered by strong feelings of identification and by defenses against these feelings, Ted's remarkable capacity for empathy may reveal itself in a perceptiveness that appears to shade off imperceptibility into his ESP abilities, as at times when he seems to know things about people—not just their characters or superficially hidden feelings, which any highly intuitive person can pick up, but things like where they may just have been, the houses they live in, and so forth—that certainly he would have no ordinary normal way of knowing. At times, in fact, he seems not to be aware that a certain piece of knowledge should not by rights be his, and he will come out with statements or appraisals of people and situations as if they sprang from his own stock of memories and associations when every indication exists that this is not and could not have been so. Ehrenwald, a psychiatrist, has hypothesized that one of the roots of the confusion of thought shown by some psychotic individuals is their inability to separate the wheat of their own normally-come-by awarenesses from the chaff of all sorts of sometimes fear-provoking material that may inundate them telepathically from the outside. But Ted shows no trace of the psychotic in his makeup, a fact again clearly borne out by his psychological test results.

Ted's seeming capacity to transcend the usual barriers between the 'I' and the 'thou' and the 'I' and the 'it,' barriers which are not fixed in any biological sense but are largely the result of training and education within given cultural contexts, might appear to be related to whatever it is that enables him to 'know' the objects he gets on film with such extraordinary accuracy and intimacy. There is, however, no way of directly testing this hypothesis. In any case, the portion of Ted's being that has to do with his awareness of self as well as with his awareness of the outer world, appears to have a fluidity that does not characterize most people in highly developed Western cultures, whose individualities are as carefully guarded as their latchkeys and can ordinarily be abrogated only chemically, by engulfment in mobs or by special techniques of brainwashing. One sometimes gets the impression that Ted runs on a double track, with continuous awareness of self at the same time as there exists a continuous awareness of the outer world. He can talk on and on about himself but suddenly leap right out of this seemingly complete self-absorption to say, "Hey, looka that robin—ain't he quite the fellow, now?" or "That sonofabitchin' mutt is gonna get himself bumped off." If you ask where he sees this he may point in directions and to locales that would not ordinarily come into the sphere of one's interest and attention, to a bird standing (now that you look at it) as if it were about to make a speech to the unseen inhabitants of a shrubbery patch about fifty feet away, or to a dog trotting uncertainly in the street two or even three blocks up ahead. His mind, no matter what it seems to be engaged in on the surface, appears always to be scanning the outer world and taking in stimuli—people and what they are doing, signs, movements of traffic well out of the range of immediate significance—that would normally be shut out of the field of attention. Almost incredibly, this sometimes seems to obtain when he is drunk. Naturally this goes for broads, in any direction, at any distance, and at all times.

Ted's empathic propensities are also associated with a chronic tendency to play Walter Mitty roles. A trench coat is not just an ordinary garment for Ted but a badge in a fraternity of private eyes to which he fantasies people imagine him to belong when he wears one. When he can be induced to get on a horse he becomes a Western bad man or a marshal. Driving along in a cap he got specially to look like a woodsy sportsman, he will say, "I betcha everyone thinks I'm a hunter," taking it for granted that people who may happen to glance his way are thinking *something* about him. When he started using a violin case for smuggling his beer into the radiology departments of the hospitals we worked at, Ted was hung up between two competing roles. At one time he was a musician who was going to play for the patients, and he thought about reinforcing the illusion by carrying sheet music in his hand on his next visit; on another occasion his fantasied role changed to that of a mobster carrying a sawed-off shotgun. "I betcha they think, 'uh-uh, here come the boys, hit the deck, everyone.' " Once, after being picked up for being drunk and disorderly, he

registered in a suburban jail, where he was not already known, as
Dr. Jule Eisenbud, psychiatrist. The following day he contritely
handed me all the papers—the summons, the personal recogni-
zance, the receipt for articles taken from him (one wrist watch,
one dollar)—made out in my name. The private cell and (according to him) somewhat deferential treatment he received as a
psychiatrist were highly gratifying, and he had been happy to
repay these courtesies when he sobered up in the morning, he
confessed, by giving a few consultations on the family problems of
the prison personnel. But although this apparently started off in
a mood of expansive *noblesse oblige,* the real Ted soon came
through. "Them assholes," he said to me in reviewing his brief
career as a psychotherapist, "I really screwed them up—but good."

It should be remarked that Ted's profanity, which has never
displayed the originality or imaginativeness of which he is otherwise capable but is altogether habitual and stereotyped, has leveled
off considerably since the early days of our work together
(as has, incidentally, his drinking; he was bone-dry during two
of his successful later sessions). Nevertheless it is still episodi-
cally strongly in evidence. When drunk he makes heroic efforts
to curb the worst of it in the presence of women and children, but
his guard may drop embarrassingly at times. Mostly, when catch-
ing himself on the verge of a slip, he can accomplish an adroit
recovery and split-second alteration of course. "Where the fu——
fur heaven's sake where is that darn gismo?" he may exclaim,
grinning coyly at the 'in' bystanders. Nevertheless, watching him
trying to navigate in polite conversation can sometimes be as
harrowing as watching a drunk weaving perilously across a heavily
trafficked thoroughfare and again and again just missing catas-
trophe by a hair's breadth.

Despite the fact that most people in Ted's world fall in the
bums-and-bastards category, towards humanity as a whole he maintains a watchful solicitude, and he would like to be able to deploy
his particular talent somehow toward furthering the cause of
peace on earth and good will among men. His sometimes expansive vision of his role, however, never extends to the blasphemous.
He knows very well who is who on earth and in heaven, and he
exhibits, as far as psychiatric scrutiny goes, nothing of the narcissistic identification with God, so manifestly observable in certain

psychotics, and so often inferrable in the dark secret places of the neurotic mind, that can make life difficult for those whose only role is to be His creatures. Ted, in fact, is a favored target for people, usually women, who find states of such obvious moral decay as his almost irresistible and who never leave off scheming and angling for the honor of being the instrument of his salvation. But with these, he is sternly reproving; and though he has no notions of ever gaining the top ranks in the heavenly hierarchy, he still, as mentioned earlier, has a pretty firm sense of his basic moral worth. He wrote recently, in answer to a 'let me be your guide' letter from an evangelistically inclined lady of his acquaintance, "Yes im a Drunk, Drifter Bum Lo i.q. Steal but . . . . i say i do good Defend cats Dogs pigons Birds and small Kidds." He might have added that if there were much about him that was different, he would, in all probability, not be the priceless boon to science that quite a few people are now ready to agree that he is.

CHAPTER XIV

The Anatomy of Resistance

UNFORTUNATELY, not everyone feels that Ted and people like him
are worth scientific study. There are still many who not only continue to turn their backs on investigations of this sort but, whether
they are aware of it or not, will do everything in their power to
sabotage any such program.

As has already been indicated, this is nothing new in the history
of psychical research. In 1901, William James described his difficulty in getting his Harvard colleagues to sit in on a session or
two with one of the most remarkable mediums of the day, the
paranormality of whose trance 'knowings' he, as well as numerous
others who were to study her intensively over a period of twenty-
five years, felt was absolutely beyond question. "For instance," he
wrote, "I invite eight of my scientific colleagues severally to come
to my house at their own time, and sit with a medium for whom
the evidence already published in our *Proceedings* has been most
noteworthy. Although it means at worst the waste of the hour for
each, five of them decline the adventure. I then beg the 'Commis-
sion' connected with the chair of a certain learned psychologist in
a neighboring university to examine the same medium, whom Mr.

Hodgson and I offer at our own expense to send and leave with them. They also have to be excused from any such entanglement. I advise another psychological friend to look into this medium's case, but he replies that it is useless, for if he should get such results as I report, he would (being suggestible) simply believe himself hallucinated. When I propose as a remedy that he should remain in the background and take notes, whilst his wife has the sitting, he explains that he can never consent to his wife's presence at such performances. This friend of mine writes *ex cathedra* on the subject of psychical research declaring (I need hardly add) that there is nothing in it; . . . and one of the five colleagues who declined my invitation is widely quoted as an effective critic of our evidence. So runs the world away! I should not indulge in the personality and triviality of such anecdotes, were it not that they paint the temper of our time, a temper which . . . will certainly be impossible after this generation." [1]

I am sorry to have to report that several generations later the type of irrational behavior that James described, and the temper of the time which permits it, is far from impossible. True, I have been able to inveigle a few more of my colleagues into at least one 'seance' with Ted (and the commitment to an attestation which was part of our terms) than James was successful in doing in the case of his medium, Mrs. Piper; but this is very likely because I have sometimes resorted to tactics that the gentle James, who was a pragmatist only in theory, would never have stooped to. Even so, the list of holdouts among my colleagues would grace any Who's Who in Science. What is interesting, moreover, is not just the number of refusals I received but the manner in which these were tendered and the excuses offered. Several people, who could just as easily have picked up a phone to let me know how they felt— or better, if it came to that, have told me face to face—went through the formality, unusual in our time (except for 'Dear John' letters), of mailing me notes excusing themselves. Already 'distancing' had set in. One man, head of a department at the Medical School, wrote that he felt antipathetic to the whole thing because of the way in which our sessions were staged, particularly the part alcohol played in the proceedings. (This man of science, I strongly suspect, might have had less objection had Ted been ground up and introduced into a solution of alcohol in colloidal suspension.) The

---

[1] "Frederic Myers' Service to Psychology."

head of another department, who on one early occasion had had the opportunity only of seeing several whities produced, wrote, in begging off a personally tendered invitation to come and see the real thing when Ted was in one of his blazing streaks, "Frankly, I do not believe that I should be a party to those experiments. . . . It would be less than honest of me to pretend that I wish to participate again." A third friend and colleague at the Medical School, who on other occasions had found the telephone no bar to communication when face-to-face encounter happened not to be convenient, wrote that he had no need to see Ted work in person (*in vivo*, as biologists say) since he could get as much from slides of Ted's pictures, which he would be very happy to have me bring over some evening. It is difficult for me to believe that this same colleague would have preferred to look at picture postcards of Niagara Falls, had he been right there, instead of just looking out the window at the real thing.

In addition to these frank 'avoidance' reactions, or non-encounters, there were sometimes encounters on the uncomfortable or distinctly unpleasant side. One physical scientist, plainly disturbed by a picture he claimed to be flatly impossible (it seemed to bear a personal reference), went into a violent temper and almost succeeded in destroying the print before I managed to get it away from him. Two others, after signing statements alleging that they could not account for results witnessed under "excellent" conditions of "unrestricted observation," but who afterward came to the conclusion that trickery must nevertheless have been involved somewhere, were responsible for the rumor, which spread like the flu among interested persons at the Medical School and elsewhere, that Ted and I had finally been exposed, Ted as a fraud and I as at best his dull-witted dupe.

I could go on with many stories of colleagues who preferred not to get 'involved' with the kind of thing Ted and I were doing, some stating this in so many words, some merely failing to respond to my personally extended invitation, some tendering excuses that would be considered feeble by any cocktail-party hostess; and I could go on also with other stories of those who, after allowing themselves to get involved to the extent of sitting in on a session, behaved with questionable rationality or honesty. But my objective is not to produce a dreary catalogue of silly excuses and minor discourtesies, nor even to demonstrate how particular persons were led to act in a manner thoroughly out of keeping with every ideal of open-mindedness (to say nothing of courage, curiosity, and creativity) that they probably would espouse and live up to in other circumstances. My purpose is to inquire into what factors behind this obvious resistance to disturbing facts is peculiar to the type of data that psychical research deals with, as over against the type of initially anomalous data that every other discipline in the history of science has without exception run up against and, where the data have been verifiable, ultimately made one or another kind of adjustment to, sometimes at enormous cost to prevailing theories and methods of investigation.

The answers usually given—that the data of psychical research remain sequestered and ignored because they do not fit into any known causal nexus or the broader contexts of science, or because no truly repeatable experiment exists—are either incorrect, or true only in a limited sense (if the nature of causal explanation, for instance, is highly restricted) or, as I have already indicated, just as applicable to data which have been assimilated by other disciplines without permanently embarrassing their pretensions or their practitioners. What is unique about the data of psychical research is that only they suggest that man has in fact within him vast untapped powers that hitherto have been accorded him only in the magic world of the primitive, in the secret fantasies of childhood, and in fairy tales and legend. But herein lies a paradox. Other violently resisted revolutionary changes in man's scientific outlook—the heliocentric astronomical system, the theory of evolution, and psychoanalysis—have all progressively chipped away at man's narcissism as they forced him severely to modify his image of himself as either the favored child of creation or as one whose special mark of his kind, his reason, made him supreme. How is it that psychical research, which would seem to enhance and gratify man's narcissism by restoring to him powers hitherto reserved for supernatural beings, should be the most fiercely resisted of all?

The answer to this must be looked for in the study of how supernatural beings came into existence. Unfortunately there is no subject more cluttered with tendentious conjecture and no subject where, because of the vast spans of empty, unyielding time in which its beginnings are lost, the appalling poverty of fact is more likely to endure.

It has been widely assumed that early man, overwhelmed by anxieties and dread in the face of an awesome array of elemental forces which he could neither comprehend nor control, developed intellectually primitive notions to account for the seemingly independent 'wills' of things outside himself. Out of these archaic animistic ideas, it is maintained, evolved a belief in spiritual entities—ghosts, demons, gods—which he could propitiate and, through one means or another, manipulate to his advantage.

However, this picture, valid as it may be in certain respects, does not take into account the supposition of some students of prehistory that very early man probably experienced a primeval identification and oneness with nature, in all her moods and with all her rigors, that modern man cannot even faintly comprehend; and that by the time he and his group (with which, according to some, he probably also merged in a way impossible for us to understand) had become separate enough from nature to stand in awe and dread of it, something had already occurred to engender the sense of the supernatural.

Various data suggest that what occurred was the alienation of man from certain aspects of himself rather than from nature. What then appeared as a progressive separation from nature, with the elaboration of more and increasingly more definite interposing forces and agencies of one kind or another—spirits, demons, gods— was basically a manifestation, by displacement, of the widening schism in early man himself brought about by the repression and projection outward of *internal* forces with which he could not come to grips.

In 1912, Freud, in his remarkable study *Totem and Taboo,* gave an unsurpassably clear and compelling exposition of the possible nature of this schism. He began with the fear of the dead, whose ubiquity, universality and, so far as our meager data go, unexceeded ancientness is one of the few things that anthropologists are agreed upon. He showed that this may very well have represented the displacement and projection of hostile feelings, notably death wishes, which he likened to similar processes in neurotics, particularly in a class of sufferers known as compulsion (or obsessional) neurotics. The reason these wishes had to be transformed and displaced, according to Freud, was that in both the primitive mind and in compulsion neurotics the wish was in some way mistaken for the deed in reality, which the sense of guilt simply could not tolerate; and the reason why the wish was thus overvalued, he claimed, was because it was a remnant of the so-called omnipotence of thought which characterized the earliest stage of man's psychosexual development, the so-called narcissistic stage of infancy. At this stage the child is still almost wholly dependent on the mother, who is its whole horizon and major source of gratification, and does not properly distinguish between itself, the mother, and the external world.

From here on, in this study, Freud developed some of the most contrived theories he ever elaborated in order to account not just for the displacement of ambivalent attitudes toward the dead onto animals, which he felt was an important factor in the development of the peculiar beliefs and practices of primitives constituting the core of totemism, but for the persistence of such powerful trends for so many millennia—right up to the Eucharist (whose derivation from early totemic practices, he modestly and quite properly pointed out in a footnote, was not an original idea with him)—in the group, which reacted as if it possessed the psyche of an individual neurotic. But although Freud gave every evidence that he himself was only too well aware of the awkwardness of some of his constructions, he kept backing and filling in an effort to patch up their obvious defects in a way he would undoubtedly have spotted as a kind of blocking and denial had he seen comparable gyrations in one of the patients on his couch.

With this part of the study, which many anthropologists have used as a reason for condemning the whole of it, we are not concerned here. Its main part, dealing with the origins of the ambivalent attitudes toward the dead which have played such a large part in the development of religions, and with the derivation of magic and taboo, is a breath of cool, clean fresh air in the fetid backrooms of scholarship without insight. Moreover, the transformation of hostile wishes, felt unconsciously to be able to produce real effects, into fears from without—frequently, by displacement, into fear of things like animals and thunder and lightning, which are easily rationalized—can be demonstrated repeatedly in the consulting room of any psychiatrist. (If the 'natural dread' theories as to the origin of the fears of the thunder and lightning and animals that have assumed such central importance in the thinking of some ethnologists concerning the origins of religious awe needed a *coup de grâce,* such was certainly provided by the London Blitz and other war experiences. It was demonstrated that children who were removed from their mothers for safety's sake developed many more, and more terrifying, 'external' fears than those who remained with their mothers and were comparatively unaffected by the bombing.) Nevertheless, what remains still to be accounted for is not only what continued to occupy Freud, the persistence in mankind in general of some sort of guilt reaction from hundreds of thousands of years ago, not only the strength and pervasiveness in the mental lives of savages and neurotics— and in the unconscious of everyone—of what is held to be merely an infantile delusion (this did not bother Freud nor has it particularly bothered anyone else), but also the fact of the intensity and persistence of the efforts of every civilized agency and institution to discredit and stamp out this delusion—even to the extent, paradoxical as it may seem, of the elaboration of delusions even more fanciful and hardly less defensible than the one everyone is at such pains to deny. Taking a leaf from Freud's own observations on the presumptive strength of the inclinations which must be behind the necessity for such severe sanctions as taboos, might one not surmise that there would hardly have to be this concerted effort on everyone's part were there not, somewhere in the background, a lurking fear of a core of reality behind what is so forcefully denied? Does a mere delusion, a remnant of infantile error, require the big battalions to be routed out?

It happens that up to very recently there existed—and, as I have already indicated, there are apparently even today scattered remnants of this—a number of primitive peoples among whom very much more than just a core of reality was ascribed to the power of thought and among whom, as a matter of fact, the belief in this power is seen in connection with its most open and awful form— the death wish. According to Lucien Lévy-Bruhl, a French 'library' anthropologist who drew a composite picture of primitive mentality from the analysis of numerous data furnished by observers of widely varying competence—missionaries, field anthropologists, explorers, traders, and contemporary primitives themselves, in many of these people the idea of death apart from somebody's wish to have someone dead, which is simply and intuitively accepted as the most natural of all causes, is largely unknown. When anyone dies, his intimates are questioned. Who had something against the 'victim'? Who envied him, was jealous of him, hated him for any of the usual reasons? If a wife dies, the husband is the obvious suspect, and vice versa. (For this reason widows are not considered good marital risks in certain tribes.) If a child dies, it is not considered at all unlikely that he was the victim of the angry thoughts of one of the parents, usually the parent of the same sex. This type of causation is taken for granted even if the victim falls into the river and is done for by a crocodile, or meets death in combat. A literal translation of the term used to describe what happens here is that the victim was 'given over' to these events by somebody. The question is: Who *made* him fall into the river? Who *made* him relax his guard for a moment or slip on a stone so that a blow which might have been parried—a mere proximal cause— became the death blow? The same type of thinking is intuitively extended to what we term inanimate nature, a notion apparently foreign to these primitives' way of thinking since to them all things are animate in so far as they are susceptible to direct human influence and are, as such, instruments of human will. If a falling boulder kills someone, the same question is pertinent: Who hated the victim enough to cause the boulder to be dislodged at that moment? Similar thinking is applied to fire, plague, and flood. Beneficent events take place solely in the absence, temporary at best, of opposing malevolent forces that are basically human in origin. At bottom no pure extrahuman agencies of any kind— spiritistic or probabilistic—are recognized. Emotions and nature are one, and at the core of everything is the simple, primary, immediately experienceable volition. This is the nature of things; this is destiny.

Now we may certainly question the degree to which the composite picture drawn by Lévy-Bruhl represents a simple homogeneous analogue of any given stage in early man's development. It is not as if we are dealing with the fossilized remains of some extinct species. Malinowski, for instance, tells us that among the Trobriand Islanders the idea of illness and death being exclusively the result of the malign influences of others is not given much credence as an abstract theory—that only in the case of oneself and one's family (when the game is for real, that is) is this generally held; and among Rose's Australian aborigines, where thought is taken for granted as transcending the carefully laid out canons of time, space, and causality that modern man is familiar with, the death and illness of enemies apparently do not figure too high any longer in the catalogue of the things that magic is good for. Nevertheless we have it on good authority from modern field anthropologists that this sort of thing has by no means vanished, and it does not seem unreasonable to suppose that the farther back we go the more widespread would we find not only the belief in the efficaciousness of one's own and the other fellow's hostile wishes, but also a much higher tolerance of such a state of affairs without the need to repress and project the possibility effective wish for someone's death. It seems plausible to suppose, in fact, that there was a stage, sometime after man's emergence from his hominid ancestors, but before objects and beings invested with the aura of the supernatural became the executors of the 'bad' thoughts of the living, when it was not necessary for man to repress his hostile feelings at all, potent as these may have been held to be when unleashed. It may be that when very early man did let fly with a death wish, he really wanted it to work and couldn't have been more pleased, or less guilty, than when it appeared to.

It may strike the reader, however, that such a state of existence would be unsupportable and in its very nature unstable, demanding resolution or progression into something far less threatening. "If we then remember," writes Lévy-Bruhl in a section on what he calls "home-bred bewitchment," "that such states of mind and such feelings may be active in a person without his even knowing it, we at once see that family life affords this malign influence constant opportunities for exercise. Who can feel certain that no feeling of jealousy or irritation or ill-will has ever been aroused in him in regard to the person with whom one lives, even those whom he most fondly loves?"

The one suggestive link, as it happens, between the very distant past, when the first split in man's psyche must have occurred, and the present, when this alienation of man from himself and from nature continues to widen and derive its force from some hidden source, is the family and a side of the drama of family life that Freud, for whatever reason, paid scant attention to at the time he wrote *Totem and Taboo*. We are coming more and more today to see that the greatest reservoir of hidden aggression, as of all neurosis, in fact, is the very situation that many indications point to as the origin of the necessity for repression which may have occasioned the initial split in man's psyche in the distant past in the first place—the all-encompassing mother-child relationship. For I think it can be said that more data point in the direction of the first projection occurring in connection with the need to repress death wishes against all-powerful and autocratic mother figures who seem, according to penetrating studies of the myths which have come down to us from the mists of prehistory, to have been the first tribal rulers to emerge from the anarchy of a swamplike precultural existence, than in connection with the sexually pre-eminent father figure that Freud hypothesized as the victim of a primordial Ides of March murder plot and as the continuing target of man's aggression and guilt. (Freud himself admitted that the fact that the great maternal deities preceded the great paternal ones did not support his thesis.)

But whether the birth of the slightest separation between man's conscious and unconscious sides, however brought about, in itself entailed a necessarily ever widening rift or whether changed conditions of family life, with perhaps a prolongation of the period of dependency on maternal security figures, made it harder and harder for man to tolerate a consciously experienced ambivalence toward these figures and thus occasioned the split in the first place, the fact is that the schism is still widening. Moreover, man behaves still as if there were a core of effectiveness to his hostile wishes and is still absurdly touchy on the subject. For once the primordial split took place, the dominant note ever since has been the ongoing, progressive need of man—not just of the priestly caste, as some anthropologists would have it, or of supraindividual entities like 'culture,' as others would have it, but of every man—to project farther and farther from himself his responsibility for the evil that goes on around him.

Anthropologists are by no means agreed on exactly what the first step in the development of this projective tendency and, concurrently, in the sense of the supernatural was. Some see an archaic forerunner of a primitive kind of supernatural power or 'whammy' as a spin-off from primarily human will and force of great potency that became attached to sticks and stones and sundry other objects which, in consequence, became invested with a magical charisma of their own. (Late residues of this *mana,* as it is called, have been found in widely distributed cultures, including the American Indian Iroquois and Dakota cultures.) According to others, this still half-material, half-psychic extrusion was for the most part bypassed in favor of a full-blown something outside oneself, something with a will—mostly an evil one—of its own. (Some etymologists trace the derivation of 'ghost' to the Old Norse *geisa,* meaning 'to rage' or 'to rave,' and to another similar root word meaning 'to bring outside oneself.') But whichever was the case, this first split-off and projection outward of aggression may well have been the real beginning of modern times—not fire, not the wheel, but man's invention of a device which enabled him to say, 'I didn't do it—that thing out there did.' [2] From here on, in any case, the course is clear: the progressive exteriorization of the will and its take-over by independent external entities and forces can be traced with unbroken continuity to the highly elaborate religions and highly sophisticated science of today, with largely impersonal gods on one hand, themselves bound by an external destiny whose laws they hardly ever seek to contravene, and completely impersonal 'forces' of greater and greater complexity and intellectual refinement on the other.

That the prototype of the concepts of force and cause was to be found in our own will—and even connected with violence and ferocity, as in the Egyptian figure-with-a-knife hieroglyph for Divine Power—has long been recognized by philosophers and grammarians of science. But, despite such contributions as Kelsen's tracing of the concept of cause to guilt and retribution for wrong done in the ancient Indian texts, from whence it was taken over into Greek jurisprudence and later science, and despite the near insights of other investigators in this area, the basic

2 According to an interesting theory personally communicated to me by Dr. L. B. Leakey of Kenya, however, the understanding of the making of fire would probably have had to precede the kind of development of abstract human speech and thinking that would presumably have been necessary for this kind of projection to have occurred.

emotional factor underlying the gradual elimination of the will from the scientific picture of the world has not been recognized. Thus the final transmutation of force and cause into field and probabilistic notions—their final abandonment, as it were—has been hailed purely as the supreme triumph of reason and not seen as an inevitable development, in which reason has of course been an indispensable instrument, in the widening schism which began with man's first device for getting himself off the hook of his own complicity in the destructive happenings around him.

It is not only as a tool of analysis, however, that the liberation of the concepts of force and cause from their lowly origins in hate and the power of thought has been manifest. With the elimination of these metaphysical artifacts from science's picture of matter and motion there took place at the same time a downgrading of man in his picture of himself in relation to the universe. Once indissolubly a part of—and through his own will the agent of—everything that happened for good or evil, man is reduced now to a helpless pawn scrounging for redemption because his 'original sin' has not yet been completely bleached out of him. He has become essentially as passive in relation to the main action of the play as a Greek chorus—free to look on, to lament and, like Cassandra, to voice his fateful prophecies, but not to stem the overwhelming tide of destruction he sees in the offing as completely outside his own volitional doing. In the final travesty of this projection from within outward, man conceives of himself as basically peace-loving but helplessly swept over the brink into faceless wars which no one wants (he claims), in which no one really hates anyone, and for which no one takes responsibility in his own heart but which occur, as a last step in the externalization of the will, by a process of what was recently referred to from on high as "blind mindless escalation."

All this was no doubt already well on its way when the Greeks, as Cornford saw it in his study of the origins of their philosophy and science, succeeded in squeezing the last traces of life out of their conceptual model of the real. And it ends now with the nothing less than remarkable claim of some physicists that their picture of ultimate particles, or of waves of probability from which anything even remotely resembling the human will has been eliminated, is somehow as close to reality as we can get. This is accompanied in philosophy by the rise of an analytic school whose disinfectant approach to truth has become detached from even the everyday problems of science, to say nothing of the dried-up carcass of reality it leaves so far as the rest of human experience goes. And topping it all is a mathematical theory of how things happen and get related to each other in the aggregate which is, as one commentator remarked in a moment of rare unconscious insight, "a kind of miracle, as esoteric to the further domains of science as the resurrection of the dead." [3] From this kind of science and philosophy, at all events, only faint vestiges of the original ambivalence to the mother out of which it grew can now be seen.[4]

It is thus in no way surprising that the data of psychical research have been rejected by science. How could it have been otherwise when one of the chief behind-the-scenes factors in the development of science has been the need for man to disavow the dark and sinister side of himself that these data threaten to disclose? From its very inception science, which presents a number of striking parallels to the kind of overmethodical scrupulosity in the thinking and behavior of compulsive neurotics which Freud showed to be a defense against death wishes, grew up brainwashed in this respect. It is hardly to be wondered that it automatically sees anything faintly suggestive of the power of thought as superstitious nonsense to be rejected firmly and out of hand. To expect anything different would be as unrealistic as to expect a temper-

3 Struik: "On the Foundations of the Theory of Probabilities."

4 A remarkably insightful discussion of these vestiges, however, can be found in *The Origins of Science*, by the physicist, E. H. Hutten.

I am by no means trying to suggest that the vicissitudes of the infantile nursing situation are solely responsible for the ills of mankind, much less that only ill has eventuated from the progressive projective externalization of the destructive drives that have their source in this situation. There is little doubt, nevertheless, that this kind of repression and projection necessarily involves in its wake drives other than the purely aggressive—the sexual, for instance—even if these were not subject to repressive forces from other sides. (For this side of things, see Freud's *Civilization and Its Discontents*, and Norman O. Brown's *Life Against Death*.) Compared to those of the primitive, at any rate, our emotional lives are a very dull gray typified by a good deal of unsatisfying pseudo-aggression and what has been aptly termed counterfeit sex, not the least counterfeit aspect of which is the cool penthouse variety aspired to by the fancy men's deodorant set. Periodic attempts to escape from this tightening emotional stranglehold have been seen in all ages, but these sporadic upthrusts from below—Dionysian cults of one sort or another, which have generally involved a recrudescence of what Nietzsche called "the natural cruelty of things"—are of course powerless to reverse the general trend.

ance worker to go out and get soused with the sinners she is trying to save from the demon rum.

The mystery behind the phenomenon of the ever-receding horizon is now solved. Science, like a well-behaved compulsive neurotic, is committed to following out blindly a conspiracy of denial and rejection that is bred into its very marrow. As a result anthropologists automatically take it for granted that the stories and legends of the occult they have been collecting these many years from their primitive informants have no basis whatever in fact. Psychiatrists and psychologists, for their part, just as automatically assume that accounts they may hear of alleged telepathic incidents or dreams from their informants must be due to mal-observation or purely chance coincidence, and unhesitatingly write off anyone manifesting an interest in the subject as suffering from a regressive need for the miraculous. And physicists, who have elaborated a model of a universe that runs by itself in the large and the small, automatically reject data which might provide a basis for a more plausible account of things as in their very nature incompatible with the miraculous 'look, Ma, no hands' model which the whole direction of the development of their science has led them to favor.

But unfortunately the rejection of the basic data and implications of psychical research does not stop here. Parapsychologists, well embedded in the scientific culture which has bred the disciplines from which they come—psychology, biology, physics, mathematics—tend themselves to be prone to the fundamentally obsessional ideals of scientific thinking which pass for the 'good' or even 'only' types of thinking in other disciplines; they are, in any case, members of a community whose approval they seek. The popular-frontist, all-spit-and-polish statistical approach to psychical research that this has engendered has, consequently, tended to play down and cause to be viewed with suspicion anything in the field that cannot be easily and comfortably quantified. The result is that one can read widely in the field today without once getting the impression that there was much of value in it before card guessing and dice throwing put it on a sound scientific basis. This 'distancing' from the threatening emotionally charged core of the subject is thus essentially supported by the same resistances that cause science automatically to reject the data of psychical research in the first place.

Notwithstanding the indubitable value—from the standpoint of conventional science—of some of the experimental work that has been done under the impetus of this trend toward gaining scientific respectability, its net effect has been counterrevolutionary and has played into the hands of the powerful and insidiously strangulating resistance from which it has sprung. It is somewhat similar to the current popular-frontist counterrevolutionary trends in psychoanalysis, which too began by revealing to man a demonic side of himself of almost limitless potency but has ended with a narrow preoccupation with the petty bookkeeping of the ego as far removed from the once-powerful kingdom of the id as are card-calling experiments from the awe-inspiring data of the great days of psychical research. In both cases a defensive compromise position has been reached, a sort of "You may hang your clothes on a hickory limb but don't go near the water" stalemate.

This need of even parapsychology to dissociate itself from the ultimate implications of its data—it is significant that in a several-day-long conference not long ago on parapsychological factors in 'unorthodox' healings not one word was mentioned of the possibility, accepted by common folk of all times and places, that these factors might also operate in the opposite direction—leaves the whole subject in a peculiar cul-de-sac, with the hope of being extricated getting dimmer all the time. The result is that were William James alive and trying to peddle his remarkable Mrs. Piper among his colleagues today, it is doubtful that he would get any further than he did at the turn of the century. And psychical research, which has been hopefully hailed for almost a century now by some of the finest scientific and philosophic intellects the world has produced as the field of investigation of greatest potential importance to mankind, is beginning to look more and more like the overage child prodigy who finally has to give up his knee pants and Lord Fauntleroy bows and admit sadly that he just hasn't made it.

CHAPTER XV

The Shapes and
Shadows of Thought

WE have seen that a possible answer to the peculiar straits in which our divided science finds itself may lie in the fact that when man began many thousands of years ago to try to wash himself clean of a blood guilt that became harder and harder to tolerate, he inevitably began to whitewash himself into a corner. Beginning with the need to project his dangerous and destructive thoughts outside himself, he at the same time divorced himself from the very essence of causality and now finds that, having got rid of this category altogether as an explanatory concept, all the king's philosophers and all the king's men cannot put body and mind together again, either in the individual animal or in nature at large.

So much for an answer to our primitive Galileo's first question—how does a large segment of mankind come to elaborate theories that are so patently false?

When we attempt to deal with our primitive's sixty-four goat or pig (or wife) question, however, we find that we are up against a much more formidable job. In essence the question is: if the power to influence material systems outside the body by purely mental means is present in all of us (just as the power to influence our own bodies is), how is it that so few of us exercise this power and that things remain pretty much what and where they are?

Let us for the moment not dispute the assumption on which the primitive bases his question; let us consider as quite plausible the possibility that something like this power is indeed latent in all of us, just as there is reason to believe that ESP capacities are. (In support of this, besides the universality and strength of the defenses against the possibility of such power breaking loose, is the fact that nature doesn't ordinarily do things by halves and that wherever a 'power' phenomenon was first discovered in isolated occurrences—the rubbing of silk on amber, the attraction of certain substances for iron, and so forth—it was ultimately found to be pervasive, however well concealed. Against such an assumption is, essentially, only an extension of the argument which would deny the existence of this power anywhere—and this we have agreed that Ted, if not others, has disproved.) The problem is: what has happened to this enormous reservoir of potential power so that it doesn't manifest itself?

I think the one supposition that we are finally forced to face as probably the most plausible is that it *is* 'manifest,' but in ways that our conventional categories of thought do not favor our being able easily to discern. Actually the primitive himself had a clue to the mystery in his sense of oneness with nature but, what with his not being an analytically minded fellow, it may not have occurred to him to do the 'power auditing' that might have led to the insight I am leading up to. This is, of course, that the latent mental power which all of us possess goes into sustaining—and is thus manifest in—all the natural processes that we see around us, from the growth of the lowliest seed to the movements of the heavenly bodies. It might thus be put down under the heading of 'general maintenance.'

Now this is what might be termed a metaphysical assumption or construct and, if the reader feels that it's a whopper, I shall have to inform him that all metaphysical constructs—except the very ones we live with and take so for granted that we are never even aware of their character as metaphysical constructs (such as that there exist other minds than our own)—are whoppers and thus run the risk of being ignored or disdained by the more down-to-earth souls of any given age. But, as Dr. Mary Hesse warns us in the very last line of *Forces and Fields,* her admirable study of action at a distance in the history of physics, "a society which is uninterested in metaphysics will have no theoretical science."

Unfortunately, however, metaphysical assumptions are just that —assumptions—and are difficult to test as such by means of the kind of procedures leading to direct confirmation or refutation that hypotheses of lesser scope may lend themselves to. Rather do they provide, in place of predictable results, important struts in an overall framework in terms of which the data integrated by these lesser hypotheses may sometimes be seen to make better sense. In the present instance, thus, all we may have to commend such an assumption is that in one stroke it seems to answer the question of where the latent power to mentally influence material systems has gone in the general run of us at the same time that it uncovers—or at least tells us where to look for—both the missing quantities long searched for by the physicists and what it is that carries out the otherwise only logically comprehensible, but not necessarily empirically workable, laws of probability.[1]

From this point of view, then, individuals like Ted and the great physical mediums are extraordinary only in that they do not play in concert with the rest of the orchestra but insist on going off on toots of their own, like the mad trumpet player who goes beserk with his discordant blasts that stand out sharply from the otherwise harmonious whole. If the curious reader would like to know, however, what would happen if the rest of us were to withdraw our power from the universe at large, all I can suggest is a simple so-called thought experiment which he can either do for himself or take my word for, as I have done it many times and can tell him exactly what will happen: the universe collapses and in fact vanishes, like the image on a television screen when the current is shut off, putting an end at once to the controversies of the cosmologists, who simply disappear in the general confusion.

Now the reason that your mind and mine may have escaped notice as nourishing sources of the 'mind' the great philoso-

---

[1] One of the people bothered by this latter question was the German philosopher and mathematician, Karl Marbe, who, in his exhaustive investigation into what makes probability run, came independently to the conclusion (just as Jordan did in the case of physics) that the answer must somehow be supplied by psychology, just how he couldn't yet fathom.

phies, particularly the Eastern ones, have always claimed to be
holding up the universe is precisely because these instruments,
your mind and mine, have—like the Devil whose cleverest trick
is to convince you he doesn't exist—always been only unobtru-
sively in the picture observing, reflecting, idly contemplating, and
now and then making assumptions about the nature of the universe; few took the trouble to see what they could do along less
familiar lines. The situation is not unlike that in the story about
the president of a large real-estate enterprise who received a phone
call from his man in charge of sales. "A terrible thing happened,"
reported the salesman. "We sold our model house today, took
away the scaffolding—and the whole house collapsed." "How many
times must I tell you!" shouted the president. "Never take away
the scaffolding until the wallpaper is up." In our universe too,
the whole structure collapses unless our thought and will—which,
like the wallpaper in the story, are the last things suspected in
this role—are there to hold everything up.

At this juncture, however, and before he gets too set up over the
idea that, like Molière's bourgeois gentleman, he has so to speak
always been talking prose without even being aware of it, there are
two directions the reader would be well advised to scout for
possible modifications to his picture. The first—and I am sure that
this has hardly escaped the majority of readers—is that much the
same sort of reasoning (at least as far as trying to find the missing
quantities of the physicists and biologists is concerned—and not a
few physicists and biologists have wound up in this camp) has
been used to arrive at the concept of a Divine Intelligence, or the
God concept. I think it worthwhile, as a matter of fact, to cite here
the statement, including a very pertinent footnote, of a not
untypical contemporary expression of this point of view. The
following is from philosopher N. K. Brahma's *Causality and
Science:*

> In the case of the universe also the creative consciousness is
> pervadingly present and is working without cessation, and it is
> because of the ceaseless work and energy of the Creator that under-
> lies the working of physical things that combinations can produce
> such wonderful results. We are liable to overlook the presence of
> this all-pervading intelligence at the source just because it works
> continuously: we do not and cannot know what would happen if

it failed to work. The creative functioning of such an Intelligence is always present as the underlying factor and we cannot prove its utility simply because it is present in all cases. Causation is proved by means of agreement in presence and absence, but as we can never show what happens in its absence, because *ex hypothesi* it is always present, we cannot demonstrate that this is the most important factor (if not also the sole determining factor) in the cause. That the sun's rays are essential to the growth and preservation of organisms can be proved because during the night we do not have them and we can study what happens in their absence. But if we could never find any instance of their absence, perhaps these also would have been ignored as wholly inessential, although we now know fully their importance.

Now follows the footnote (with Brahma's italics) from Bridgman's classic *The Logic of Modern Physics:*

Thus in the case of the bell, all our experiments were made in the presence of the atmosphere. The causal connection between the striking of the bell and the sound should have been always recognized in principle as relative to the presence of the atmosphere. Indeed, later experiments in the absence of the atmosphere show that the atmosphere does play an essential part. Now as a matter of fact, the atmosphere is so comparatively easy to remove that we readily include the atmosphere in the chain of causal connection. *But if the atmosphere had been impossible to remove, like the old ether of space, our idea of the causal connections between the striking of the bell and its sound might have been quite different.* In actual physical applications of the causality concept, the constant background which is maintained during all the variations by which the causal connection is established usually has to be inferred from the context.

According to this point of view then, the question of what keeps the universe running—the question of who or what is in the back of the Big Store—admits of an answer that is not only sublimely simple but in principle unassailable: just look for the throne behind the power. (The reader can see that, so far as the God of the metaphysicians goes, the rumors of his death, like Mark Twain's, have been grossly exaggerated.)

The other direction of thought which is likely to compel some modification of man's image of himself as the Creator (a doctrine

which has, incidentally, had a long history in the annals of
mysticism) not only robs man of a good deal of his newly acquired
governing status in order to pay out at the other end of the line
but, some may feel, also leaves the argument for a Supreme Power
unaltered since it merely delegates to intermediaries some of the
executive detail but not the ultimate responsibility or authority.
Even neglecting this latter consideration, however, it soon becomes
apparent that, once we admit mind into the very innards of things
in the way that we have, sentient mental entities in the universe
other than man—gnats and mites and mealy bugs—are going to
want in on the act; and before you know it, you may even find
some Copernicus in one of these orders—which are very likely
closer to the pulse of things than we are and perhaps able to make
observations and reflections on a more appropriate scale—extend-
ing the privilege to sticks and stones with the observation that
what we (mites) do when we think and exert our will is, after all,
only a special case of what all these other things do when they just
exist and go through *their* motions. If, some mite may muse, sticks
and stones were endowed with anything corresponding to our
consciousness, they might, not being subject to a mitocentric bias
but having one of their own, elaborate a perfectly consistent
though in the final analysis also insufficient picture of reality that
would center around *their* own behavior. "Because *I* do what I do
(fall through the air, break in two, or perform some equally
physical act)," one of these sticks or stones might think, "that mite
over there, which hitherto supposed itself to be actuated only by
its own fancy, now takes it into its head to fly hither and yon in
perfect correspondence to what I am doing; and that human over
there—I am going to influence him in a moment or two to pick me
up and throw me into the pond, for I feel like a bit of a skip on it
and then a nice quiet snooze on the bottom."

Now such a view of things, or any view similarly developed by
other self-conscious participants in the world drama, would clearly
be as parochially biased as would be an anthropo-psychocentric view
developed by man. Better no doubt would be some universal
calculus that could express the relationships between events (which
after all is perhaps the only way we can begin adequately to
define 'mind') in an invariant way true for all points of departure
into that innermost crucible of nature where all processes melt

into one. However, lacking such a device with which to encompass in one economical description events as seen by the electron, the gnat, the tree, the human, and the far-off wandering suns of space, we might do worse than fall back on the makeshift devices of the poet [2] while noting, nevertheless, that we have come back to a picture not too different after all from the one the physicists from Newton on have, with modifications here and there, insisted on as most adequately fitting the facts—except that we have somewhere along the line managed to smuggle 'mind' into the picture, the very mind that thoughtful physicists have insisted should have been there all along. Something not too unlike this picture, as a matter of fact, was already reflected in a widely held and influential medieval doctrine (inherited or borrowed, I believe, from the ancient Chinese); and, despite the increasing befuddlement of later Western philosophy over just what to do with mind, this point of view has never really lost its appeal. (The philosophy of Alfred North Whitehead, for instance, is steeped in it.)

However, if we are going to sneak mind back into our picture of how the world's work gets done, we have to bring back that part of mental activity—its destructive aspect—which was responsible for its having been deleted from the world picture to begin with. This may bring us back into somewhat closer alignment with the great pre-Christian cosmological myths, and with the ancient gods that were both destructive as well as creative, and not just gods of love and mercy.

Now while we are hardly suggesting a return to the world

[2] Goethe and the Vedantic poets have managed very admirably to express such a conception of things, as has of course Wordsworth, especially in his incomparable Tintern Abbey lines:

> . . . . For I have learned
> To look on nature, not as in the hour
> Of thoughtless youth; but hearing oftentimes
> The still, sad music of humanity,
> Nor harsh nor grating, though of ample power
> To chasten and subdue. And I have felt
> A presence that disturbs me with the joy
> Of elevated thoughts; a sense sublime
> Of something far more deeply interfused,
> Whose dwelling is the light of setting suns,
> And the round ocean and the living air,
> And the blue sky, and in the mind of man;
> A motion and a spirit, that impels
> All thinking things, all objects of all thought,
> And rolls through all things.

of the primitive (not that this option is open to us in any case), it may nevertheless be feared that even this direction of thinking must lead inevitably to a too-shockingly paranoid world picture, not too far, perhaps, from the one from which we fled into the supernatural and thence to religion and science. It need scarcely be pointed out, however, that reality as it is, not just our rather denatured picture of it, has become something of a Hieronymus Bosch nightmare that could match the elaborations of the most far-gone psychotic anyway. A moment's reflection will show us, too, that the raw facts are in any case what they are and will not change with a mere alteration in our theoretical picture. We would simply be exchanging one kind of paranoid picture for another, but not one entry in the actuarial tables would be different.

As to building blocks for a theoretical structure that might bridge the gulf on other fronts between the mental and the physical, and which might, as I believe an adequate theory should, encompass the data of what we might term creation as well as the data of perception and cognition, I can't think of a better place to begin than right where Ted is (and hopefully where others like him will in time be). For in a study of images and imagery of this sort—and in phenomena like the dream, the hallucination, and the apparition, which are really as remarkable as, even if more familiar than, Ted's images—we are confronted by various grades of organized entities with one leg in the world of reality and one leg in that part of the world of reality that we term the world of appearance. As important as thoughtographic data in investigating the role of the unconscious in linking perception and creation, it seems to me, might be what we might glean from the study of apparitions, more familiarly known as ghosts. Unfortunately these strange creatures are almost as hard to come by as individuals like Ted; but I am inclined to believe that they occur more frequently than is generally allowed and are simply kept in the family closet, which in our culture is by all odds the safest place for aberrant creatures of this sort. (If the reader, by the way, has never had the pleasure of the company of one of these entities and doesn't even believe there are such things, I suggest that he start his study with Tyrrell's unexcelled survey, in his *Apparitions*, of their ins and outs and ups and downs which, whether he believes them true or not, he cannot help but find fascinating.) At any rate, H. H. Price, an English philosopher, has the following to say of the apparition as a possible bridge between appearance and reality:

A hallucinatory entity, the celebrated pink rat, for instance, is composed of sense-data or appearances (cognita) just as a 'real' object is. What is wrong with it, what inclines us to call it 'unreal,' is the fact that there are not *enough* of them. For instance, the hallucinatory rat can be seen from the front but not from the back; it is visible but not tangible; it can be perceived by one percipient but not by more; and it endures only for a minute or so. But some hallucinations do better than this. Apparitions, for example, are sometimes public to several percipients, can be seen from several different points of view, and endure for considerable periods of time—though not as long as they would if they were 'real' human beings. Now suppose there was an apparition which had unrestricted publicity, i.e., was public to an indefinite number of points of view and an indefinite number of observers: suppose that there are tangible as well as visible particulars among the appearances (or 'cognita') which are its constituents; suppose it endures for half an hour and then disappears. We should not know whether to call it an unusually prolonged and complex hallucination, or a very queer 'real object' (queer, because we should not know how it got into the room, or why it abruptly vanished into thin air). In point of fact, it would be something intermediate between the two, a complex system of 'cognita,' but not quite complex enough to count as a complete material object . . . Now imagine this process pushed to the limit, so to speak. We might expect that occasionally a complete material object or a complete physical event would be produced by purely mental causes.[3]

To give this point of view a specific reference, and at the same time to link it up with the role of the unconscious in both perception and creation, I can report that not too long ago I had the opportunity of studying an 'appearance' which manifested itself in parts over a period of many months to a group of seven people in a rural community in the following ways: to two, visually, to five, auditorily, and to five, tactually; and sometimes to several persons together in more than one modality. To all seven the apparition was a definite and compelling presence with a highly

[3] Preface to Whateley Carington's *Matter, Mind and Meaning.*

marked indivuality and identity. There was every indication, however, that Becky (for that was what the apparition called itself) was
the joint unconscious elaboration of the persons involved in this
extravaganza (just as if all were sharing a dream, which is sometimes seen, or a psychotic delusion—the well known *folie à deux*
or *à trois*), while there was no evidence whatsoever that this extremely well-organized visible, audible, and in other ways experienceable entity had any existence apart from these persons. (If
Becky still on rare occasions puts in an appearance and carries on
with her high jinks, I do not take this as an indication of an independent existence but merely that my all-too-brief psychotherapy
was not completely successful, and that, as is so often the case,
residual conflict material remains to be teased out to the light and
worked through; one sometimes sees the same sort of incomplete
result in cases of multiple personality and in fact in the psychotherapy of all types of cases.)

Now one cannot help wondering whether there is much difference in principle between this kind of apparition, or the endow-
ing of a purely mental image with a quasi-reality by the sort of
thing Ted does, and all manner of creations and occurrences that
might be lost in the general stream of life and happening because
we have no ready means of disentangling them from the environ-
mental context into which they can so smoothly blend. Remember
Bridgman's bell, and what would happen if we had no means of
producing a vacuum.

At all events, one might think of Ted conjuring up and capturing on film, as it were, very much the kind of apparition Professor
Price is talking about, and giving it a publicity that it would not
otherwise enjoy. Such would be, like apparitions which have been
multiply experienced in several modalities, perhaps an embryonic
foreshadowing of the complete material object or event that
Professor Price envisages as conceivably produced by purely
mental causes if the process of adding sensorially perceivable
dimensions were pushed to the limit. (In Ted's case, who knows
but what this might result in the materialization of film emulsion
and print paper that some critics have demanded as practically the
only criterion of genuine paranormality they would accept.) If we
are inclined to think this too farfetched, let us consider a statement of Einstein. "It is not a long step," he is reported to have

said, "from thinking of matter as an electronic ghost to thinking of it as the objectified image of thought." [4]

But before we get to imagining that we may be only just around the corner from being able to think or will ourselves into a mysterious appearance in the environs of the planet of some receding sun far out in space (whose inhabitants, perhaps thousands or millions of their astral years behind us in development, may just have discovered the multiple uses of the projection of aggression into demons), let us pause and take stock. The fact is that the step referred to by Einstein as "not long" is really an immense one if, generation after generation, only a handful of people are ever girding themselves to take it, and if even these, becoming drowsy in the magic wood of 'reason,' begin to imagine that such a step can itself, in its purely intellectual form (however inspired), carry us over the ever-receding horizon.

So we come back to Ted, and the hope of more Teds, as providing the faintest promise of a more workable wedge into the forces of resistance than what is now on the scene. But who knows how long Ted will be able to continue to pile up the data he has been providing these last few months of feverish activity, ever haunted by the fear that the curtain will one day come down, as he says, "kerboom, and that's all, brother!" If Jean Laffite knows the answer to this one, let him kindly step forward (or downward, as the case may be) and speak his piece.

There are of course many directions one would like to move with Ted, if we could only count on his ideally 'producing' like a uranium pile or Old Faithful. There are areas that have not been explored at all, and many 'experiments'—some extremely simple in execution—that undoubtedly will appear to some readers as warranting priority over the type of things we have done. Unfortunately, whatever it is in Ted that does the 'producing' doesn't lend itself always to the type of procedure that I (or others) might think desirable; and if I try to pressure Ted into some direction

---

[4] Quoted by Brahma, *op. cit.* Many Vedantists have held that the power of desire leads to the creation of matter and that the force of imagination is the basis of energy. The physical universe is conceived of as a projection of mind.

An information-theory approach to the integration of mental images into the structure of physical and cosmological theory has been put forth by the late C. C. L. Gregory, a physicist, and Anita Kohsen, an ethologist, in two of their joint works. See also Bergson.

when that something in him is just not willing or ready, I soon find out who is boss, as Ted once put it, in terms of foot dragging, obstructiveness, and ultimately negative results. This is why for a long time Ted was encouraged to take the reins while I and others simply stood by ready to pick up whatever data came our way. I have no apologies for this policy, however, as these chips fell not only in considerable profusion at times but sometimes fell out as if Ted were following an unconscious plan to give me what I wanted without my saying anything, at times even without my consciously knowing that this or that bit of data was precisely what I *should* have wanted were I a clever experimenter follow-ing some program of sequential analysis.

A project I should very much like to see explored with Ted (or with others like Ted who might turn up; I believe the entire program could best be integrated by a group of university teams) is along the lines of something we tried several months back but left along the wayside with the hope of returning to it some day after a few other problems had been investigated and Ted was thoroughly rested. (For the next few months Ted wants a sabbati-cal, which he shall have with my blessing.) The idea was to see if an arrangement could be worked out whereby Ted and I (or Ted and other 'stooges') might experience the illusion of 'togetherness' while the spatial distance between us was extended stepwise until terrestrially considerable distances had been achieved. With this in mind, Ted and I worked one evening at a local television broad-casting studio, Ted viewing me holding a camera and ready to snap at his signal in one monitoring box while I was looking at him in another where I was stationed about thirty feet away. Al-though Ted and I were facing in the same direction, with our monitoring boxes parallel to each other at this distance, the size and position of our images were arranged to conform as closely as possible to how we would appear to each other if I were holding a camera about three or four feet from Ted and he were facing me and looking straight into the lens, as he customarily does, and preparing to give me the signal to shoot. The systems were wired for sound so that there was perfect 'togetherness' and feedback in this dimension, with Ted instructing me to move the camera a bit to this side or that as he usually does when we work from the vis-à-vis position. Our hope was for Ted to become thoroughly accustomed to getting images in this manner, when we could gradually increase the distance between us until the illusion of being together and in face-to-face communication could be achieved while Ted and I were first in different parts of the building, next in different buildings, then perhaps in different parts of town and finally in different cities.[5]

Unfortunately on this one occasion Ted was anything but in the mood for work (he had been having a last fling before entering a hospital the following morning for 'the cure'), but he was game to have a go at it anyway because all arrangements with the crew of the television studio had been made and the necessary personnel and equipment were on hand and ready to shoot. The sole results, with Ted rather woodenly going through the motions of concentrating on the camera I was holding before him on the screen, were a half-dozen blackies out of about fifty tries, but these, more or less bunched together, were absolutely perfect and indicated that the method might have promising possibilities. Not a sign of the effect of light could be detected on these prints although from about fifteen feet away several thousand watts were streaming into the unobstructed lens of the camera I was triggering. (The flash of the wink light indicated that the shutter had been opened.)

Prior to the actual run at the studio, a curious anomaly of sorts turned up during attempts to accustom Ted to working from an image of me holding the camera instead of facing me directly in the flesh. In three practice sessions given over to this manner of shooting Ted and I arranged ourselves to form a four-foot equilateral triangle with a line in the center of a three-foot-high mirror. Ted stood facing an image in the mirror of me holding the camera while I looked back at him in the mirror from where I stood. Several series of trials were run with a screen placed between us so that each would have no peripheral vision of the other. In not one of more than a hundred trials done this way was there any evidence of the slightest alteration of the photographic image from what would normally be expected, while in a large percentage of the controls done when Ted and I would swing around

---

[5] A series of experiments done with Ted in Chicago and several spotters in Denver, checking on the closed cameras they set out at specified times led to results which in several instances were provocative but inconclusive because of the ambiguous nature of the images and our difficulty in convincing ourselves that every possibility of these having been artifactually produced had been eliminated.

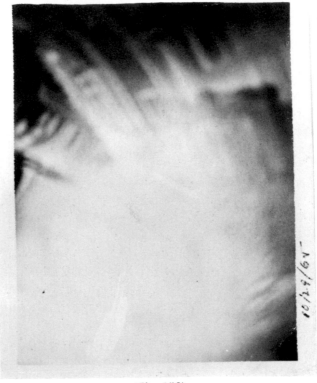

(Fig. 150)

and face each other instead of the mirror there were signs of either beginning imagery or the occurrence of partial or complete blackies. To find out whether he was cooking, during one of these sessions, I asked him to try for a target picked from a magazine that happened to be lying at hand. Ted merely threw a brief glance at this—the picture (which the magazine involved does not wish reproduced) shows merely the windows and chimneys of some row houses in a Welsh town—and came up practically immediately with the jumbled but definite correspondence shown in fig. 150. When we returned to the mirror directly afterward—nothing, absolutely nothing. When the seeming constancy of the difference between the two situations became manifest, a more formal method of randomization was used to obviate the likelihood of this difference being due to chance, but the discrepancy continued without variation. The possibility was considered that perhaps

Ted was not used to viewing me and the camera as a reversed image, but when a second mirror was brought in to re-reverse the image the results continued negative. So far as we could see, not a molecule on the emulsion of any print obtained in this way was where it shouldn't have been. At the end, Ted was glowering at the mirror as at a personal enemy, but his fiercest looks (and vilest profanity) failed to move it.

There was thus this added psychological hurdle for Ted to take when he went up against the television tube at the studio. He told me later that it reminded him of all "them cameras" glaring at him in his nightmares (and latterly in his bouts of severe intoxication). But with the blackies—especially in front of a dozen close observers who simply could not figure out how such a result could possibly have been obtained under the circumstances—he feels better about continuing with this line of investigation at a future time. (The mirror anomaly too should clearly be run to the ground, as any result this constant must be of significance.)

If Ted can get used to getting images in this manner at any appreciable distance, all indications from the cumulative data on psi phenomena point to the possibility of his being able to come through from halfway around the globe, or from out in space. If and when that day arrives it might be interesting to have Ted try for a target like a phrase thought up on the spot and written in the handwriting of one of the observers on the camera end of the setup, some phrase, perhaps, like 'What man [or maybe Ted] hath wrought.' The only trouble is that on the one occasion we tried something like this (getting handwriting of the deceased was a stunt of some of the 'spirit photographers'—and a damned good one) Ted didn't come up with the handwriting or even the phrase chosen but with two different series of images that could very well have been associatively derived from the phrase. With a handwritten target, thus, like 'What man hath wrought,' Ted could very well come up with a picture of Winged Mercury looking for all the world as if he had just come to life and stepped down off his pedestal, or even of Samuel F. Morse looking slightly puzzled and as if he were wondering what in God's name was going on around here anyway; and then where would we be?

Problems.

A note on the pictures.

Every effort has been made to reproduce Ted's pictures with fidelity, except in several instances where contrast was sharpened to bring out detail. No other alterations have been made. Unfortunately, the deep, velvety quality peculiar to Ted's blacks and shadows cannot adequately be achieved in reproduction. Some slight variation from the standard $2\frac{7}{8}$ by $3\frac{3}{4}$ inch print size of the series 95 Polaroid Land camera has sometimes occurred in the process of assembling the pictures for publication.

At Dr. Gersten's

With Dr. Paley

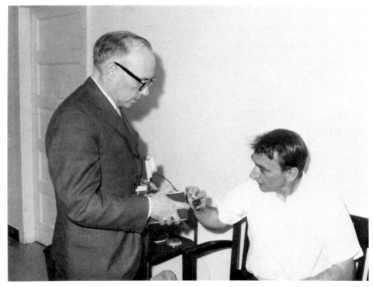

Ted by Ted

ACKNOWLEDGMENTS

I wish to express my appreciation and indebtedness to the following persons, organizations and institutions. Dr. Arthur Robinson of the Department of Biophysics of the University of Colorado Medical School, for a study of Ted's genetic structure; Dr. Harold Elrick of the Department of Medicine, University of Colorado Medical School, for a study of Ted's hormonal system; Dr. Paul Polak of the Fort Logan Mental Health Center, for medical laboratory studies of Ted; Dr. Harl Young of the U.S. Veteran's Administration Hospital, Denver, and Dr. Margaret Thaler Singer of Berkeley, California, for projective and other psychological studies of Ted; Dr. David R. Metcalf of the University of Colorado Medical School, for electroencephalographic studies of Ted; Dr. Martin M. Alexander, for medical examinations of Ted; Mr. James A. Hurry of the Research and Development Division of the Gates Rubber Company, Denver, for the use of the Faraday cage in his laboratory; Mr. Wesley J. Anderson and Mr. Albert J. Hazle of the Colorado State Department of Public Health, for whole body radiation studies of Ted; the Departments of Radiology of St. Luke's and General Rose Memorial Hospitals, Denver; the Westinghouse Electric Corporation, X-ray Division; Mr. James Davis, Western History Division of the Denver Public Library, and the staffs of the Denver Public Library, main branch, and the Denison Memorial Library of the University of Colorado Medical

School; Mr. Simeon Edmunds, London, England, for his help in connection with the Westminster Abbey picture; Mrs. Pauline Oehler for permission to print the Queen Elizabeth picture and for many other courtesies; Mr. Curtis Fuller for permission to print the Air Division, Royal Canadian Mounted Police picture and for many other courtesies; Miss Elizabeth Parfet and the staff of the Printing Service of the University of Colorado Medical School, for aid in the preparation of the manuscript; Mr. Billie Wheeler and the staff of the Department of Audio-visual Education of the University of Colorado Medical Center, for invaluable photographic help; Mr. Jack A. Schlaefle and the staff of Channel 6, KRMA-TV, Denver; Mrs. Laura A. Dale, Long Island, N.Y., for bibliographic help; Mr. W. E. Cox, Southern Pines, N.C., for help in matching the picture shown in Figure 12 a; Dr. Siegwalt O. Palleske, for identification of the picture shown in figure 115; and ENIT-Rome, for the picture used in figure 91.

Finally, I wish to express my appreciation to all those who sat through long, often fatiguing, and sometimes unrewarding sessions with Ted, and especially to Drs. Henry Frey, Henry Lehrburger, Johann Marx, F. Bruce Merrill, Aaron Paley, and David Starrett, without whose invaluable and sustained help this work could not easily have been carried on.

BIBLIOGRAPHY

Allport, Floyd H., *Theories of Perception and the Concept of Structure*. New York: John Wiley & Sons, 1955.

Bachofen, Johann Jakob, *Das Mutterrecht*, Vols. II and III of Collected Works. Basel: Schwabe & Company, 1948. The myths of prehistory from which the role of the mothers is deduced. Unfortunately, no English translation exists.

Backman, Alfred, "Experiments in Clairvoyance." *Proc. Soc. Psychic. Res.*, Part 19, Vol. VII, July, 1891.

———"Further Information as to Dr. Backman's Experiments in Clairvoyance." *Ibid.*, Part 22, Vol. VIII, July, 1892.

Barrett, W. F., *On the Threshold of the Unseen*. New York: E. P. Dutton & Company, Inc., 1917. A firsthand account by a physicist of major physical psi phenomena.

———and others, "First Report of the 'Reichenbach' Committee." *Proc. Soc. Psychic. Res.*, Part 3, Vol. I, July, 1883.

Beattie, John, "A Description of Remarkable Experiments in Photography." *Brit. Jour. Photog.*, June 28, 1872.

———"Spirit Photography." *Ibid.*, July 11, 1873.

Becker, R. O., "The Biological Effects of Magnetic Fields—a Survey." *Med. Electron. Biol. Engng.*, Vol. I, 1963.

Beloff, John, *The Existence of Mind*. New York: The Citadel Press, 1964.

Berger, Hans, *Psyche*. Jena, Germany: Gustav Fischer, 1940.

350   *Bibliography*

Bergson, Henri, *Matter and Memory*. London: George Allen & Unwin,
    Ltd., 1950. Shorn of its fuzz, an amazingly farsighted theory.
    Should be read by those who are convinced that *all* aspects of
    mental functioning can be—or need be—explained in terms of the
    brain.
Biographical Dictionary of Parapsychology. New York: Helix Press,
    1964.
Boas, Franz, *The Mind of Primitive Man*. New York: The Macmillan
    Company, 1938.
Brahma, Nalini Kanta, *Causality and Science*. London: George Allen
    and Unwin, Ltd., 1939.
Bridgman, P. W., *The Logic of Modern Physics*. New York: The Mac-
    millan Company, 1946. A provocative approach to 'light,' among
    other things.
Broad, C. D., *Religion, Philosophy and Psychical Research*. New York:
    Harcourt, Brace & Company, 1953.
———*The Mind and its Place in Nature*. New York: Harcourt, Brace,
    1925. London: Routledge & Kegan Paul, 1949.
Brown, Norman O., *Life Against Death*. Middletown, Conn.: Wesleyan
    University Press, 1959.
Carington, Whateley, *Matter, Mind and Meaning*. New Haven: Yale
    University Press, 1949.
Carrington, Hereward, *Modern Psychical Phenomena*. New York:
    Dodd, Mead & Company, 1919.
Chappell, V. C., *The Philosophy of Mind*. Englewood Cliffs, N. J.:
    Prentice-Hall, Inc., 1962.
Coates, James, *Photographing the Invisible*. Chicago: Advanced
    Thought Publishing Company, 1911. The best survey of its day.
Cohen, Sydney, *The Beyond Within*. New York: Atheneum, 1965.
Cornford, F. M., *From Religion to Philosophy. A Study in the Origins
    of Western Speculation*. New York: Harper & Row (Torchbook
    20), 1957.
Crawford, W. J., *Experiments in Psychical Science*. London: Watkins,
    1919.
———*The Psychic Structures of the Goligher Circle*. New York: E. P.
    Dutton & Company, Inc., 1921.
Crookall, Robert, *The Study and Practice of Astral Projection*. Lon-
    don: The Aquarian Press, 1961.
———*More Astral Projections*. London: The Aquarian Press, 1964.
Crookes, William, "Experimental Investigation of a New Force."
    Quart. Jour. Sci., Vol. VIII, July, 1871.
———"Some Further Experiments in Psychic Force." *Ibid.*, Oct., 1871.

———"Notes on an Enquiry into the Phenomenon Called Spiritual during the Years 1870-73." *Ibid.,* Vol. XI, Jan., 1874.

———*Researches in the Phenomena of Spiritualism.* Manchester: Two Worlds Publishing Co., 1926.

Descartes, René, *Philosophical Works.* Abridged Edition. New York: Dover Publications, 1955.

Dewey, John, *Experience and Nature.* New York: W. W. Norton & Company, 1929.

Dobbs, H. A. C., "Time and Extrasensory Perception." *Proc. Soc., Psychic. Res.,* Part 197, Vol. LIV, 1965.

Dodds, E. R., *The Greeks and the Irrational.* Berkeley: University of California Press, 1951. A discussion of forces behind the development of a guilt culture in ancient Greece.

Doyle, Arthur Conan, *The Case for Spirit Photography.* New York: George H. Doran Co., 1923. Among other matters, The Case of the Purloined Plates (or the investigators investigated). A real thriller.

Ducasse, C. J., *Nature, Mind and Death.* La Salle, Ill.: Open Court Publishing Company, 1951.

———"Paranormal Phenomena, Nature, and Man." *Jour. Amer. Soc. Psychic. Res.,* Vol. XLV, No. 4, 1951.

Eastman, Margaret, "Out-of-the-Body Experiences." *Proc. Soc. Psychic. Res.,* Part 193, Vol. LIII, Dec., 1962.

Eccles, John Carew, *The Neurophysiological Basis of Mind.* Oxford: Oxford University Press, 1953.

Eddington, A. S., *The Nature of the Physical World.* New York: The Macmillan Company, 1929.

Ehrenwald, Jan, *New Dimensions in Analysis: A Study of Telepathy in Interpersonal Relationships.* London: George Allen and Unwin, Ltd., 1954.

Einstein, Albert, and Infeld, Leopold, *The Evolution of Physics.* New York: Simon & Schuster, 1938.

Eisenbud, Jule, "Analysis of a Presumptively Telepathic Dream." *Psychiat. Quart.,* Vol. XXII, Jan., 1948.

———"Psi and the Nature of Things." *Int. Jour. Parapsychol.,* Vol. V, No. 3, 1963.

Eliade, Mircea, *Patterns in Comparative Religion.* New York: Sheed and Ward, 1958.

———*Shamanism: Archaic Techniques of Ecstasy.* New York: Bollingen Series LXXVI, Pantheon Books, 1964.

Feilding, Everard, Baggally, W. W., and Carrington, Hereward, "Report on a Series of Sittings with Eusapia Palladino." *Proc. Soc.*

Psychic. Res., Vol. XXIII, 1909. Reprinted: *Sittings with Eusapia Palladino and Other Studies.* New Hyde Park: University Books, Inc., 1963.

Fisher, Charles, "A Study of the Preliminary Stages of the Construction of Dreams and Images." *Jour. Amer. Psychoanal. Assoc.*, Vol. V, No. 1, 1957.

Flew, Antony, *Body, Mind and Death.* New York: The Macmillan Company, 1964.

Fodor, Nandor, *Encyclopaedia of Psychic Science.* London: Arthurs Press Ltd., 1933. Reprinted: New Hyde Park, N.Y., University Books, 1966.

Freud, Sigmund, *Civilization and Its Discontents.* Vol. XXI, Complete Psychological Works, Standard Edition. London: Hogarth Press, 1961.

——*The Interpretation of Dreams,* Vols. IV and V, Complete Psychological Works, Standard Edition. London: Hogarth Press, 1953.

——*Totem and Taboo.* Vol. XIII, Complete Psychological Works, Standard Edition. London: Hogarth Press, 1955.

Fukurai, Tomokichi, *Clairvoyance and Thoughtography.* London: Rider and Company, 1931.

Geley, Gustave, *From the Unconscious to the Conscious.* New York: Harper and Brothers, 1920.

Gerloff, Hans, *The Crisis in Parapsychology.* Tittmoning, Obb., Germany: Walter Pustet, 1965.

Gibson, J. J., *The Perception of the Visual World.* Boston: Houghton Mifflin Company, 1950. A mathematical approach to visual perception.

Girden, E., "A Review of Psychokinesis (PK)." *Psychol. Bull.*, Vol. LIX, Sept., 1962.

Glendinning, Andrew, *The Veil Lifted.* London: Whittaker & Company, 1894.

Grad, Bernard, "Some Biological Effects of the 'Laying on of Hands': A Review of Experiments with Animals and Plants." *Jour. Amer. Soc. Psychic. Res.*, Vol. LIX, No. 2, 1965.

Gregory, C. C. L. and Kohsen, Anita, "A Cosmological Approach to a Theory of Mental Images. *Proc. Soc. Psychic. Res.*, Part 187, Vol. LII, Oct., 1958. Tough going, but there it is for the hardy, like Everest.

——*Physical and Psychical Research.* Reigate, Surrey: The Omega Press, 1954.

Gurney, E., Myers, F.W.H., and Podmore, F., *Phantasms of the Living.* Abridged Edition. New York: E. P. Dutton & Company, 1918. Reprinted: New Hyde Park: University Books, Inc., 1962. An excellent case book of spontaneously occurring telepathy. A classic.

Hansel, C. E. M., *ESP—A Scientific Evaluation.* New York: Charles Scribner's Sons, 1966.

Hawkins, David, *The Language of Nature.* San Francisco: Freeman & Company, 1964. Some uses of information theory. Not for the lazy.

Hays, H. R., *In the Beginnings.* New York: G. P. Putnam's Sons, 1963. A popular account of the beginnings of magic and religion.

Hesse, Mary B., *Forces and Fields.* London: Thomas Nelson & Sons, 1961. The author arrives at the very brink of the point of view touched upon in the last chapter of the present volume in her study of power accounting systems in the history of physics.

Hoffman, B., "ESP and the Inverse Square Law." *Jour. Parapsychol.* Vol. IV, 1940.

Hook, Sidney, ed., *Dimensions of Mind.* New York: Collier Books, 1961.

Hutten, Ernest H., *The Origins of Science.* London: George Allen & Unwin, Ltd., 1962.

Hyslop, James H., "Some Unusual Phenomena in Photography." *Proc. Amer. Soc. Psychic. Res.,* Part 3, Vol. VIII, 1914.

James, E. O., *Prehistoric Religion.* London: Thames & Hudson, 1957. An excellent survey of paleolithic burial rituals and discussion of the cult of the dead in antiquity.

James, William, "Frederic Myers' Service to Psychology." *Proc. Soc. Psychic. Res.,* Part 42, Vol. XVII, May, 1901. Reprinted in *William James on Psychical Research,* eds. Murphy, Gardner, and Ballou, Robert O. New York: The Viking Press, 1960.

Jammer, Max, *Concepts of Force.* New York: Harper and Brothers (Torchbook 550), 1962.

Jeans, Sir James, *The Mysterious Universe.* New York: The Macmillan Company, 1944.

Jordan, Pascual, *Physics of the Twentieth Century.* New York: Philosophical Library, 1944. One of the pioneers of quantum physics invites us to consider "whether the whole world—and we with it—be not possibly only a dream of God."

———"Reflections on Parapsychology, Psychoanalysis and Atomic Physics." *Jour. Parapsychol.,* Vol. XV, 1951.

———*Verdrängung und Komplementarität.* Hamburg: Strom-Verlag-Bergedorf, 1947. No English translation.

Jung, C. G., *Psychology and Religion.* New York: Pantheon Books, 1958. The relationship of phallic worship and the worship of trinities.

Kelsen, Hans, *Society and Nature.* Chicago: University of Chicago Press, 1943.

Kuhn, Thomas S., *The Structure of Scientific Revolutions.* Chicago: University of Chicago Press. Vol. 2, No. 2, Foundations of the Unity of Science, International Encyclopedia of Unified Science, 1962.

Lévy-Bruhl, Lucien, *Primitives and the Supernatural.* New York: E. P. Dutton & Company, 1935.

Lodge, Oliver J., Experience of Unusual Physical Phenomena Occurring in the Presence of an Entranced Person (Eusapia Palladino). *Jour. Soc. Psychic. Res.,* Vol. VI, Nov., 1894. A masterfully written report by an eminent physicist.

Lowie, Robert H., *Primitive Religion.* New York: Grosset & Dunlap, 1952.

Maimonides, Moses, *Guide for the Perplexed.* (Trans. S. Pines.) Chicago: University of Chicago Press, 1963.

Malinowski, Bronislaw, *Magic, Science and Religion.* Garden City, New York: Doubleday Anchor Book, 1948.

Marbe, Karl, *Die Gleichförmigkeit in der Welt.* Munich: Beck, 1916. Unfortunately no English translation of this provocative work exists.

Margenau, Henry, "Physical Versus Historical Reality." *Phil. Sci.,* Vol. XIX, 1952.

Meerloo, Joost A. M., *Hidden Communion: Studies in the Communication Theory of Telepathy.* New York: Helix Press, 1964.

Morgan, Richard G., "Outline of Cultures in the Ohio Region." In: *Archeology of Eastern United States,* edited by James B. Griffin. Chicago: University of Chicago Press, 1952.

Morse, J. J., *A Brief History of Spirit Photography.* Manchester: Two Worlds Publishing Company, 1909.

Mumler, William H., *Personal Experiences of William H. Mumler in Spirit Photography.* Boston: Colby & Rich, 1875.

Murphy, Gardner and Ballou, Robert O., *William James on Psychical Research.* New York: Viking Press, 1960. The observations and opinions of one of the great masters of psychology, philosophy, and prose. Absorbing reading.

Murray, Margaret A., *The God of the Witches.* London: Faber & Faber, Ltd., 1931. Glimpses into the disreputable recent past of the Creator.

Myers, F. W. H., *Human Personality and Its Survival of Bodily Death.* New York: Longmans, Green, & Company, 1904. (Abridged: New Hyde Park: University Books, Inc., 1961.) A wide ranging and deeply probing examination of data on 'subliminal' states of consciousness. *The* classic of psychical research.

Oehler, Pauline, "The Psychic Photography of Ted Serios." *Fate,* December, 1962.

Osis, Karlis, "ESP Over Distance: A Survey of Experiments Published in English." *Jour. Amer. Soc. Psychic. Res.,* Vol. LIX, No. 1, 1965.

———and Fahler, Jarl, "Space and Time Variables in ESP." *Jour. Amer. Soc. Psychic. Res.,* Vol. LIX, No. 2, 1965.

Owen, A. R. G., *Can We Explain the Poltergeist?* New York: Helix Press, 1964.

Piaget, Jean, *The Child's Conception of the World.* New York: Humanities Press, 1951.

Price, G. R., "Science and the Supernatural." *Science,* Vol. CXXII, No. 3165 (Aug. 26, 1955).

Prince, Walter Franklin, "The Doris Case of Multiple Personality." *Proc. Amer. Soc. Psychic. Res.,* Vol. IX, 1915; Vol. X, 1916. An absolute must for all students of personality, single or multiple.

———*Noted Witnesses for Psychic Occurrences.* Boston: Boston Society for Psychic Research, 1928. Reprinted: New Hyde Park, N.Y., University Books, 1963.

Proceedings of Four Conferences of Parapsychological Studies. New York: Parapsychology Foundation, Inc., 1957.

Puharich, Andrija, *The Sacred Mushroom.* New York: Doubleday & Company, Inc., 1959.

Radin, Paul, *Primitive Religion.* New York: Dover Publications, 1957. The author favors an economic interpretation of religious and cultural development, with the medicine man as the Tammany boss throughout. The psychology used tends to be somewhat on the too-primitive side.

Rhine, J. B., *The Reach of the Mind.* New York: William Sloane Associates, Inc., 1947.

Rhine, Louisa E., *Hidden Channels of the Mind.* New York: William Sloane Associates, Inc., 1961.

———"Spontaneous Physical Effects and the Psi Process." *Jour. Parapsychol.,* Vol. XXVII, No. 2, June, 1963.

Richet, Charles, *Thirty Years of Psychical Research.* London: Collins & Sons, 1923. A no-holds-barred account by a Nobel Prize winner in physiology and medicine.

Robertson, A. J. B., "Telepathy and Electromagnetic Waves." *Jour. Soc. Psychic. Res.,* Vol. XXXIV, 1947.

Rose, Ronald, *Living Magic.* New York: Rand McNally & Company, 1956.

Rush, J. H., "Some Considerations as to a Physical Basis of ESP." *Jour. Parapsychol.*, Vol. VII, 1943.

Russell, Bertrand, *Human Knowledge.* New York: The Macmillan Co., 1921.

———*The Analysis of Mind.* New York: Simon and Schuster, 1948.

Ryle, Gilbert, *The Concept of Mind.* New York: Barnes and Noble, 1949. A persuasive attempt to exorcise the 'ghost in the machine' concept of mental functioning.

Schrenck-Notzing, Albert Baron Von, *Phenomena of Materialization.* London: Kegan Paul, Trench, Trubner & Company, 1920.

Schroedinger, Erwin, *Mind and Matter.* Cambridge University Press, 1959.

———*What is Life?* New York: The Macmillan Company, 1945.

Scott, George Ryley, *Phallic Worship.* Westport, Connecticut: Mental Health Press, N.D.

Servadio, Emilio, "A Presumptively Telepathic-Precognitive Dream During Analysis." *Int. Jour. Psycho-anal.*, Vol. XXXVI, 1955.

Sherrington, Sir Charles, *Man On His Nature.* Cambridge University Press, 1963. A great neurophysiologist and confirmed dualist wonders how nature managed to get mind into things as if *it* were a monist.

Sidgwick, Mrs. Henry, "On Spirit Photographs; a Reply to Mr. A. R. Wallace." *Proc. Soc. Psychic. Res.*, Part 19, 1891.

Smith, Susy, *The Mediumship of Mrs. Leonard.* New Hyde Park, New York: University Books, Inc., 1964.

Soal, S. G. and Bateman, F., *Modern Experiments in Telepathy.* New Haven: Yale University Press, 1954.

Stratton, F. J. M., "An Out-of-the-Body Experience Combined with ESP." *Jour. Soc. Psychic. Res.*, Vol. XXXIX, No. 692, June, 1957.

Struik, Dirk, "On The Foundations of the Theory of Probabilities." *Phil. Sci.*, Vol. I, No. 1, 1934.

Taetzsch, Robert, "Design of a Psi Communications System." *Int. Jour. Parapsychol.*, Vol. IV, No. 1, 1962.

Tenhaeff, W.H.C., "The Method of Introspection and Depth-Psychological Background of Spontaneous Paragnostic Experiences." *Proc. Parapsychol. Inst. of the Univ. of Utrecht.*, No. 3, Jan., 1965.

Thigpen, Corbett H. and Cleckley, Hervey M., *The Three Faces of Eve.* New York: McGraw-Hill Book Company, Inc., 1957.

Tromp. S. W., *Psychical Physics.* New York: Elsevier Publishing Co., Inc., 1949. A mine of information.

Tylor, Edward Burnett, *Religion in Primitive Culture.* Part II of *Primitive Culture.* New York: Harper and Brothers, 1958. A classic by a great pioneer who saw himself as a crusader against the occult superstitions which he so beautifully described.

Tyrrell, G. N. M., *Apparitions*. New York: Collier Books, 1963. A must for anybody before he answers the question, "Do you believe in ghosts?"

———*Science and Psychical Phenomena*. New York: Harper and Brothers, 1938. Reprinted: New Hyde Park, N.Y., University Books, 1961. One of the best all-around primers of psychical research.

Vasiliev, L. L., *Experiments in Mental Suggestion*. Authorized translation by ISMI Publications, Church Crookham, Hampshire, England, 1963. First published in 1962 by Leningrad State University. Reprinted: *The Mysterious Phenomena of the Human Psyche*. Translated by Sonia Volochova. New Hyde Park, N.Y., University Books, 1965.

Walker, Roland, "Parapsychology and Dualism." *Sci. Monthly*, Vol. LXXIX, No. 1, 1954.

Wallace, A. Russell, *Miracles and Modern Spiritualism*. London: James Burns, 1874. Of historical interest for those interested in a major preoccupation of the godfather of the theory of evolution. A small section on spirit photography, including the author's personal experience with it.

Warcollier, René, *Experiments in Telepathy*. New York: Harper and Brothers, 1938. A fascinating account of telepathic drawing experiments in which interesting parallels to the data of ordinary perception are revealed.

West, Louis J., ed., *Hallucinations*. New York: Grune & Stratton, 1962. A group of essays summarizing the latest data on a trick of the brain somewhat like 'thoughtography'—the registration of objects which are not present according to other avenues of information.

Whitehead, Alfred North, *Process and Reality*. New York: The Macmillan Company, 1929.

Whiteman, J. H. M., "The Process of Separation and Return in Experiences Fully 'Out of the Body.' " *Proc. Soc. Psychic. Res.*, Vol. L, 1956.

———*The Mystical Life*. London: Faber & Faber, 1961. A provocative section on 'light' as it figures in the experiences of mystics.

Wiener, Norbert, *Cybernetics*. New York: John Wiley & Sons, Inc., 1948. A pioneering attempt, among other provocative things in this classic, at a mathematical approach to certain aspects of visual perception.

Wordsworth, William, *The Complete Poetical Works*. New York: Houghton Mifflin Company, 1904.

INDEX

A NOTE ABOUT THE AUTHOR

A native New Yorker, Dr. Eisenbud was educated at Columbia College and Columbia College of Physicians and Surgeons, where he received both the Doctor of Medicine and the Doctor of Medical Science degrees. From 1938 until 1950, he engaged in private practice of psychiatry and psychoanalysis in New York City and served as Associate in Psychiatry at the Columbia College of Physicians and Surgeons. During that same period, he taught at the New York School of Social Work and other institutions. Since 1950 Dr. Eisenbud has been a resident of Denver, Colorado, in which city he has continued his private practice and is a member of the faculty of the University of Colorado Medical School as Associate Clinical Professor of Psychiatry. A Fellow of the American Psychiatric Association and a member of both the American Psychoanalytic Association and the American Society for Psychical Research, he has been throughout his professional career a steady contributor to psychiatric, psychoanalytic and parapsychological journals and books in this country and abroad. Dr. Eisenbud is married and has three children.